# Education in Sport and Physical Activity

Sport and physical activity are embedded in our education systems and in wider society. This book takes the broadest possible look at this topic, across every key discipline and on different continents, opening up important new directions for the future development of sport and physical activity education.

The book examines education in sport coaching, sport management, PE teacher training, physical activity and health promotion, and the emerging discipline of outdoor studies, considering how trends such as globalisation, digitalisation, and privatisation are having a profound impact on education programs. It identifies some of the most important societal issues that must be addressed by sport and physical activity educators, including healthy lifestyles, inequality, intercultural aspects, human rights, and emerging technologies, and looks at how sport and physical activity education in Europe, North America, Latin America, Asia, and Australasia is evolving to meet these challenges.

Designed to invite self-reflection, to provoke debate and to open up new cross-disciplinary and international perspectives within sports organisations and higher education institutions, this book is fascinating reading for advanced students, researchers, teachers, and policy makers with an interest in sport and physical activity.

**Karen Petry** is Senior Researcher and Deputy Head of the Institute of European Sport Development and Leisure Studies at the German Sport University Cologne and Vice President of the European Network of Sport Education (ENSE). She is responsible for the research activities in Sport Policy, Sport and Society and Sport for Development. In 2011, she received the Alberto-Madella-Award for her outstanding engagement in Sport Education. Karen has published on European and international sport policy, education in sport, sport and development, sport and social work, and sport and gender.

**Johan de Jong** is Professor of Healthy Lifestyle, Sports & Physical Activity at the Hanze University of Applied Sciences Groningen, Netherlands and Board Member of the European Network of Sport Education (ENSE). Furthermore, he represents Hanze University in the Health Enhancing Physical Activity Europe Network (HEPA) and the European Citizen Science Association (ECSA). His main research objective is to develop and evaluate approaches that stimulate people, from young to old, to become more physically active as part of a healthy lifestyle. Johan has published in different sport, physical activity and health related journals.

# Education in Sport and Physical Activity

## Future Directions and Global Perspectives

Edited by
Karen Petry and Johan de Jong

LONDON AND NEW YORK

First published 2022
by Routledge
2 Park Square, Milton Park, Abingdon, Oxon OX14 4RN

and by Routledge
605 Third Avenue, New York, NY 10158

*Routledge is an imprint of the Taylor & Francis Group, an informa business*

© 2022 selection and editorial matter, Karen Petry and Johan de Jong; individual chapters, the contributors

The right of Karen Petry and Johan de Jong to be identified as the authors of the editorial material, and of the authors for their individual chapters, has been asserted in accordance with sections 77 and 78 of the Copyright, Designs and Patents Act 1988.

All rights reserved. No part of this book may be reprinted or reproduced or utilised in any form or by any electronic, mechanical, or other means, now known or hereafter invented, including photocopying and recording, or in any information storage or retrieval system, without permission in writing from the publishers.

*Trademark notice:* Product or corporate names may be trademarks or registered trademarks, and are used only for identification and explanation without intent to infringe.

*British Library Cataloguing-in-Publication Data*
A catalogue record for this book is available from the British Library

*Library of Congress Cataloging-in-Publication Data*
A catalog record has been requested for this book

ISBN: 978-0-367-43360-4 (hbk)
ISBN: 978-1-032-20606-6 (pbk)
ISBN: 978-1-003-00266-6 (ebk)

DOI: 10.4324/9781003002666

Typeset in Goudy
by KnowledgeWorks Global Ltd.

# Contents

| | |
|---|---|
| *List of contributors* | viii |
| *List of abbreviations* | xii |
| | |
| Introduction | 1 |
| KAREN PETRY AND JOHAN DE JONG | |

**PART I**
**Current issues in sport education**      **9**

1 The challenge of doing coach education and development
  in the 21st century: Past, present, and future trends     11
  SERGIO LARA-BERCIAL AND JOHN BALES

2 International sport management education: Curricula, trends,
  and challenges     24
  THOMAS GIEL, REI YAMASHITA, DARYOUSCH ARGOMAND,
  AND KIRSTIN HALLMANN

3 The need for T-shaped sport, physical activity,
  and health professionals     38
  JOHAN DE JONG AND THOMAS SKOVGAARD

4 Outdoor education as a deep education for global sustainability
  and social justice     49
  HEATHER PRINCE AND JEAN CORY-WRIGHT

vi Contents

## PART II
## New trends in sport education

61

5 Sport education from a global perspective

63

RICHARD BAILEY AND BETTINA CALLARY

6 The utility of new technologies in the future of sport education

75

JONATHAN ROBERTSON AND MARGARET BEARMAN

7 Industry alignment: Fit-for-purpose sport education

84

STEVEN OSBORNE AND ELIZABETH LEWIS

## PART III
## Education in sport and physical activity around the globe

97

8 European perspectives on qualifications in sport

99

STEFAN WALZEL, RUTH CRABTREE, AND KAREN PETRY

9 Sport development and delivery in Canada, México, and
the United States: Commonalities, differences, and future needs

110

HANS VAN DER MARS, TIM HOPPER, GORD INGLIS, EDTNA JÁUREGUI-ULLOA,
JUAN RICARDO LÓPEZ-TAYLOR, MARTIN FRANCISCO GONZÁLEZ-VILLALOBOS

10 Education in sport and physical activity across the Pacific

126

DEAN DUDLEY, JOHN CAIRNEY, AUE TE AVA, AND JACKIE LAUFF

11 Education in sport and physical activity: Current trends,
developments, and challenges in Latin America

137

MIGUEL A. CORNEJO AND ALEXANDER CÁRDENAS

12 Physical education and school sport in Eastern Asia

148

EMI TSUDA, YOSHINORI OKADE, TAKAHIRO SATO, AND YUNG-JU CHEN

## PART IV
## Education in sport and physical activity
## in a changing world

161

13 Sport, physical activity, and health promotion:
Implications for the education of future professionals

163

CATHERINE WOODS, MARIE MURPHY, AND ENRIQUE GARCÍA BENGOECHEA

Contents vii

14 Being active as a sports or PA student in an era
of wearable technology 173
CHARLOTTE VAN TUYCKOM AND STEVEN VOS

15 Sport, diversity, and inequality: Intersecting challenges
and solutions 183
KAREN PETRY, MARIANNE MEIER, AND LOUIS MOUSTAKAS

16 Human rights in sport education 195
DANIELA HEERDT AND WILLIAM ROOK

17 Developing intercultural sport educators in Europe:
Opportunities, challenges, and future directions 206
LOUIS MOUSTAKAS, ELEFTHERIA PAPAGEORGIOU, AND KAREN PETRY

18 Careers of European athletes: Who is ultimately responsible? 216
STEFAN WALZEL, NIKLAS A. ROTERING, AND RUTH CRABTREE

19 Transforming coach education for the 21st century 228
CHRISTIAN THUE BJØRNDAL, TYNKE TOERING, AND SIV GJESDAL

*Index* 238

# Contributors

**Daryousch Argomand** is a Master's Student in Sport Management and a former Research Assistant at the Institute of Sport Economics and Sport Management at the German Sport University Cologne, Germany.

**Richard Bailey** teaches in the Centre for Academic Partnerships and Engagement at the University of Nottingham Malaysia. Prior to moving to Asia, he was head of research at the International Council of Sport Science and Physical Education, based in Berlin, Germany, and held Full Professorships in several UK universities.

**John Bales** is the President of the International Council for Coaching Excellence (ICCE), Canada.

**Margaret Bearman** is Research Professor at the Centre of Research in Assessment and Digital Learning (CRADLE), Deakin University, Australia.

**Enrique García Bengoechea** is Researcher affiliated with the Physical Activity for Health Research Cluster, Health Research Institute, Department of Physical Education and Sport Sciences at the University of Limerick, Ireland.

**Christian Thue Bjørndal** is Associate Professor at the Department of Sport and Social Sciences, Norwegian School of Sport Sciences, Oslo, Norway.

**John Cairney** is Professor and Head of School in the School of Human Movement and Nutrition Sciences at the University of Queensland, Australia.

**Bettina Callary** teaches in the Sport and Physical Activity Leadership programme at Cape Breton University, Canada, focusing on coaching and sport psychology.

**Alexander Cárdenas** is affiliated with the Open University of Catalonia in Spain and is the founder of the *Plataforma Deporte para el Desarrollo y la Paz*.

**Yung-Ju Chen** is Assistant Professor in the Department of Teacher Education and Kinesiology at the Minot State University, USA.

**Miguel A. Cornejo** is Associate Professor and Researcher in the Physical Education Department at University of Concepción, Chile and is former Vice President of the Latin American Association for Social Studies of Sports (ALESDE).

Contributors   ix

**Jean Cory-Wright** is a Senior Academic teaching education for sustainability at the Ara Institute of Canterbury, Ōtautahi Christchurch, Aotearoa New Zealand.

**Ruth Crabtree** is Vice President of the World Association of Sport Management and leads on global teaching excellence at Northumbria University, UK.

**Dean Dudley** is Associate Professor of Health and Physical Education in the Macquarie School of Education at Macquarie University, Australia and an Honorary Associate Professor in the School of Human Movement and Nutrition Sciences at the University of Queensland, Australia.

**Thomas Giel** is Researcher and Lecturer at the Institute of Sport Economics and Sport Management, German Sport University Cologne, Germany and the programme coordinator of the Master of Science in Sport Management offered by the university.

**Siv Gjesdal** is Associate Professor at the Department of Sport and Social Sciences, Norwegian School of Sport Sciences, Oslo, Norway.

**Martin Francisco González-Villalobos** is Associate Professor and Teacher's Coordinator of the Department of Human Movement Sciences, Sports, Education, Recreation and Dance of the Health Sciences Center at the University of Guadalajara, México.

**Kirstin Hallmann** is Researcher and Senior Lecturer at the Institute of Sport Economics and Sport Management, German Sport University Cologne, Germany. She has published in areas such as sport participation, sport volunteering, elite sports, and sport tourism.

**Daniela Heerdt** is Research Officer for the Centre for Sport and Human Rights and Independent Consultant in the field of Sport and Human Rights.

**Tim Hopper** is Leader for the Physical Education Teacher Education program in the School of Exercise Science, Physical and Health Education at the University of Victoria, Canada.

**Gord Inglis** is Chair of the Bachelor of Sport Management and Bachelor of Sport & Fitness Leadership programs at Camosun College, Canada. Previously, he served as Chair of the Kinesiology & Sport Studies program at Red Deer College, Canada.

**Edtna Jáuregui-Ulloa** is Coordinator of the Physical Activity and Lifestyle Master Degree Program and Associate Professor of the Health Sciences Center at the University of Guadalajara, Mexico.

**Sergio Lara-Bercial** is Reader in Sport Coaching at Leeds Beckett University, UK, and the Manager for Strategy and Development of the International Council for Coaching Excellence.

x Contributors

**Jackie Lauff** is the Chief Executive Officer of Sport Matters, Australia.

**Elizabeth Lewis** is Senior Lecturer, Programme Director and Academic Team Leader for Sport Management at Cardiff Metropolitan University, UK, and is also Director of an awarding winning gymnastics social enterprise in the United Kingdom.

**Juan Ricardo López-Taylor** is Chair of the Department of Human Movement Sciences, Sports, Education, Recreation and Dance of the Health Sciences Center at the University of Guadalajara, México.

**Marianne Meier** is Researcher and Lecturer specialized in sport, diversity, and sustainability at the Interdisciplinary Centre for Gender Studies (ICFG) at the University of Berne, Switzerland.

**Louis Moustakas** is Researcher and Lecturer at the Institute of European Sport Development and Leisure Studies at the German Sport University Cologne, Germany and the Secretary General of the European Network of Sport Education (ENSE).

**Marie Murphy** is Chair of Exercise and Health, Dean of Postgraduate Research and Director of the Doctoral College at Ulster University, Northern Ireland.

**Yoshinori Okade** is Professor in the Department of Sport Studies for International Community at Nippon Sport Science University, Japan.

**Steven Osborne** is Principal Lecturer in employability at Cardiff Metropolitan University, UK, and is also involved as the European Association of Sport Management (EASM) working group chair for employability and UK Professional Development Board member for the sport and physical activity industry.

**Eleftheria Papageorgiou** is Primary School Teacher and PhD student at the University of Thessaly, Greece. Her research focuses on intercultural education training and sport pedagogy.

**Heather Prince** is Professor of Outdoor and Environmental Education at the University of Cumbria, UK.

**Jonathan Robertson** is Lecturer in Deakin Business School's sport management program at Deakin University, Australia.

**William Rook** is Deputy Chief Executive and Chief Operating Officer at the Centre for Sport and Human Rights, Switzerland, Senior Advisor at the Institute for Human Rights and Business, UK, and a Solicitor qualified to practise in England and Wales.

**Niklas A. Rotering** is Research Assistant at the Institute of Sport Economics and Sport Management of the German Sport University Cologne, Germany.

**Takahiro Sato** is Professor at the Faculty of Health and Sport Sciences at the University of Tsukuba, Japan.

**Thomas Skovgaard** is assigned to head up Active Living research at Department of Sports Science and Clinical Biomechanics, University of Southern Denmark. He also serves as the President of the European Network of Sport Education (ENSE).

**Aue Te Ava** is Lecturer in the School of Pacific Arts, Communication, and Education at the University of the South Pacific, Fiji.

**Tynke Toering** is Lecturer and Senior Researcher at the Institute of Sport Studies, Hanze University of Applied Sciences, the Netherlands.

**Emi Tsuda** is Assistant Professor in the College of Physical Activity and Sport Sciences at the West Virginia University, USA.

**Hans van der Mars** is Professor in Physical Education and Sport Pedagogy at Arizona State University in the Mary Lou Fulton Teachers College, USA.

**Charlotte van Tuyckom** is affiliated as Lecturer/Researcher with Howest University of Applied Sciences, Department of Sports and Movement Sciences, Belgium.

**Steven Vos** is Professor in the Department of Industrial Design at Eindhoven University of Technology, the Netherlands, and Head of Research at the School of Sports Studies, Fontys University of Applied Sciences, the Netherlands.

**Stefan Walzel** teaches and researches at the Institute of Sports Economics and Sports Management at the German Sport University Cologne, Germany. His research focuses on sports sponsorship and social responsibility in the field of sports.

**Catherine Woods** is Chair of Physical Activity for Health (PAfH) and Director of the PAfH Research Cluster, Health Research Institute, Department of Physical Education and Sport Sciences, at the University of Limerick, Ireland.

**Rei Yamashita** is Assistant Professor in the Faculty of Sport Sciences at Waseda University, Japan and the Secretariat General of the Asian Association for Sport Management.

# Abbreviations

**Chapter 1**
CD          coach developer
CED         coach education and development
CPD         continuing professional development
EU          European Union
ICDF        International Coach Developer Framework
UK          United Kingdom

**Chapter 2**
FIFA        Fédération Internationale de Football Association
IOC         International Olympic Committee
PA          physical activity
SDGs        Sustainable Development Goals
TOCOG       Tokyo Organising Committee of the Olympic and Paralympic Games
TOP         The Olympic Partner
UN          United Nations

**Chapter 3**
GAPPA       Global Action Plan on Physical Activity
LL          Living Labs
NGO         Non-Governmental Organization
WHO         World Health Organization

**Chapter 4**
CŠOD        Centre for School and Outdoor Education (Center šolskih in obšolskih dejavnosti)
DOC         Department of Conservation
EOE         European Institute of Outdoor Adventure Education and Experiential Learning
EONZ        Education Outdoors New Zealand

| | |
|---|---|
| NCEA | National Certificate in Educational Achievement |
| NZ | New Zealand |
| UK | United Kingdom |
| YMCA | Young Men's Christian Association |

**Chapter 5**

| | |
|---|---|
| ICCE | International Council for Coaching Excellence |
| ISCJ | International Sport Coaching Journal |
| MINEPS | International Conferences of Ministers and Senior Officials Responsible for Physical Education and Sport |
| OECD | Organisation for Economic Co-operation and Development |
| PISA | Program for International Student Assessment |
| WHO | World Health Organisation |

**Chapter 6**

| | |
|---|---|
| LMS | learning management system |
| MOOC | Massive Open Online Course |
| OUA | Open University Analytics |

**Chapter 7**

| | |
|---|---|
| ASOIF | Association of Summer Olympic International Federations |
| CDL | Career Development Learning |
| ESSA-Sport | European Sector Skills Alliance for Sport and Physical Activity |
| OECD | Organisation for Economic Co-operation and Development |
| PI | Professional Identity |
| PID | Professional Identity Development |
| PPI | pre-professional identity |
| USEM | Understanding Skills Efficacy Metacognition |
| WBL | Work-Based Learning |
| WRL | Work-Related Learning |

**Chapter 8**

| | |
|---|---|
| EHF | European Handball Federation |
| EQF | European Qualifications Framework |
| ESSDCSL | European Sectoral Social Dialogue Committee for Sports and Active Leisure |
| EU | European Union |
| GDP | gross domestic product |
| ICT | information/communication technology |
| UEFA | Union of European Football Associations |
| XG HR | Expert Group on Skills and Human Resources and Development in Sport |

xiv  Abbreviations

**Chapter 9**

| | |
|---|---|
| AYSO | American Youth Soccer Association |
| CDE | Centros deportivos escolares |
| CONADE | National Commission of Physical Culture and Sport |
| CPR | cardio-pulmonary resuscitation |
| LTAD | Long-Term Athlete Development |
| LTDSPA | Long-Term Development in Sport and Physical Activity |
| NBA | National Basketball Association |
| NCCP | National Coaching Certification Program |
| NFSHSA | National Federation of State High School Associations |
| NGBs | National Governing Bodies |
| NSO | National Sport Organizations |
| OTP | Own the Podium |
| PAA | Physical Activity Alliance |
| PHE | Provincial and National Physical and Health Education |
| PHE | Physical Health Canada |
| PSO | Provincial/Territorial Sport Organizations |
| USDHHS | United States Department of Health and Human Services |

**Chapter 10**

| | |
|---|---|
| AIS | Australian Institute of Sport |
| ASC | Australian Sport Commission |
| ECHO | Pacific Ending Childhood Obesity Network |
| GSHS | Global School-based Student Health Survey |
| MVPA | moderate-to-vigorous physical activity |
| NCD | non-communicable disease |
| NOC | National Olympic Committee |
| NSO | national sports organisation |
| ONOC | Oceania National Olympic Committees |
| OSEP | Pacific Islanders |
| OSFO | Organisation of Sport Federations of Oceania |
| PACREF | Pacific Regional Education Framework |
| PICT | Pacific Island Countries and Territory |
| RST | Regional Sport Trust |
| SPAPE | Pacific Sport, Physical Activity and Physical Education |
| SSO | state sports organisation |
| WHO | World Health Organization |

**Chapter 11**

| | |
|---|---|
| EYFS | Early Years Foundation Stages |
| GDP | gross domestic product |
| OAS | Organization of American States |

Abbreviations xv

| | |
|---|---|
| OECD | Organisation for Economic Co-operation and Development |
| SDGs | Sustainable Development Goals |
| UNESCO | United Nations Educational, Scientific and Cultural Organization |

**Chapter 12**

| | |
|---|---|
| AJHSAF | All Japan High School Athletic Federation |
| JSPO | Japan Sport Association |
| MEXT | Ministry of Education, Culture, Sports, Science and Technology-Japan |
| MOE | Ministry of Education Republic of China |
| NCEE | National Centre on Education and the Economy |
| NJHSPCA | Nippon Junior High School Physical Culture Association |
| OECD | Organisation for Economic Co-operation and Development |
| PE | physical education |

**Chapter 13**

| | |
|---|---|
| CSPPA+ | Children's Sport Participation and Physical Activity plus |
| HDI | Human Development Index |
| MVPA | moderate-to-vigorous intensity physical activity |
| PA | physical activity |
| PE | physical education |
| SDGs | United Nation's Sustainable Development Goals |
| WHO | World Health Organization |
| WISH | Walking In ScHools |

**Chapter 14**

| | |
|---|---|
| ACSM | American College of Sports Medicine |
| PA | physical activity |
| VAR | video assistant referee |

**Chapter 15**

| | |
|---|---|
| SDGs | Sustainable Development Goals |
| SRM | sports role model |
| UN | United Nations |

**Chapter 16**

| | |
|---|---|
| FIFA | Fédération Internationale de Football Association |
| HRC | UN Human Rights Council |
| HRW | Human Rights Watch |
| IHRB | Institute for Human Rights and Business |
| IOC | International Olympic Committee |
| LOCOG | London's Organising Committee of the Olympic Games |
| MSEs | mega-sporting events |

| | |
|---|---|
| **OECD** | Organisation for Economic Co-operation and Development |
| **SC** | Supreme Committee |
| **SDP** | sport for development and peace |
| **SGBs** | sports governing bodies |
| **UNESCO** | UN Educational, Scientific and Cultural Organization |
| **UNGPs** | United Nations Guiding Principles on Business and Human Rights |

**Chapter 17**

| | |
|---|---|
| **EDU:PACT** | Intercultural Education through Physical Activity, Coaching and Training |

**Chapter 18**

| | |
|---|---|
| **HPAs** | high-performance athletes |

# Introduction

*Karen Petry and Johan de Jong*

Education in sport and in physical activity has a long tradition in most parts around the globe. Recently, higher education and non-university education settings in the sport sector are growing, both in numbers and in importance. Since a couple of years, the idea of making projections about the future of education in the sport and physical activity sector was first discussed with selected members of the European Network of Sport Education (ENSE). One important conclusion of these debates was that education in sport and physical activity contributes significantly to the quality of life of global citizens in the context of a greener, more health-conscious set of policies. Furthermore, considering recent complex societal developments, there is a need to create awareness of the important role of education in the sport and physical activity sector around the globe. As a result, this book aims to present a comprehensive, global, and multidisciplinary overview of education in sport and physical activity with a focus on current and future developments in the sport and physical activity and related sectors from a cross-national perspective.

The diversity of approaches which are introduced in this book focuses on four different dimensions: (1) on selected disciplines (such as Coaching, Physical Education, Sport Management, Physical Activity and Health, and the Outdoor Education sector), (2) on future trends in education and the effects on the sport and physical activity sector (such as globalisation and digitalisation), (3) on the status of sport and physical activity on different continents (Europe, Asia, North America, Australia/Oceania, and Latin America), and (4) on the future challenges in a changing world and the responsibility of education in sport and physical activity. These four dimensions are taken up in the four parts of this book, namely:

Part I: Current Issues in Sport Education
Part II: New Trends in Sport Education
Part III: Education in Sport and Physical Activity Around the Globe
Part IV: Education in Sport and Physical Activity in a Changing World

DOI: 10.4324/9781003002666-1

## Part I: Current issues in sport education

Part I comprises four different chapters about the current and future status of education in the sub-sectors Coaching, Sport Management, Physical Activity and Health, and Outdoor Education.

In the first chapter, Lara-Bercial and Bales discuss the main current challenges in coach education and describe the latest thinking on coach education and development (CED). The challenge of balancing the education and development of a workforce that includes volunteer, part-time, and full-time workers and what this means for educational offerings and the evolving role of coach developers are considered. The chapter concludes with an overview of what CED may look like in the future.

The second chapter, written by Giel, Yamashita, Argomand, and Hallmann, presents the status quo of sport management education and gives an outlook for its future directions. Core components of sport management education are outlined, and the congruency and heterogeneity of contents among current degree programmes of several universities from all six continents are presented. Recent trends, developments, and challenges affecting the sports industry such as sustainability and social responsibility, digitalisation, internationalisation and intercultural management, as well as integrity and good governance are finally discussed.

Chapter 3 describes the need for T-shaped Sport, Physical Activity and Health professionals. The authors de Jong and Skovgaard give insights on how to stimulate exercise and physical activity behaviour and counter sedentarism from a socioecological perspective. This perspective considers the complexity and systems thinking necessary to promote an active lifestyle for health. Furthermore, recommendations for a T-shaped Sport, Physical Activity, and Health professional that is educated in real-life situations ("Living Labs") are made. From inside the classroom to outside in practice, the approach is a more congruent way of experiencing and learning how to deal with complex Sport, Physical Activity and Health challenges.

Chapter 4, written by Prince and Cory-Wright, is titled "Outdoor Education as a Deep Education for Global Sustainability and Social Justice". This chapter includes perspectives on Outdoor Education from the United Kingdom and New Zealand and illustrates similarities, differences, and trends from these two countries on two separate continents. Also, recommendations for future education in the outdoor sector are made and state that the sector should concentrate more on optimising the benefits of activities and experiences in local places and spaces such as parks and gardens in a creative and active way. This would also improve equitable and inclusive access for participants from different socio-economic groups.

## Part II: New trends in sport education

The focus of the second part of the book is to describe and analyse current and future trends in sport with an emphasis on understanding the effects of globalisation, the impact of new teaching and learning technologies, as well as the importance of employability and lifelong learning.

Chapter 5 is about sport education from a global perspective. Bailey and Callary focus on the concepts of internationalisation, which refers to an awareness of ideas and developments from around the world, and globalisation, or the ways in which different educational systems are increasingly connected. This chapter analyses these phenomena within the contexts of school physical education and sport coaching and seeks to identify some of the dominant trends through which internationalisation and globalisation are expressed in practices around the world.

In Chapter 6, Robertson and Bearman analyse the utility of new technologies in the future of sport education. Both authors provide a review of the role digital learning environments play in higher education in sport and specifically how technology may support the teaching and learning in an increasingly digitalised higher education sector. The chapter ends with an outlook on sport-related education in 2035 by extrapolating current trends in technology to stimulate discussion about the future of sport education in terms of widely adopted versus exceptional technological usage.

Chapter 7 is about "Industry Alignment: Fit-For-Purpose Sport Education", written by Osborne and Lewis. Employers are requesting that sport educationalists engage in discussions to develop a robust sports workforce to meet the industry's immediate and future demands. The chapter introduces new employability and lifelong learning frameworks that can assist the career development of current and future sports professionals. The authors argue that the sectoral progression towards professionalisation of key sports roles, the influence of digitally enabled education, and an increasing interface between industry professionals and higher education institutions may require educationalists to move beyond traditional models of delivery.

## Part III: Education in sport and physical activity around the globe

Part III outlines continental educational specificities in sport and physical activity in Europe, Middle and North America, South and Latin America, as well as Asia and the Pacific Region.

Chapter 8 starts with the European perspectives on qualifications in sport. Walzel, Crabtree, and Petry present a systematisation of the qualification landscape in sport in Europe, including three dimensions: job category, occupational level, and qualification provider. The authors discuss the challenges and opportunities for the sports qualification systems in Sport Management and Coaching and the employability of professionals in the field. The chapter concludes with future developments and challenges in providing high-quality qualifications in sport in Europe.

"Sport Development and Delivery in Canada, México, and the United States: Commonalities, Differences, and Future Needs" is then outlined in **Chapter 9**. The team of authors (van der Mars, Hopper, Inglis, Jáuregui Ulloa, López-Taylor, and González-Villalobos) represents all countries and highlights the following topics: type and prevalence of sport education delivery (e.g., physical education, youth sport, club sport), the governance of and policies specific to sport, and the role and possible impact of coach education. To some extent, the three North American countries overlap in how sport is delivered and experienced. However, differences are present in how sport generally is defined, the role that the government plays in the delivery and its oversight, and the degree to which there is equity in creating quality access to sport for all children and youth.

In Chapter 10, Dudley, Cairney, Te Ava, and Lauff give an overview of the education in sport and physical activity across the Pacific region. The authors explore the physical activity and sport participation data that is prevailing across Australia, New Zealand, and the broader Pacific Island Nation States. The chapter also includes a synopsis of the relevant policy and social sports structures within these nations. Furthermore, some recent education innovations and projects being pursued across the Western Pacific region with regard to increasing and improving sports participation and sports experience are outlined. The chapter concludes with a commentary on how the concept of Physical Literacy is being used as an educative solution in sport across the region against the backdrop of a broader international sporting agenda.

Chapter 11 focuses on trends, developments, and challenges in education in sport and physical activity in Latin America. Cornejo and Cárdenas provide a general description of the educational system across the continent and introduce the promotion of healthy lifestyles, well-being, and physical activity of school children. Also, the roles of higher education institutions and sport federations in contributing to the advancement of education in sport and physical activity in Latin America are discussed. The chapter concludes with the discussion of challenges, like the lack of access to physical education programmes for people with disabilities and the limited understanding of the importance of sport as a vehicle to support education. Finally, the potential of sport and physical activity to tackle social problems or as contribution to the Sustainable Development Goals are addressed.

In Chapter 12, Tsuda, Okade, Sato, and Chen describe and discuss the systems and current trends of physical education and school sport in three Eastern Asian countries: Japan, South Korea, and Taiwan. The authors highlight the roles of physical education in the school curriculum as well as extracurricular activities. However, children's and adolescents' physical activity levels are still low, and teachers have been struggling to provide context-specific quality physical education. Furthermore, overemphasis on competition in school sport has been causing various issues in the field (e.g., teachers' overwork, physical, verbal, and sexual harassment abuse).

## Part IV: Education in sport and physical activity in a changing world

The final part of the book aims to describe the most important and relevant global developments which will have an impact on education in sport and physical activity in the coming decades. The developments and issues addressed are health promotion, technology, diversity and inequality, human rights, dual career for high-performance athletes, intercultural education, and coach education.

The issue of health promotion and the role of sport are described in Chapter 13. Woods, Murphy, and García Bengoechea reflect on the implications for the education of future professionals concerning the relevant aspect of health promotion. The authors argue that encouraging participation in sport represents one way to increase physical activity levels in the population. A summary of the evidence linking sport participation and physical activity levels is given, and the characteristics of sport activities and programmes that are conducive to increased physical activity are outlined. Finally, nine recommendations for effective strategies and policy actions are provided to optimise the health promoting potential of sport in a variety of settings.

In Chapter 14, Van Tuyckom and Vos discuss the topic of "Being Active as a Sports or PA Student in an Era of Wearable Technology". They argue that knowledge about sport and physical activity (PA)-related wearable devices should be a core component of the curriculum of sport and PA students. After presenting four main roles of sport- and PA-related wearable devices and the adapting role (and skills) of sports and PA professionals in the current digital era, they discuss some of the opportunities and challenges inherent to wearable technology in sport and PA, and they stress the importance of interdisciplinary collaboration between sport, humanities, and technology.

Chapter 15 is titled "Sport, Diversity, and Inequality: Intersecting Challenges and Solutions", written by Petry, Meier, and Moustakas. Structural changes, growing diversity, the dissolution of boundaries in media and communication, the individualisation of lifestyles, and increased mobility in a globalised world have led to more diversity in all areas of society. This has been accompanied by fundamental changes that have privileged market-based approaches and reduced government provision of social services, leading to growing inequality both within and between countries. The authors discuss how inequality takes form in sport and present specific examples through a gender-focused lens. Finally, they critically assess how sport can help to tackle inequalities and conclude by highlighting the importance of training sport educators.

The importance of including aspects of Human Rights in sport education is presented by Heerdt and Rook in Chapter 16. Sport has a unique power to promote human rights but at the same time carries numerous human rights risks. In the past decade, the human rights discourse has infiltrated the world of sport as a result of a recent trend among stakeholders such as athletes, sponsors, and civil society organisations raising awareness of the importance of human rights to sport and to sports governing bodies. The authors argue that sport and human rights should be integrated in sport-related education at all levels so that future professionals and those already working in the world of sport can continue and consolidate the trend to make it more sustainable.

In Chapter 17, Moustakas, Papageorgiou, and Petry present the EU-funded project "Intercultural Education through Physical Activity, Coaching and Training"

(EDU:PACT). The project aimed to prepare physical education teachers and coaches for inclusive intercultural education in and through sport. The challenges and opportunities inherent to intercultural sport education are discussed, and future avenues for the development of intercultural sport education are presented.

In Chapter 18 Walzel, Rotering, and Crabtree reflect about the careers of athletes under a dual career perspective. While athlete's dual careers have been well researched from the athletes' perspective, comparatively little attention has been paid to the benefits of universities offering specific sport science study programmes to high performance athletes (HPA). This chapter shows that HPAs have several advantageous skills and experiences that are especially functional for jobs in sport or related to sport.

And finally, Chapter 19 is about "Transforming Coach Education for the 21st Century". Bjørndal, Toering, and Gjesdal critically discuss the scientific and cultural premises on which current coach education in sport is based and offer reflections on how this education can be developed and improved. The authors suggest that current sport science models, characterised by separate silos of knowledge, may limit holistic approaches to sport coaching. Additionally, these systems of knowledge are created by power dynamics that are explicitly and implicitly valued in coach education, leading to the production of normative ideas about sport coaching and athlete development. This limited view may lead to blind spots in coach expertise development and hinder the improvement of coaching and coach education. They conclude by sharing some ideas that may contribute to the transformation of coach education through the use of more transdisciplinary approaches in coaching courses.

## Conclusion on future directions of education in sport and physical activity

This book comprises several future developments in the subsequent chapters: nowadays, but also in the future, sport and physical activity are considered important agents to address and contribute to complex societal challenges like inequity between genders, socio-economic status, and health status. Furthermore, sport and physical activity are also considered as important means to positively contribute to a substantial number of the 17 Sustainable Development Goals (SDGs) as declared by the United Nations.

Digital and technological developments will increasingly impact not only education in general but also the field of sport and physical activity education. Examples of this are flipping the classroom, digital feedback to students but also how to use wearables and other technological devices to enrich educational tasks and learning. Along with this growing technological and digital development, more emphasis on the global and international perspective will emerge in education since distance barriers and borders disappear.

Education in sport should be more responsive to many rapid changes that are foreseen in the coming decades. This means that education should be based more and better on the changes in students' and target groups' needs, the job market and practical field, and demographic and societal changes in the countries worldwide. Ways for the educational system to adapt to these changes could be through experimenting with blended learning and more teaching in real-life, practical settings with other professionals to learn how to work in a multidisciplinary way, since many complex challenges in the field of sport, physical activity, and health require multidisciplinary approaches. With this book, we explore this multidisciplinary examination of sport education, encompassing sociology, economics, management, health, coaching, outdoor education, physical education, and sport development.

The book features a mix of 47 authors across the disciplines representing around 20 countries worldwide. A big thanks goes to the teams of authors who followed our ideas and contributed with 19 interesting chapters. We all know that each of the mentioned and discussed aspects could have been elaborated on in a much more detailed way. The forward-looking approach makes it hopefully an important reading for those with an interest in the development of modern sport and physical activity and its education.

Karen Petry and Johan de Jong

## Acknowledgements

We are grateful to Helena Gey and Nina Seibert for their support on the manuscript of this book.

# Part I

# Current issues in sport education

Chapter 1

# The challenge of doing coach education and development in the 21st century

## Past, present, and future trends

*Sergio Lara-Bercial and John Bales*

### Introduction

Over the last 50 years, sport has experienced a democratisation process which has made it accessible to more and more citizens around the world. Long gone are the days when sport was the prerogative of elite athletes or the upper class. National governments (SASCOC, 2012; Sport Canada, 2012; Sport England, 2016; Sport New Zealand, 2020) and international agencies (UNESCO, 2016; Council of the European Union and the Representatives of Governments of Member States, 2017a) have identified the potential benefits of sport for individuals and society and thus invested in its promotion to an ever-wider audience. Every day, hundreds of millions of children, young people, adults, and senior citizens take part in athletic pursuits. Sports participation is a pervasive feature of 21st century societies globally.

Many forms of sports participation have one thing in common – the presence of a coach. Only recently, however, have authorities realised the actual size and impact of the coaching workforce. Estimates in the European Union (EU) put the number of coaches at anything between five and nine million (Lara-Bercial et al., 2017). Similar figures would be expected across most of the developed world and increasingly in developing countries, too. Coaches therefore make up one of the biggest workforces across the planet. This population has been shown to have specific demographic characteristics which have the potential to affect its function and capacity. The vast majority of coaches are unremunerated volunteers who are unqualified or hold low-level qualifications (North, 2009; Rankin-Wright et al., 2017; Lara-Bercial et al., 2020). This compromises the quality of delivery and may have a negative impact on the participants' experience and contribute to their dropping out of sport for good.

Moreover, the precarious nature of the coaching workforce is also reflected in the observed high turnover of coaches, especially at the grassroots level (Cuskelly et al., 2006; Paiement, 2007; Busser and Carruthers, 2010). Local authorities and clubs need to recruit a substantial number of new coaches every year, many of whom lack the skills required for the job (EOSE, 2019). In addition, the coaching workforce, at all levels, suffers from an underrepresentation of female coaches

DOI: 10.4324/9781003002666-3

(Reade, Rodgers and Norman, 2009) and coaches from minority ethnic backgrounds (Bradbury, 2013). This poses another significant risk – the alienation and non-sports participation of these populations who do not see themselves represented in the coaching workforce.

Consequently, organisations with competence over the delivery of sport at national and international levels have begun to question whether this haphazard and fragile workforce can serve the needs of participants and society (Council of the European Union and the Representatives of Governments of Member States, 2017a). Issues of identification, recruitment, and most importantly education, development, and retention are increasingly considered both in the academic literature (Lyle and Cushion, 2017; North *et al.*, 2019) and in policy circles (ICCE, ASOIF and LBU, 2013; Council of the European Union and the Representatives of Governments of Member States, 2017b, 2020). Recent research across the EU member states indicates that there is a trend towards the regulation and/or professionalisation of coaching (Lara-Bercial *et al.*, 2020; Moustakas, Petry and Lara-Bercial, 2020). Although the extent to which each country has made progress in this respect varies substantially, this tendency is characterised by the existence of:

- A clear definition of the coaching role
- Laws pertaining to the access and right to practice
- An organisation with the mandate to lead and regulate coaching
- A set of professional standards
- A coach licensing system
- Coaching qualifications aligned with the National Qualifications Framework and referenced to the European Qualification Framework for Lifelong Learning (EQF) (EQF, 2008)

A key driver of the improvement and/or professionalisation of coaching is coach education and development (CED). For the purpose of clarity, coach education typically refers to formal courses leading to a recognised and accredited qualification, whereas coach development normally refers to the overall journey of the learning coach regardless of the type of learning opportunities accessed (also known as Long-Term Coach Development) (ICCE, ASOIF and LBU, 2013). This chapter will explore the past and present of CED and offer glimpses of future developments. First, current literature on the nature of coaches' learning and how it can be facilitated will be explored. Second, the evolving nature and role of the coach developer (CD) will be examined. Third, the highly topical issue of assessment and certification will be reviewed. And fourth, the challenge of balancing the education and development of a workforce that includes volunteer, part-time, and full-time workers will be considered. The chapter will conclude by taking all four areas into account to offer an overview of what CED may look like in the future and what areas appear to be most important for stakeholders to consider going forward.

## How do coaches learn?

The study of "how coaches learn" has received increasing attention over the last two decades. A number of different foci can be identified, such as types of learning opportunities, learning preferences, coaching expertise development, types of knowledge, coach career development pathways, the learning process, or the impact of CED programmes. A full review of these topics is beyond the scope of this chapter (Cushion and Nelson, 2013; Lyle and Cushion, 2017; Trudel, Milestetd and Culver, 2020). Instead, we will summarise the key notions stemming from these varied approaches to researching coach learning and draw some conclusions and recommendations.

CED, similarly to other fields, has been influenced by contemporary theories of learning (i.e., constructivism and its many variations, social learning, etc.) and educational policy (i.e., the EQF) (European Commission, 2008). Perhaps the most significant change has been the move away from educational practices that were based on knowledge transfer and inputs (i.e., hours of learning, curriculum) to a learning outcomes and competence-based model. The latter emphasises the acquisition of not only knowledge but also the skills and attitudes required to perform the tasks of the job. This is reflected in reference documents such as the International and European Sport Coaching Frameworks (ICCE, ASOIF and LBU, 2013; Lara-Bercial *et al.*, 2017). To facilitate the work of those tasked with developing coaches, these documents define the core functions of the coach and the associated competencies required to fulfil a variety of coaching roles.

Another recent departure point for CED is the realisation that coaches learn from a variety of opportunities. These have been typically characterised as formal (Eshach, 2007) – follows a set curriculum, assessed, accredited; non-formal – outside of formal education, flexible curriculum, non-assessed, non-accredited, intentional; and informal – non-intentional, part of daily life. Moon (2004) offers an alternative classification by putting the focus on whether the learning is mediated or not. Mediated learning is facilitated by another person or a specific medium. In CED terms, it would incorporate courses and awards, clinics and seminars, e-learning, and formal mentoring. By contrast, unmediated learning is initiated by the learner who decides what is to be learnt and how and seeks information on the topic. Examples of this in coaching include observing other coaches, reading books on a particular subject, or casual conversations with other coaches. Finally, Moon also acknowledges the existence of "internal learning" through conscious (deliberate) as well as unconscious (incidental) reflection on our lived experiences.

Regardless of what classification we use, research has shown that coaches learn from a variety of opportunities and experiences (Lara-Bercial and Mallett, 2016; Stodter and Cushion, 2019). More importantly, the value they attach to each of these opportunities appears to be a function of personal preference and developmental stage. For instance, and paradoxically, formal education appears to be highly valued by successful high-performance coaches (Lara-Bercial and Mallett, 2016) and most useful to lay a foundation of knowledge for beginner coaches (Trudel, Culver and Werthner, 2013). By contrast, a variety of studies concluded that coaches favour non-formal and informal education over formal education as it is more grounded on personal needs and practical experience (Nelson, Cushion and Potrac, 2006; Mesquita, Isidro and Rosado, 2010). These preferences may also be influenced by the coaches' previous experiences as an athlete (Côté, Duffy and Erickson, 2013), their level of general education (Lara-Bercial and Mallett, 2016), and a variety of personal circumstances (i.e., time availability, external pressures, etc.) (Mesquita et al., 2010).

Therefore, no form of CED is better than another, but its effectiveness depends on how well it meets the needs of the specific coach at a particular point in time (Lyle and Cushion, 2017). Recent research into the actual process of coach learning has provided further evidence of this. In their study of youth football coaches, Stodter and Cushion (2017) found that coaches attending the same learning opportunity experienced completely different outcomes based on their previous knowledge, experiences, biographies, and practice/working contexts. These factors lead to the rejection, adoption, or adaptation of the new ideas and concepts they are exposed to in a variety of formal, non-formal, and informal opportunities. In sum, CED is not a one-size-fits-all solution and consideration of how CDs may account for this is required.

The understanding of CED as a highly individualised, context-bound, long-term process influenced by myriad internal and external factors presents a series of challenges. The two most significant ones include:

- The inability of the set curricula and standardised delivery typical of formal education to account for coaches' varying individual needs, stages of development, and working contexts
- The realisation that, in a way, coach development tends to effectively take place in the periods between episodes of formal education, and thus the need to re-conceptualise formal learning, increase the available offer of non-formal learning, and support coaches to maximise their learning throughout all these opportunities

Not an easy undertaking.

To meet this challenge, organisations and CDs are drawing on adult learning theory (Knowles, 1968; Lave and Wenger, 1991; Merriam, 2001; Jarvis, 2006) to shape CED in new and more effective ways. Some of the principles or strategies incorporated include problem-based learning, situated learning, reflection, mentoring or recognised prior learning. The implications of CED's transition towards these pedagogies on the role of CDs will be explored in the next section.

## The emerging role of coach developers

CDs have recently emerged as a significant factor in the evolution and improvement of coach education globally. Some countries, for example Ireland, the United Kingdom (UK), Canada, and Finland, have trained tutors or learning facilitators to deliver their CED programmes for over 20 years. In many other countries, however, coach education programmes have just tended to recruit subject matter experts to deliver their content knowledge. Whether that has been a successful coach describing their practical experiences, or a sport science expert teaching aspects of physiology, psychology, or biomechanics, the emphasis has been on knowledge transfer – providing information to coaches to expand their depth of understanding of key theories and practice principles.

Improved knowledge remains essential to learning and is the foundation of CED. However, the desire to close the gap between acquiring knowledge and its application has resulted in the emergence of the role of CDs and a shift from knowledge-based and instructor-centred strategies to application-focused and learner-centred approaches (Paquette and Trudel, 2018a and 2018b; Dohme, Rankin-Wright and Lara-Bercial, 2019).

The International Coach Developer Framework (ICDF) (ICCE ASOIF & LBU, 2014) describes the roles of CDs (p. 8):

> Coach developers are not simply experienced coaches or transmitters of coaching knowledge. They are trained to develop, support and challenge coaches to go on honing and improving their knowledge and skills to provide positive and effective sports experiences for all participants.

CDs should be first and foremost experts in learning and then have:

- Expertise in coaching and
- In either a stage of athlete development or
- A related discipline such as an aspect of sports science or medicine, coaching pedagogy, or technology

The umbrella term "coach developer" encompasses a range of roles and functions including:

- Facilitating
- Assessing
- Mentoring
- Programme design and evaluation
- Leadership and personal development

CDs respond to coaches' needs and the context in which they operate by providing and facilitating a range of formal and non-formal learning opportunities."

Stimulated by the publication of the ICDF, organisations realised that to enhance the effectiveness of their coaching programmes, they needed to address

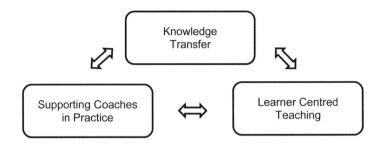

*Figure 1.1* Evolution of coach education and development and the role of the coach developer.

both how coaching courses were taught and how to help coaches apply the acquired knowledge to their coaching practice. This transition has been supported by an emerging body of literature within education showing the value of learner-centred and active learning methods in improving the application and transfer of knowledge (Weimer, 2013). As explained by Winfrey (2016, p. 132), "the teacher needs to understand what the students know and how they know it. Beginning with reality as the student views it, rather than from the teacher's perspective, provides the base from which a different and deeper reading of reality can develop".

With the above in mind, CED and the role of the CD can be said to have experienced an evolution towards a three-prong profile: knowledge transfer, learner-centred delivery, and in-practice support (Figure 1.1).

Supporting coaches in practice broadens the role of CDs beyond formal courses to assist coaches in the interpretation and application of their new learning and to help coaches practice the behaviours and approaches required to put the new learning into practice. This can include such activities as mentoring, practical observation of the coach and feedback on their practice, and organising informal learning situations like job shadowing or participating in another coach's training session. Elements of the learning programme can also be shifted from a course or workshop approach to on-the-job, in-situ learning where the coach is directly applying the knowledge in his or her work environment. Moreover, as coaching is becoming more professional, examples of CDs being hired by organisations and clubs to raise the quality of coaching and to be directly available to support the coaches in practice are emerging.

## Coach assessment

Another important issue in the evolution of CED and the emergence of CDs is the role of coach assessment. As the field transitions from knowledge transfer to problem-based learning and in-practice support, a few questions arise:

- What role does coach assessment play?
- How can we best determine if coaches have achieved the learning objectives set for a particular course?

- Can we certify that coaches who have completed a coaching course have achieved the required standard or competencies?
- And perhaps most importantly, do the coach assessment procedures contribute to or inhibit coach learning?

Research answering these questions in the CED field to help CDs design optimal coach assessment procedures is scarce. A wide variety of approaches is being used in different coach education programmes. These range from attendance with no assessment, to knowledge tests, to assessment of specified coaching competencies in practice, and any combination of the above.

Over the last two decades, there has been a global trend in education to move from input- to outcome-based education. Rather than focusing on knowledge transfer and hours of learning, the emphasis has shifted towards the development of competencies required to fulfil specific functions or jobs. In CED, programmes that have adopted a competency or outcomes-based methodology attempt to show that a coach, upon completion of the programme, can demonstrate the prescribed competencies and be certified as "competent" to fulfil a specific role. The course design process thus focuses not just on knowledge transfer but on what the coach can do with the knowledge – developing the specific skills for the coach to demonstrate competence.

Table 1.1 compares a traditional content-based programme with one designed to develop competencies.

However, two main concerns are often expressed about coach assessment. First, for adult learners, who have often been out of formal education for many years, assessment processes may be intimidating and discourage them from participating in coach education. This may be exacerbated in CED aimed at volunteer coaches. This concern has, for instance, prompted Sport New Zealand to make drastic changes to their coach education system. They have shifted the emphasis from formal competency assessment to lifelong learning with a "focus on continuous learning rather than formal accreditation" (Eade and Reid, 2015, p. 350).

This points to the second concern – whether the competency assessments being used are valid. Collins *et al.* (2014) argue that competency-based approaches face inherent limitations and are only valuable at the beginner coach stage and for the more basic roles. These limitations include the oversimplification of practice, a lack of relevance and ecological validity, a misinterpretation of the skills needed to be effective in the field, and a lack of focus on lifelong learning. They thus advocate for the consideration of an alternative expertise-based approach focused on the development of decision-making and professional judgement capacities and an understanding of the why of coaching, not only the what and how. This view is supported by recent research in the Canadian context wherein certified and uncertified coaches report that "perceiving the evaluation as rehearsed or artificial convinced some coaches that there is no noticeable difference between being certified and uncertified and that evaluation is not a true reflection of coaching ability" (Gurgis, Kerr and Stirling, 2020).

18 Sergio Lara-Bercial and John Bales

*Table 1.1* Comparison of Content-Based and Competence-Based Training

| *Content-based training* | | *Competence-based training* | |
|---|---|---|---|
| **Focuses on** | | **Focuses on** | |
| • Knowledge | | • Skills and behaviours | |
| • What people know | | • What people can do with what they know | |
| **Advantages** | **Disadvantages** | **Advantages** | **Disadvantages** |
| • Easier to deliver as knowledge can be presented to large numbers | • Assesses text book knowledge not application or ability to do the job | • Tailored to on-the-job needs (skills and behaviours) | • Time needed to identify required competences and under-pinning criteria |
| • Quicker and cheaper to access | • Assessment is pass or fail, latter requiring a complete re-sit | • Learner-focused and paced | • Assessment requires observed performance |
| | | • Encourages self-assessment rather than competition | • More costly and time consuming |
| | | • Learner is either competent or not yet competent | |
| | | • Multiple chances to prove competence | |
| | | • Appraisals linked to competence | |

Source: Crisfield (2015).

Despite the above concerns, the competency-based approach remains the most common assessment choice for many coach education programmes. Although there are multiple activities that can be used for a coach to demonstrate his or her competence (i.e., case studies, portfolios, knowledge tests), an observation of actual coaching practice is usually needed to assess several predetermined competencies. This involves a trained assessor using a competency checklist to observe the coach and judge whether the coach is "competent" or "not yet competent". The cost of such procedures in broad-based programmes can be prohibitive, creating a financial burden on the coach and resulting in the assessment often being comprised of a single or small number of observations of the coach by a single coach assessor.

Additional research into the validity of such processes, and whether this type of assessment is better used as a formative assessment – for learning – rather than summative – of learning, is required. The questions of how to assess and certify the competency of coaches and the impact of coach assessment on learning remain largely unanswered and present a significant challenge which CDs, with the assistance of coaching researchers, need to address.

## A volunteer workforce

Despite substantial progress in CED over the last two decades, the truth remains that in many countries and different sport, most coaches are non-remunerated volunteers (Rankin-Wright *et al.*, 2017; Lara-Bercial *et al.*, 2020). Volunteer coaches typically coach only a few hours a week and tend to stay in coaching for a limited period of time. They also have limited time to dedicate to learning and development. Perhaps unsurprisingly, these coaches may perceive CED as less important than their full- or part-time remunerated counterparts (Wiersma and Sherman, 2005). Moreover, those deploying volunteer coaches may also consider it less imperative to invest time and money developing this casual and transitory workforce. Therefore, national and international organisations have a challenge in increasing the demand for and attendance to CED opportunities for these sections of the coaching workforce. Several strategies are being implemented currently at different levels to ameliorate this issue.

From a regulatory perspective, an ever-growing number of countries have developed laws pertaining to coaching which define the role of the coach and the minimum requirements to be able to fulfil this role (Lara-Bercial *et al.*, 2020; Moustakas, Petry and Lara-Bercial, 2020). The attainment of a coaching qualification at a specific level, often aligned with the national qualifications framework, is now a prerequisite to become a coach in many countries (European Commission, 2020). In addition, national coaching lead organisations – tasked with regulating and developing coaching – and national sport federations have developed licensing systems whereby coaches require not only a qualification but also the acquisition of several continuous professional development credits on a regular basis to maintain their "active status" and thus be allowed to coach in regulated competitions. This regulatory approach has contributed to an increase in the number of qualified coaches, yet at times has become a barrier and even created resentment. Coaches have felt coerced into attending coaching qualifications and continuing professional development (CPD) that in some instances were expensive, difficult to access, not relevant, or low in quality (Nelson, Cushion and Potrac, 2006; Mesquita et al., 2010).

To solve some of these issues, alternative strategies have been proposed to increase the number of development opportunities available to coaches and to facilitate and encourage access. For example, in some national federations, there is a move towards a horizontal learning approach which, rather than trying to get coaches to complete lengthy and expensive coaching qualifications – vertical progression, encourages them to complete shorter, modular courses which over time may accumulate into a formal qualification – or not. This has proven particularly successful in encouraging coaches to develop at their current level of practice as opposed to progressing to the level above (i.e., from youth sport to professional sport). This shorter, modular nature also aids to solve some of the other identified issues. For instance, it lends itself better to allowing coaches to access these opportunities at a time of need and in a place that suits them – for instance online or in a blended manner that reduces financial and time pressures. Moreover, this also allows for the learning opportunity to become more relevant to the needs of the coaches and potentially to increase their actual and perceived quality.

Finally, a complementary strategy is the improvement in the positioning of coaching in the sport system. Recent research shows how in Europe there is a historical divide between East and West (Moustakas *et al.*, 2021). In the East, coaching has long been a fully regulated profession requiring high-level qualifications, and, as a result, coaches have enjoyed higher levels of recognition as well as expectation – albeit with a high emphasis on performance sport. By contrast, in many Western countries, coaching has traditionally been a volunteer activity and only recently has it come to the fore in terms of requirements to be a coach and the recognition coaches get – be it financial or social. Improving the positioning and recognition of coaching and the expectations placed upon coaches may be used to foster a sense of duty to participate in CED activities and a genuine desire to do so.

## Conclusions and future directions

This chapter has explored CED's past, present, and future. Sport coaching is a paradoxical occupation. Society is demanding coaches to fulfil ever more complex roles as both people developers and community anchors, yet the workforce is largely voluntary and on average holds low-level qualifications. Nonetheless, sport coaching is making substantial strides worldwide towards professionalisation, or at least towards what North and colleagues (2019) refer to as occupational improvement. This progress can be exemplified by the following trends:

- A move towards reality/problem-based learning which emphasises the transfer and generation of knowledge to the developing coach's practice
- The broadening of the CED offering to include not only traditional formal learning opportunities but also informal and non-formal ones
- The increased tailoring of the coach's learning pathway to their specific needs and stage of development rather than the use of "one size fits all" models
- The growing recognition of the CD as a central piece in the CED landscape and the acknowledgement that CDs must be identified, recruited, and developed according to the multiplicity of roles they play nowadays
- A realisation that there is a need to balance the use of competency and expertise-based approaches to coach assessment

In summary, CED is progressing, yet the difficulty of implementing the required changes within a largely volunteer workforce and within different national contexts and systems has been highlighted. The problem is complex and the solution multi-pronged. CED is still playing to catch up to the growing demands of society and the marketplace and to developments in adult learning theory and practice. The progressive regulation of the role in many countries – be it soft or hard – and the efforts to improve its social standing and recognition have, however, started to be prioritised.

## References

Busser, J. A. and Carruthers, C. P. (2010) 'Youth sport volunteer coach motivation', *Managing Leisure*,15, pp. 128–139.

Bradbury, S. (2013) 'Institutional racism, whiteness and the underrepresentation of minorities in leadership positions in football in Europe', *Soccer & Society*,14(3), pp. 296–314.

Collins, D. *et al.* (2014) 'The illusion of competency versus the desirability of expertise: Seeking a common standard for support professions in sport', *Sports Medicine*, 45, pp. 1–7.

Council of the European Union and the Representatives of Governments of Member States (2017a) *Conclusions of the council and of the representatives of the governments of the member states, meeting within the council, on the role of coaches in society.* Brussels: Council of the European Union.

Council of the European Union and the Representatives of Governments of Member States (2017b) *European Union work plan for sport 2017–2020.* Brussels: Council of the European Union.

Council of the European Union and the Representatives of Governments of Member States (2020) *Conclusions of the council and of the representatives of the governments of the member states meeting within the council on empowering coaches by enhancing opportunities to acquire skills and competences.* Brussels: Council of the European Union.

Côté, J., Erickson, K. and Duffy, P. (2013) 'Developing the expert performance coach', in Farrow, D., Baker J. and MacMahon, C. (eds.) *Developing elite sport performance: Lessons from theory and practice.* 2nd edn. New York, NY: Routledge, pp. 17–28.

Crisfield, P. (2015) *Learning programme design. Nippon Sport Science University Coach Developer Academy e-module 9.* Leeds: ICCE.

Cushion, C. and Nelson, L. (2013) 'Coach education and learning: Developing the field', in Potrac, P., Gilbert, W. and Denison, J. (eds.) *Routledge handbook of sport coaching.* London: Routledge, pp. 329–374.

Cuskelly, G. *et al.* (2006) 'Volunteer management practices and volunteer retention: A human resource management approach', *Sport Management Review*, 9, pp. 141–163.

Dohme, L., Rankin-Wright, A. and Lara-Bercial, S. (2019) 'Beyond knowledge transfer: The role of CDs as motivators for lifelong learning', *International Sport Coaching Journal*, 6, pp. 317–328.

Eade, A. and Reid, B. (2015) 'The role of the coach developer in supporting and guiding coach learning – a commentary', *International Sport Coaching Journal*, 2, pp. 350–351.

EOSE (2019) *European labour market and workforce development priorities for the sport and physical activity sector.* Brussels: European Observatoire of Sport Employment.

Eshach, H. (2007) 'Bridging in-school and out-of-school learning: formal, non-formal, and informal education', *Journal of Science Education and Technology*, 16(2), pp. 171–190.

European Commission (2008) *The European qualifications framework for lifelong learning.* Brussels: European Commission.

European Commission (2020) *Guidelines regarding the minimum requirements in skills and competences for coaches.* Brussels: European Commission.

Gurgis, J., Kerr, G. and Stirling, A. (2020) 'Investigating the barriers and facilitators to achieving coaching certification', *International Sport Coaching Journal*, 7, pp. 189–199.

International Council for Coaching Excellence (ICCE), the Association of Summer Olympic International Federations (ASOIF), and Leeds Beckett University (LBU) (2013) *International sport coaching framework, version 1.2.* Champaign, IL: Human Kinetics.

International Council for Coaching Excellence (ICCE), the Association of Summer Olympic International Federations (ASOIF), and Leeds Beckett University (LBU) (2014) *International coach developer framework.* Leeds: ICCE.

Jarvis, P. (2006) *Towards a comprehensive theory of human learning. Lifelong learning and the learning society, volume 1.* London: Routledge.

Knowles, M. S. (1968) 'Andragogy, not pedagogy', *Adult Leadership*, 16(10), pp. 350–352.

Lara-Bercial, S. and Mallett, C. J. (2016) 'The practices and developmental pathways of professional and Olympic serial winning coaches', *International Sport Coaching Journal*, 3(1), pp. 221–239.

Lara-Bercial, S. *et al.* (2017) *European Sport Coaching Framework.* Champaign, IL: Human Kinetics.

Lara-Bercial, S. *et al.* (2020) *The EU coaching landscape baseline report 2020: A report of project CoachForce21.* Leeds: Leeds Beckett University.

Lave, J. and Wenger, E. (1991) *Situated learning: Legitimate peripheral participation.* Cambridge: Cambridge University Press.

Lyle, J. and Cushion, C. (2017) *Sports coaching concepts: A framework for coaches' practice.* London: Routledge.

Merriam, S. B. (2001) 'Andragogy and self-directed learning: Pillars of adult learning theory', *New Directions for Adult and Continuing Education*, 89, pp. 3–13.

Mesquita, I., Isidro, S. and Rosado, A. (2010) 'Portuguese coaches' perceptions of and preferences for knowledge sources related to their professional background', *Journal of Sports Science and Medicine*, 9, pp. 480–489.

Moon, J. A. (2004) *A handbook of reflective and experiential learning: Theory and practice.* New York, NY: Routledge.

Moustakas, L. *et al.* (2021) The Sport Coaching System in the European Union: State of the Nation(s). *International Journal of Sport Policy and Politics.* Ahead of print. doi: 10.1080/19406940.2021.1987291

Moustakas, L., Petry, K. and Lara-Bercial, S. (2020) *Policy, education, knowledge in coaching (PEAK) research report.* Cologne: German Sport University.

Nelson, L. J., Cushion, C. J. and Potrac, P. (2006) 'Formal, nonformal and informal coach learning: A holistic conceptualisation', *International Journal of Sports Science & Coaching*, 1(3), pp. 247–259.

North, J. (2009) *The UK coaching workforce 2009–2016.* Leeds: Sports Coach UK.

North, J. *et al.* (2019) 'The professionalization of sport coaching', in Thelwell, R. and Dicks, M. (eds.) *Professional advances in sports coaching: Research and practice.* London: Routledge, pp. 3–21.

Paiement, C. (2007) 'Youth sport coaches: Factors that predict satisfaction with the coaching experience', *Research Quarterly for Exercise & Sport*, 78(1), pp. Axxvi–Axxviii.

Paquette, K. and Trudel, P. (2018a) 'Learner-centered coach education: Practical recommendations for coach development administrators', *International Sport Coaching Journal*, 5, pp. 169–175.

Paquette, K. and Trudel, P. (2018b) 'The evolution and learner-centered status of a coach education program', *International Sport Coaching Journal*, 5, pp. 24–36.

Rankin-Wright, A. J. *et al.* (2017) *Audit of the children's coaching workforce in seven European countries: An output of project iCoachKids*. Leeds: Leeds Beckett University.

Reade, I., Rodgers, W. and Norman, L. (2009) 'The under-representation of women in coaching: A comparison of male and female Canadian coaches at low and high levels of coaching', *International Journal of Sports Science & Coaching*, 4(4), pp. 505–520.

SASCOC (2012) *Sport for life: South African model for long-term participant development*. Johannesburg: SASCOC.

Sport Canada (2012) Canadian Sport Policy. Sport Canada: Ottawa. Available at https://sirc.ca/wp-content/uploads/files/content/docs/Document/csp2012_en.pdf (Accessed: 25 August 2020).

Sport England (2016) *Towards and active nation: Strategy 2016–2021*. London: Sport England.

Sport New Zealand (2020) *Every body active*. Wellington: Sport New Zealand.

Stodter, A. and Cushion, C. J. (2017) 'What works in coach learning, how, and for whom? A grounded process of soccer coaches' professional learning', *Qualitative Research in Sport, Exercise and Health*, 9(3), pp. 321–338.

Stodter, A. and Cushion, C. J. (2019) 'Evidencing the impact of coaches' learning: Changes in coaching knowledge and practice over time', *Journal of Sports Sciences*, 37(18), pp. 2086–2093.

Trudel, P., Culver, D. M. and Werthner, P. (2013) 'Looking at coach development from the coach-learner's perspective: Considerations for coach development administrators', in Potrac, P., Gilbert, W. and Denison, J. (eds.) *Routledge handbook of sport coaching*. London: Routledge, pp. 375–387.

Trudel, P., Milestetd, M. and Culver, D. M. (2020) 'What the empirical studies on sport coach education programs in higher education have to reveal: A review', *International Sport Coaching Journal*, 7(1), pp. 61–73.

UNESCO (2016) *The power of sport values*. Paris: UNESCO Publishing.

Weimer, M. (2013) *Learner-centered teaching – Five key changes to practice*. 2nd edn. San Francisco, CA: Jossey-Bass.

Wiersma, L. D. and Sherman, C. P. (2005) 'Volunteer youth sport coaches' perspectives of coaching education/certification and parental codes of conduct', *Research Quarterly for Exercise and Sport*, 76(3), pp. 324–338.

Winfrey, N. (2016) 'Where do we go from here?', *Adult Learning*, 27(3), pp. 131–133.

Chapter 2

# International sport management education

## Curricula, trends, and challenges

*Thomas Giel, Rei Yamashita, Daryousch Argomand, and Kirstin Hallmann*

### Introduction

Early sport managers used to have some background in sport or business and they mostly learned from experience gained in the industry (Crosset and Hums, 2015). As sport managers today need knowledge of sport and business as well as the ability to apply management functions in sports contexts (Baker and Esherick, 2013; Babiak, Heinze and Thibault, 2019), Pitts and Zhang (2017) claim specialised academic preparation as essential for future sport managers. Thus, sport managers require a systematic and formal sport management education (Gregg, Pitts and Pedersen, 2019). In order to meet the demand for well-trained sport managers, sport management as an academic field and sport management curricula were developed (Crosset and Hums, 2015). The Ohio University's master's degree programme from 1966 is considered the first sport management curriculum as a systematic educational path (Baker and Esherick, 2013; Pedersen and Thibault, 2019).

Sport management research and education are discussed worldwide at (bi) annual conferences of one global and six continental academic associations, founded from the 1980s onwards (Crosset and Hums, 2015; Pitts and Zhang, 2017). The associations' objective is to drive and develop sport management, provide platforms of scientific cooperation, and offer educational services. Students can participate in seminars and workshops, be part of the community networks, and attend the associations' conferences (EASM, 2020; NASSM, 2020b; SMAANZ, 2020). Thus, sport management education is constantly evaluated by the associations' activities to meet the needs of the globalised sports industry. Education is becoming increasingly sophisticated for aspiring sport managers (Miragaia and Soares, 2017; Pedersen and Thibault, 2019). As education in sport management also became more important outside the university context, sport federations, for instance, started offering further training and specialised certificates either independently or cooperating with universities. This branch of sport management education is further explored in Chapter 8 of this book.

The current chapter presents the status quo of sport management education by mapping out core areas of sport management degree programmes from different

DOI: 10.4324/9781003002666-4

continents. Building on that, current trends, developments, and challenges are discussed, and potential topics for future sport management education curricula are suggested.

## Sport management degree programmes

As the sports industry grows, sports organisations become more market-driven (Crosset and Hums, 2015; Pedersen and Thibault, 2019). Consequently, the number of sport management degree programmes has increased worldwide (Floyd Jones, Brooks and Mak, 2008; Baker et al., 2017; Miragaia and Soares, 2017; NASSM, 2020a). Albeit several attempts to standardise sport management education (Parkhouse, 1987; NASPE-NASSM Joint Task Force, 1993; Cingiene et al., 2006; COSMA, 2016; DeLuca and Braunstein-Minkove, 2016), the curricula of sport management degree programmes vary among universities (Baker et al., 2017). For instance, the NASPE-NASSM Joint Task Force (1993) on Sport Management Curriculum and Accreditation researched curricula and consulted academics, practitioners, and professional associations to evaluate core components.

Petry, Froberg and Madella (2006) focused on analysing and comparing European university programmes and developed model curriculum structures for different sports programmes, including a chapter on sport management authored by Cingiene et al. (2006). Although recommendations already exist, examining the content of sport management degree programmes remains relevant: "a comparison across several countries is [...] important to understand the evolution of sport management in different contexts" (Miragaia and Soares, 2017, p. 13). Table 2.1 presents the identified core components (NASPE-NASSM Joint Task Force, 1993; Cingiene et al., 2006) of selected sport management degree programmes from six continents exemplarily.

All examined sport management degree programmes offer an introduction to sport management in modules such as managing sports organisations, leadership in sport, sports administration, or general (strategic) management. Additionally, to management applied to sport, law/legal aspects, (sports) marketing, (sports) finance, and (sport) economics are often considered as fundamental areas of sport management (NASPE-NASSM Joint Task Force, 1993; Cingiene et al., 2006; Baker and Esherick, 2013; Pedersen and Thibault, 2019). Knowledge in these areas combined with the affiliated skills and abilities is needed to be competitive and suitable for the sports industry (Baker and Esherick, 2013; Masteralexis, Barr and Hums, 2015; Pitts and Zhang, 2017). Most degree programmes include modules relating to those components. In contrast, a different pattern becomes evident when assessing the prevalence of the modules in ethics, sociological aspects, and field experience. Although recommended as core components (NASPE-NASSM Joint Task Force, 1993; Cingiene et al., 2006), these modules are integrated only by a few degree programmes. For example, field experiences or internships mainly accumulate in North American degree programmes (within the limited selected sample).

*Table 2.1* Corresponding Modules of Current Sport Management Master's Degree Programmes Worldwide Compared to Recommended Curricula and Core Contents for Sport Management Master's Degree Programmes

| Continent | University (country) | Degree programme's name (specialisation) | ItSM | RM | LAW | SMK | SF/SE | Ethics | SOC | FIELD |
|---|---|---|---|---|---|---|---|---|---|---|
| Africa | Kenyatta University (Kenya) | Recreation and Sport Management | ✓ | ✓ | ✓ | × | × | ✓ | × | × |
| Asia | University of Tsukuba (Japan) | Sport and Olympic Studies | ✓ | ✓ | × | ✓ | ✓ | × | ✓ | ✓ |
| | Waseda University (Japan) | Sport Science (Sport Management) | ✓ | ✓ | × | ✓ | ✓ | ✓ | ✓ | × |
| | Seoul National University (South Korea) | Global Sport Management | (✓) | (✓) | (✓) | (✓) | (✓) | (✓) | × | × |
| | Kasetsart University (Thailand) | Sports Management | ✓ | ✓ | (✓) | ✓ | ✓ | × | × | (✓) |
| Europe | German Sport University Cologne (Germany) | Sport Management | ✓ | ✓ | ✓ | ✓ | ✓ | × | ✓ | × |
| | Russian International Olympic University (Russia) | Sport Administration | ✓ | ✓ | × | ✓ | ✓ | × | × | ✓ |
| | Loughborough University (the United Kingdom) | Sport Management | ✓ | ✓ | ✓ | ✓ | ✓ | × | × | × |
| | The International Centre for Sport Studies (the United Kingdom, Italy, Switzerland) | FIFA Master – Management, Law and Humanities of Sport | ✓ | ✓ | ✓ | ✓ | ✓ | ✓ | × | × |
| North America | University of Windsor (Canada) | Human Kinetics (Sport Management) | ✓ | ✓ | ✓ | ✓ | × | × | ✓ | ✓ |
| | Ohio University (the United States) | Sports Administration | ✓ | × | ✓ | ✓ | ✓ | × | × | ✓ |
| | University of Massachusetts (the United States) | Sport Management | ✓ | (✓) | ✓ | ✓ | ✓ | × | ✓ | ✓ |
| | University of South Florida (the United States) | Sport and Entertainment Management | ✓ | × | ✓ | ✓ | ✓ | ✓ | ✓ | ✓ |

*(Continued)*

| Continent | University (country) | Degree programme's name (specialisation) | ItSM | RM | LAW | SMK | SF/SE | Ethics | SOC | FIELD |
|---|---|---|---|---|---|---|---|---|---|---|
| Oceania | Deakin University (Australia) | Master of Business (Sport Management) | ✓ | (✓) | ✓ | ✓ | ✓ | × | × | (✓) |
| | Griffith University (Australia) | Master of Business (Sport Management) | ✓ | (✓) | × | × | (✓) | × | × | (✓) |
| | La Trobe University (Australia) | Master of Management (Sport Management) | ✓ | (✓) | ✓ | ✓ | ✓ | × | × | × |
| | Auckland University of Technology (New Zealand) | Master of Business (Sport Leadership and Management) | ✓ | ✓ | × | ✓ | × | × | × | × |
| South America | Nove de Julho University (Brazil) | Sports Administration | ✓ | (✓) | × | ✓ | × | × | × | × |
| | University of Externado (Colombia) | Communication and Sport Management | ✓ | ✓ | ✓ | ✓ | ✓ | × | ✓ | × |

Notes: ✓ = module is part of the degree programme; (✓) = contents are included in some module(s) or available as elective; × = content is not part of the degree programme in form of a module, a course, or an elective; Modules: ItSM = Introduction to Sport Management, RM = Research Methods, LAW = Legal Aspects; SMK = Sport Marketing; SF/SE = Sport Finance/Sport Economics; SOC = Sociological Aspects; FIELD = Field experience or internship.

The inclusion of a research methods module in the curriculum is dependent on the type of degree. While most business-oriented degree programmes, like a Master of Business Administration, offer research methods as one course within a module or as a small module, more research-oriented degree programmes, such as a Master of Science, tend to include more than one research-related module. However, research methods are part of almost every degree programme in the limited selected sample. This finding relates to the competencies required in the work environment a graduate aspires, including evidence-based decision-making, developing and gathering relevant knowledge, and thinking critically (Agha, Dixon and Dwyer, 2019; Andrew, Pedersen and McEvoy, 2020).

In addition to university-based education, some countries also offer non-university education in sport management, including the dual education system of vocational training. Particularly in German-speaking countries, vocational training is not only on-the-job training, but it also combines theory in vocational schools with the real-life working environment in organisations (Federal Ministry of Education and Research, 2020). In Germany, for instance, the Chamber of Commerce and Industry offers a three-year vocational training in cooperation with different sports organisations to become a management assistant for sport and fitness (IHK, 2020). The vocational training aims to prepare the sports administration trainees, including programming and scheduling, accounting and controlling, general management, marketing, and human resources management for occupations in sports associations, sports clubs, or fitness companies. The vocational training is rather practice-oriented and focuses on teaching operation management. Additionally to the teaching, vocational training offers a practical component. Trainees work in a sports organisation where they apply academic learning outcomes. This includes advising and supporting customers as well as taking on administrative tasks (IHK, 2020).

## Trends and challenges in sport management

### Sustainability and social responsibility

The United Nations (UN) announced the "Sustainable Development Goals" (SDGs) in 2015. They are considered as a blueprint to achieve a better and more sustainable future for all by 2030. Consisting of 169 targets and 17 goals, these SDGs cover poverty, inequality, climate change, environmental degradation, peace, and justice.

The UN outlined an overview of what sport can do to create a sustainable society:

> Sport is also an important enabler of sustainable development. We recognise the growing contribution of sport to the realisation of development and peace in its promotion of tolerance and respect and the contributions it makes to

the empowerment of women and young people, individuals and communities as well as to health, education and social inclusion objectives.

(UNOSDP, 2016, p. 2)

Nowadays, international sport federations are looking into how they fill their social roles. The International Olympic Committee (IOC) announced its sustainability strategy in the Olympic Agenda 2020 (IOC, 2014) and its Sustainability Report includes 18 objectives (IOC, 2018). The Fédération Internationale de Football Association (FIFA) documented official sustainability reports from the latest World Cups in Russia 2018 and France 2019 for the men's and the women's tournament respectively (FIFA World Cup France 2019, 2018; FIFA World Cup Russia 2018, 2015). In the 2022 Qatar report, four core sustainability areas, namely human, social, environmental, and economic development, are presented (FIFA World Cup Qatar 2022, 2019).

The Tokyo Organising Committee of the Olympic and Paralympic Games (TOCOG) is also taking sustainability trends into account in their action plans. For the Tokyo 2020 Games (hosted in 2021), the basic principle is that "sport has the power to change the world and our future" and to "showcase a model of sustainable society which humankind pursues and work integrally on sustainability challenges" (TOCOG, 2018, p. 2). Toyota, a Japanese automobile manufacturer and one of The Olympic Partner (TOP) sponsors of the IOC, will bring various mobility forms to the Tokyo 2020 Games that enable transporting attendees, including staff and visitors. They will introduce electric vehicles to reduce the environmental burden of the Games (Toyota, 2019).

International sport federations as well as professional sports teams and organisations take their stance regarding sustainability and social responsibility. For example, the Arizona Diamondbacks, a professional Major League Baseball team, donated nine tons of leftovers from the stadium concession to the locals to prevent food loss. They also introduced hand dryers instead of paper towels in the washrooms, reducing about 600 kilometres of paper (Shimbun, 2018). Another example is the Mercedes-Benz Stadium located in Atlanta, Georgia, which uses approximately 4,000 solar panels, annually creating the energy to host ten National Football League games (Mercedes-Benz Stadium, 2017; Shimbun, 2018). The sports goods manufacturer Adidas aims to reduce and replace cotton to 100% with sustainable cotton. They are working on a new supply chain using ocean plastic waste only for shoes and clothing until 2024 (Adidas, 2019). According to Forbes (2019), Adidas produced one million pairs of shoes made from ocean waste in 2017 and this number increased to 11 million pairs in 2019.

These trends in the industry should be reflected in sport management education. One example for the potential focus of sustainability modules in sport management curricula is introduced through the findings of Trail and McCullough (2020). They found no guidelines for sports organisations on how to increase consumers' awareness of sustainable activities in general. To fill this gap, Trail and McCullough (2020) introduced the "Sport Sustainability Campaign Evaluation

Model" that helps sports organisations evaluate their campaign based on a range of dimensions such as activation, motivation, or attitudes and engage their fans and participants in developing environmental sustainability. Future sport managers need to be aware of these issues and need to know how to address them, how to assess sustainability, and, in this specific context, sustainability campaigns.

### Digitalisation

Another trend within the sports business industry – like in every other industry – relates to new technologies. Digitalisation, robotics, and the use of large volumes of data have led to increasing demand for sports analytics, business intelligence in sport, and artificial intelligence in sport (Fried and Mumcu, 2017b; Ratten and Dickson, 2020). Digitalisation has changed commerce within a brick-and-mortar environment to e-commerce using various platforms (Yrjölä et al., 2017). Thereby, institutionalised trust is crucial for experienced and inexperienced consumers alike when purchasing products from unfamiliar vendors (Stouthuysen et al., 2018).

Data have always been used in the sports industry, particularly to understand performance and its outcomes (Fried and Mumcu, 2017a). The development of sports apps creates new data, real-time data on social media, and advanced informatics availability provides new opportunities for the sports business (Ratten and Usmanij, 2020). As statistics and analytics offer insights into competitive practices and facilitate decision-making, they are essential for the sports industry (Ratten and Dickson, 2020). This includes areas such as marketing, finance, performance, talent analysis, or facility management. Multiple sources of information are used as part of business intelligence to accumulate knowledge and integrate different perspectives (Ratten and Dickson, 2020).

Moreover, combining humans and machines' power can increase business performance (Daugherty and Wilson, 2018). A systematic literature review in the tourism and hospitality industry has revealed that research on the use of robots is increasing – though there is still a focus on engineering (Ivanov et al., 2019). The human-robot interaction happens at the "servicescape" (Ivanov et al., 2019), which is also important for the sports business industry. Consumer behaviour changes due to technological advancements and, therefore, business intelligence. This offers insights into the changes in the market, which is essential for sports organisations (Ratten and Dickson, 2020).

Advantages of robotics, artificial intelligence, and service automation technologies include services offered around the clock, a high and constant level of service quality, and doing routine work repeatedly (Ivanov, 2019). The drawbacks of using these technologies include a lack of a creative and personal approach (Ivanov, 2019).

There are several conclusions for sport management education relating to digitalisation and data use. Data literacy should be a core element of degree programmes. Future decision-makers need to know how to derive value from data and how data can inform evidence-based decisions (Fried and Mumcu, 2017a). Using data also helps decision-makers manage the organisation more efficiently and create competitive advantages (Mumcu, 2017). Therefore, exercises where students can learn quantitative analytical skills should be incorporated into degree programmes (Ratten and Usmanij, 2020). This could be achieved through a Business Analytics module or more credits awarded for statistical competencies seminars.

Moreover, digital fandom and eSport are becoming more popular (Ratten and Dickson, 2020). Business knowledge in these areas is important for future graduates and should be added to management and/or marketing degree programmes as seminars, papers, or entire modules. Finally, electives in robotics or machine learning could offer new insights and a crucial skillset for graduates.

### *Internationalisation and intercultural management*

According to sport management experts, digitalisation is also a key driver for the trend of internationalisation (Wohlfart and Adam, 2019), which can be regarded as an effect of globalisation (Baker *et al.*, 2017). Over several European countries, almost three out of four experts in the sport management labour market (73%) assume that internationalisation already affects their working area or will do so in the future (Wohlfart and Adam, 2019). Also, a systematic review of research topics and trends in higher education in sport management identified globalisation and internationalisation to belong to these relevant research themes (Miragaia and Soares, 2017).

People in general and particularly students are more and more interconnected through technological advancements, having permanent access to the internet, which is also true for sport (Miragaia and Soares, 2017; Pitts and Zhang, 2017). It is easily possible to follow sports competitions worldwide or order sports goods from companies abroad online. Especially sports clubs and sports corporations increasingly operate on an international scale and perceive internationalisation as necessary to remain competitive in the sports market (Wohlfart and Adam, 2019). Besides international sport federations such as the FIFA or the IOC, which are operating worldwide, also national sports leagues include large numbers of foreign players and, at times, clubs and franchises in professional leagues belong to foreign owners and league matches are hosted abroad (Baker *et al.*, 2017). The influence of cultural variables on communication styles and purchasing behaviour should, therefore, not be underestimated.

However, internationalisation benefits sport to remain competitive or to approach new target groups (Wohlfart and Adam, 2019), but sport can also be seen as a universal language facilitating human interactions and communications while promoting intercultural understanding within and across cultures (Baker *et al.*, 2017). Intercultural communication is of growing importance when societies are not only defined by national and geographic borders anymore and in which sport management students can study international degree programmes abroad (Miragaia and Soares, 2017). As national cultures still affect every citizen, including researchers, teachers, and students, management practices are often culturally dependent and what works in one country or culture does not necessarily work in another as well (Hofstede, 1997).

A lack of awareness or competency in terms of intercultural management might cause problems for organisations. Toyota gives a good example of intercultural marketing. The brand adapted its car name "MR2" to "MR" in France because otherwise it would create negative associations in the French language (Thomas, Kinast and Schroll-Machl, 2010). Similar things also occur in sport: Real Madrid adapted its logo on some merchandising sold in some countries in the Middle East in a way that it is not featuring the traditional Christian cross (Corrigan, 2017). Hofstede (1997) identified five distinct cultural dimensions: power distance, individualism, masculinity, uncertainty avoidance, and long-term orientation, distinguishing national cultures from each other. As the interaction with stakeholders from different cultures in the global marketplace is a key aspect of modern management, there is a need to incorporate intercultural communication into sport management curricula.

Many universities already realised the relevance of internationalisation and tried to provide international perspectives for their students, preparing them for globalised markets and supporting them in becoming global citizens (Danylchuk, 2011; Danylchuk et al., 2015). As a result of the increasing globalisation of sport, internationalisation needs to be reflected in sport management education, ensuring that research and teaching incorporate global perspectives and diverse international topics (Danylchuk, 2011; Miragaia and Soares, 2017). Sport managers must understand that sport is often strongly connected to the cultural background of the respective nation and that specific types of sport are of diverse importance around the world. Additionally, they need to be aware of the different international sport systems, their peculiarities, and their consequences for both, the grassroots sport as well as the professional sport.

Furthermore, at least some of the sport management courses should be offered in English as it is the dominant international language used in sports organisations (Wohlfart and Adam, 2019), especially since the language and cultural differences in learning are primary challenges among international graduate students in sport management (Danylchuk et al., 2015). As sport itself is internationalised, sport management students need to be(come) aware of the consequences of globalisation for sport. Students need to develop intercultural competence and knowledge in intercultural communication to increase their career opportunities and cope with the global marketplace.

### Integrity and good governance

Good governance can be defined as "ethically informed standards of managerial behaviour" (Henry and Lee, 2004, p. 25). In recent years, particularly representatives of large international sport federations had to face accusations or even

International sport management education    33

investigations of corruptive behaviour. Consequently, the European Commission has identified the integrity of sport as a major threat in Europe. It is one of three main areas of activity of the responsible Directorate General for Youth, Sport, Education, and Culture in sport (European Commission, 2020). Future sport managers must understand the key principles of good governance and their relevance to apply them in their future job. Generally, there are seven principles of good organisational governance: transparency, accountability, democracy, responsibility, equity, effectiveness, and efficiency (Henry and Lee, 2004).

Evidence suggests that corruption exists in sport (Manoli, Antonopoulos and Bairner, 2019), which might also resemble the general lack of integrity existent in society (Manoli, Bandura and Downward, 2020). However, the lack of integrity in sport influences neither active nor passive sports participation (yet) (Manoli, Bandura and Downward, 2020). Nonetheless, knowledge of good governance, integrity, and how to run sports organisations sustainably should be part of the curriculum of seminars or papers relating to sports organisations' management.

## Conclusion

While a "learning by doing"-approach characterised early sport managers, gradually more sport management degree programmes were offered, reflecting the growing importance of a profound education in sport management. Nowadays, various degree programmes exist with some congruent contents across the programmes and partial heterogeneity in their curricula. In addition to that, the sport management degree programmes can establish their specific unique selling points and concrete approaches in sport management education. The heterogeneity in education reflects the diversity of career opportunities in the sports business industry available for graduates in sport management. The growing demands for sustainability, business intelligence, internationalisation, and integrity require sport management education to reflect these trends and challenges affecting the sports industry. While challenging, it is important to proactively follow sport management trends and include them in the curriculum. One strategy to foster such a proactive approach might be implementing accreditation processes every couple of years to discuss and critically reflect the overall alignment of the respective sport management degree programme.

## References

Adidas (2019) *Adidas to Produce More Shoes Using Recycled Plastic Waste 2019*. Available at: https://www.adidas-group.com/en/media/news-archive/press-releases/2019/adidas-to-produce-more-shoes-using-recycled-plastic-waste/ (Accessed: 31 January 2021).

Agha, N., Dixon, J. C. and Dwyer, B. (2019) 'Sport management research', in Pedersen, P. M. and Thibault, L. (eds.) *Contemporary sport management*. Champaign, IL: Human Kinetics, pp. 442–462.

Andrew, D. P. S., Pedersen, P. M. and McEvoy, C. D. (2020) 'Research methods and design', *in Sport management*. Champaign, IL: Human Kinetics.

Babiak, K., Heinze, K. and Thibault, L. (2019) 'Management concepts and practice in sport organizations', in Pedersen, P. M. and Thibault, L. (eds.) *Contemporary sport management*. Champaign, IL: Human Kinetics, pp. 70–93.

Baker, R. E. *et al.* (2017) 'Internationalized sport management education: Bridging the gaps', in Pitts, B. and Zhang, J. J. (eds.) *Global sport management. Contemporary issues and inquiries*. Oxford, New York, NY: Routledge, pp. 18–37.

Baker, R. E. and Esherick, C. (2013) *Fundamentals of sport management*. Champaign, IL: Human Kinetics.

Cingiene, V. *et al.* (2006) 'Curriculum model development – sport management', in Petry, K., Froberg, K. and Madella, A. (eds.) *Thematic network project AEHESIS report of the third year*. Cologne: Institute of European Sport Development and Leisure Studies, German Sport University Cologne, pp. 171–200.

Corrigan, D. (2017) *Real Madrid Remove Cross from Club Crest in Middle Eastern Clothing Deal*. Available at: https://www.espn.com/soccer/real-madrid/story/3045880/real-madrid-remove-cross-from-club-crest-in-middle-eastern-clothing-deal (Accessed: 31 January 2021).

COSMA (2016) *About Cosma*. Available at: https://www.cosmaweb.org/accreditation-manuals.html (Accessed: 31 January 2021).

Crosset, T. W. and Hums, M. A. (2015) 'History of sport management', in Masteralexis, L. P., Barr, C. A. and Hums, M. A. (eds.) *Principles and practice of sport management*. Sudbury: Jones & Bartlett Learning, pp. 3–26.

Danylchuk, K. (2011) 'Internationalizing ourselves: Realities, opportunities, and challenges', *Journal of Sport Management*, 25(1), pp. 1–10. doi: 10.1123/jsm.25.1.1.

Danylchuk, K. *et al.* (2015) 'Supervising international graduate students in sport management: Perspectives of experienced advisors', *Sport Management Education Journal*, 9, pp. 51–65. doi: 10.1123/SMEJ.2014-0006.

Daugherty, P. R. and Wilson, J. H. (2018) *Human + machine. Reimagining work in the age of AI*. Harvard: Harvard Business Press.

DeLuca, J. and Braunstein-Minkove, J. (2016) 'An evaluation of sport management student preparedness: Recommendations for adapting curriculum to meet industry needs', *Sport Management Education Journal*, 10, pp. 1–12. doi: 10.1123/SMEJ.2014-0027.

EASM (2020) *Student Seminar*. Available at: https://www.easm.net/student-seminar/ (Accessed: 31 January 2021).

European Commission (2020) *About Sport Policy*. Available at: https://ec.europa.eu/sport/policy_en (Accessed: 31 January 2021).

Federal Ministry of Education and Research (2020) *Education: The German Vocational Training System*. Available at: https://www.bmbf.de/en/the-german-vocational-training-system-2129.html (Accessed: 31 January 2021).

FIFA World Cup France 2019 (2018) *Sustainability Strategy "Dare to shine" on All Fronts*. Available at: https://resources.fifa.com/image/upload/sustainability-strategy-for-the-fifa-women-s-world-cup-france-2019.pdf?cloudid=r2sks010xbbqhhobnkql (Accessed: 31 January 2021).

FIFA World Cup Qatar 2022 (2019) *Sustainability Strategy*. Available at: https://resources.fifa.com/image/upload/fifa-world-cup-qatar-2022tm-sustainability-strategy.pdf?cloudid=p2axokh26lzaafloutgs (Accessed: 31 January 2021).

FIFA World Cup Russia 2018 (2015) *Sustainability Strategy*. Available at: https://resources. fifa.com/image/upload/sustainability-strategy-for-the-2018-fifa-world-cup-2666950.pdf?-cloudid=h0ysulsujvogspqmnbhl (Accessed: 31 January 2021).

Floyd Jones, D., Brooks, D. D. and Mak, J. Y. (2008) 'Examining sport management programs in the United States', *Sport Management Review*, 11(1), pp. 77–91. doi: 10.1016/S1441-3523(08)70104-9.

Forbes (2019) *Adidas Challenges the Fashion Industry in Sustainability, Pledging Only Recycled Plastic by 2024*. Available at: https://www.forbes.com/sites/pamdanziger/2019/07/18/adidas-challenges-the-fashion-industry-in-sustainability-pledging-only-recycled–plastic-by-2024/#4501cc071049 (Accessed: 31 January 2021).

Fried, G. and Mumcu, C. (2017a) 'Introduction', in Fried, G. and Mumcu, C. (eds.) *Sport analytics. A data-driven approach to sport business and management*. Oxford, New York, NY: Routledge, pp. 1–14.

Fried, G. and Mumcu, C. (2017b) *Sport analytics. A data-driven approach to sport business and management*. Oxford, New York, NY: Routledge.

Gregg, E. A., Pitts, B. and Pedersen, P. M. (2019) 'Historical aspects of the sport business industry', in Pedersen, P. M. and Thibault, L. (eds.) *Contemporary sport management*. Champaign, IL: Human Kinetics, pp. 50–69.

Henry, I. & Lee, P. C. (2004) Governance and ethics in sport. In J. Beech & S. Chadwick (Eds.), *The Business of Sport Management* (pp. 25–42). Pearson Education.

Hofstede, G. (1997) 'Organization culture', in *The IBM handbook of organizational behavior*, pp. 193–210.

IHK (2020) *Sport- und Fitnesskaufmann/-frau [Management Assistant for Sports and Fitness]*. Available at: https://www.ihk-koeln.de/Sport_und_Fitnesskaufmann__frau.AxCMS (Accessed: 31 January 2021).

IOC (2014) Olympic Agenda 2020 - 20+20 Recommendations. Available at: https://stillmed. olympic.org/Documents/Olympic_Agenda_2020/Olympic_Agenda_2020-20-20_Recommendations-ENG.pdf (Accessed: 06 December 2021).

IOC (2018) *IOC Sustainability Report – Sharing Progress on Our 2020 Objectives*. Available at: https://stillmed.olympic.org/media/Document%20Library/OlympicOrg/IOC/What-We-Do/celebrate-olympic-games/Sustainability/IOC%20Sustainability %20Report_Final%20Rev1.pdf #_ga=2.63589615. 1161813183.1591695721-236760653. 1588319092 (Accessed: 31 January 2021).

Ivanov, S. (2019) 'Ultimate transformation: How will automation technologies disrupt the travel, tourism and hospitality industries?', *Zeitschrift für Tourismuswissenschaft*, 11(1), pp. 25–43. doi: 10.1515/tw-2019-0003.

Ivanov, S. *et al.* (2019) 'Progress on robotics in hospitality and tourism: A review of the literature', *Journal of Hospitality and Tourism Technology*, 10(4), pp. 489–521. doi: 10.1108/JHTT-08-2018-0087.

Manoli, A. E., Antonopoulos, G. A. and Bairner, A. (2019) 'The inevitability of corruption in Greek football', *Soccer & Society*, 20(2), pp. 199–215. doi: 10.1080/14660970.2017.1302936.

Manoli, A. E., Bandura, C. and Downward, P. (2020) 'Perceptions of integrity in sport: Insights into people's relationship with sport', *International Journal of Sport Policy and Politics*, 12(2), pp. 207–220. doi: 10.1080/19406940.2020.1747101.

Masteralexis, L. P., Barr, C. A. and Hums, M. A. (2015) *Principles and practice of sport management*. 5th edn. Sudbury: Jones & Bartlett Learning.

Mercedes-Benz Stadium (2017) *4,000+ Georgia Power Solar Panels in Place at Mercedes-Benz Stadium.* Available at: https://mercedesbenzstadium.com/4000-georgia-power-solar-panels-place-mercedes-benz-stadium/ (Accessed: 31 January 2021).

Miragaia, D. and Soares, J. (2017) 'Higher education in sport management: A systematic review of research topics and trends', *Journal of Hospitality, Leisure, Sport & Tourism Education*, 21, pp. 101–116. doi: 10.1016/j.jhlste.2017.09.001.

Mumcu, C. (2017) 'An introduction to analytics and data', in Fried, G. and Mumcu, C. (eds.) *Sport analytics. A data-driven approach to sport business and management.* Oxford, New York, NY: Routledge, pp. 17–32.

NASPE-NASSM Joint Task Force (1993) 'Standards for curriculum and voluntary accreditation of sport management education programs', *Journal of Sport Management*, 7(2), pp. 159–170.

NASSM (2020a) *Academic Programs.* Available at: https://nassm.com/Programs/AcademicPrograms (Accessed: 26 February 2020).

NASSM (2020b) *Student Services.* Available at: https://www.nassm.com/StudentServices (Accessed: 31 January 2021).

Parkhouse, B. L. (1987) 'Sport management curricula: Current status and design implications for future development', *Journal of Sport Management*, 1, pp. 93–115.

Pedersen, P. M. and Thibault, L. (2019) 'Managing sport', in Pedersen, P. M. and Thibault, L. (eds.) *Contemporary sport management.* Champaign, IL: Human Kinetics, pp. 4–29.

Petry, K., Froberg, K. and Madella, A. (2006) *Thematic network project AEHESIS report of the third year.* Cologne: Institute of European Sport Development and Leisure Studies, German Sport University Cologne.

Pitts, B. G. and Zhang, J. J. (2017) 'Introduction. The WASM Foundation Stone', in Pitts, B. and Zhang, J. J. (eds.) *Global sport management. contemporary issues and inquiries.* Oxford, New York, NY: Routledge, pp. 3–17.

Ratten, V. and Dickson, G. (2020) 'Big data and business intelligence in sport', in Ratten, V. and Hayduk, T. (eds.) *Big data and business intelligence in sport.* Oxford, New York, NY: Routledge, pp. 25–35.

Ratten, V. and Usmanij, P. (2020) 'Statistical modelling and sport business analytics', in Ratten, V. and Hayduk, T. (eds.) *Statistical modelling and sports business analytics.* Oxford, New York, NY: Routledge, pp. 1–9.

Shimbun, A. (2018) なぜスポーツに持続可能性? *[Why Sustainability in Sports?].* Available at: https://www.asahi.com/articles/ASL7N3Q09L7NUTQP00C.html (Accessed: 31 January 2021).

SMAANZ (2020) *SMAANZ HDR STUDENTS.* Available at: http://smaanz.org/students/ (Accessed: 31 January 2021).

Stouthuysen, K. *et al.* (2018) 'Initial trust and intentions to buy: The effect of vendor-specific guarantees, customer reviews and the role of online shopping experience', *Electronic Commerce Research and Applications*, 27, pp. 23–38. doi: 10.1016/j.elerap.2017.11.002.

Thomas, A., Kinast, E.-U. and Schroll-Machl, S. (2010) *Handbook of intercultural communication and cooperation.* 2nd edn. Goettingen, Oakville: Vandenhoeck & Ruprecht.

TOCOG (2018) Tokyo 2020. *Tokyo 2020 Olympic and Paralympic Games. Sustainability Plan. Version 2.* Available at: https://gtimg.tokyo2020.org/image/upload/production/jyt3ocxciw8shkus9vqd.pdf (Accessed: 31 January 2021).

Toyota (2019) *Toyota Provides Diverse Mobility for Tokyo 2020, Including a Full-Line-up of Electrified Vehicles.* Available at: https://global.toyota/en/newsroom/corporate/29232815.html (Accessed: 31 January 2021).

Trail, G. T. and McCullough, B. P. (2020) 'Marketing sustainability through sport: Testing the sport sustainability campaign evaluation model', *European Sport Management Quarterly*, 20(2), pp. 109–129. doi: 10.1080/16184742.2019.1580301.

UNOSDP (2016) *Sport and Sustainable Development Goals*. Available at: https://www.un.org/sport/sites/www.un.org.sport/files/ckfiles/files/Sport_for_SDGs_finalversion9.pdf (Accessed: 31 January 2021).

Wohlfart, O. and Adam, S. (2019) *New Age of Sport Management Education in Europe: Research Project under the Erasmus + Programme*.

Yrjölä, M. *et al.* (2017) 'Consumer-to-consumer e-commerce: Outcomes and implications', *The International Review of Retail, Distribution and Consumer Research*, 27(3), pp. 300–315. doi: 10.1080/09593969.2017.1314864.

Chapter 3

# The need for T-shaped sport, physical activity, and health professionals

*Johan de Jong and Thomas Skovgaard*

## Introduction

Sufficient levels of physical activity (PA), exercise, and sport are of evident importance for health (Blair, 2009; Lee *et al.*, 2012). Moreover, sedentary behaviour such as sitting too long and too often has proven to be a crucial risk factor for several health problems (Katzmarzyk *et al.*, 2009; Bouchard, Blair and Katzmarzyk, 2015). That is why stimulating sport and PA aside with decreasing sedentary behaviour on a population wide scale is a major ambition of many nations worldwide. But this is more easily said than done, since modern lifestyle has changed a lot of things in our lives such as transportation and communication which are accompanied by undoubted improvements in living conditions. However, it has unintentionally created a mismatch between human beings' evolutionary history and the environment to which humans have adapted (e.g., humans are not designed to sit all day). Because of technology, a person can now eat, work, shop, bank, and socialise without having to move or be physically active. The effect of the Covid-19 pandemic showed a significant decline of the total number of steps per day because of the lockdowns (Fitbit, 2020). At the same time, it magnifies the importance of PA for physical, mental, and social health.

It is estimated that PA causes 6–10% of premature mortality through non-communicable diseases worldwide. Sufficient PA lowers the risk of getting Diabetes Type 2, coronary heart disease, and breast and colon cancer and increases life expectancy (Lee *et al.*, 2012). Furthermore, PA positively affects depressive symptoms and anxiety and increases feelings of energy level and quality of life (Bartholomew, Morrison and Ciccolo, 2005; Puetz, 2006; Martinsen, 2008; Yau, 2008; Conn, Hafdahl and Brown, 2009; Mead *et al.*, 2009). The consequences of sitting too much for too long are now recognised as a unique health hazard that has greatly contributed to non-communicable diseases (Blair, 2009; Henson *et al.*, 2016). Sedentary behaviour includes sitting during commuting, at the workplace, in leisure time, as well as in connection with community events (Owen *et al.*, 2010). Katzmarzyk *et al.* (2009) conducted the first comprehensive study exploring the health effects of sitting. They found that, independently from the amount of PA and cardiorespiratory fitness of a person, too much sitting is negatively related

DOI: 10.4324/9781003002666-5

to their health condition. However, Ekelund et al. (2016) reported that high levels of moderate intensity PA (i.e., 60–75 minutes per day) seem to eliminate the increased risk of death associated with sitting time. These apparently contradictory results require further research. Such findings have potential implications for the emerging area of research on using socio-ecological models to understand sedentary behaviour. Those models attribute significant roles to socio-economic and cultural factors as well as the built environment.

## Socio-ecological framework for sport, PA, and health

During the last decades, many studies have emphasised the importance of raising awareness, education, and designing interventions with the potential to change determinants that influence sport, PA, and sedentary behaviour. However, data from cross-sectional studies aiming for individual behavioural change illustrate that such approaches only explain 20–40% of the variance in PA behaviour (Spence and Lee, 2003; Olander et al., 2013). This confirms the importance of a wide variety of factors when dealing with behavioural change (Biddle, Mutrie and Gorely, 2015). Sallis and colleagues (2006) adapted principles of general socio-ecological models to their model on four domains of active living (see Figure 3.1).

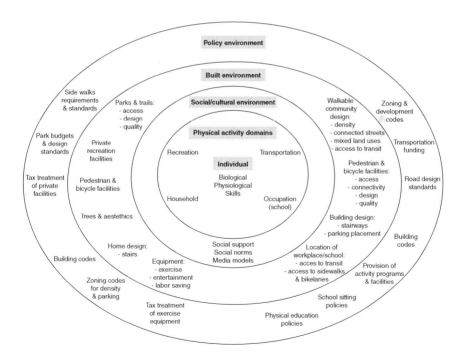

*Figure 3.1* Socio-ecological model of four domains of active living (adapted from Sallis et al., 2006, p. 301).

This model points out how much behaviour is influenced by a range of determinants (individual physical environment, social/cultural environment, built environment, and policy environment) at multiple levels instead of only a narrow range of psychosocial variables (McLeroy et al., 1988; Sallis and Owen, 2002). Together with others, Sallis et al. (2006) makes it clear that behavioural interventions are most effective if multiple levels are combined and integrated. Therefore, using socio-ecological models and approaches is becoming more common in PA research. The four domains of active living, as described in the model, are: active recreation, household activities, occupational activities, and active transport. These domains cover how people are physically active throughout their day and life.

## Socio-ecological model and three levels of determinants

In this context, it is about using PA in health promotion processes. This ambition is evident in, e.g., large-scale initiatives such as the WHO's Global Action Plan on Physical Activity (GAPPA), which aims at reducing physical inactivity by 10% by 2025 and 15% by 2030 (WHO, 2018). In line with other similar initiatives, this strategy points to a broad range of determinants of health enhancing PA.

### Determinant factors of PA

Often a distinction is made between individual, social, and environmental determinants of health behaviour. A general starting point is that the main drivers of human behaviour – for example in relation to PA and exercise – are to be found in, firstly, personal characteristics such as gender, age and individual skills, knowledge, attitudes, and experiences. Secondly, behaviour is conditioned by, for instance, social support and family relations, together with the local and wider environments in which the individual lives (Biddle et al., 2015).

### Individual determinants

Until rather recently, both practice and research focused on identifying individual determinants of PA and subsequently combining and evaluating intervention strategies at this level. A primary aim has been to support the individual's belief that habits and routines can be changed and that these changes will be sustainable over time. It has, however, become clear that there is a need to assess how the various frameworks surrounding and shaping our daily lives contribute to the actual and perceived formation of opportunities and limitations for PA. Such "framework thinking" helps to avoid overly individualising the responsibility for lifestyle factors such as PA. It is also suitable for supplementing the individual-oriented intervention strategies at a point where these often fall short – namely in the efforts to develop effective strategies for physical inactive or less active parts of the population. Efforts to activate the sedentary sections of the population do not go far (enough) by focusing predominantly on promoting individual lifestyle changes via personal resources that may be available or which can be cultivated. Emphasis must also be placed, and perhaps even more so, on altering the social and physical frameworks that contribute to active living.

In a nutshell: We should not throw everything we know about health promotion aimed at individual determinants out the window, but rather combine this knowledge with attempts to design PA-stimulating social and structural conditions to amplify the measures' effects.

### Social determinants

The relationships between PA and social factors have been studied for quite some time. The picture is not clear-cut, but a fair amount of evidence suggests that the likelihood of getting a reasonable amount of PA is enhanced among those being in social environments displaying a positive attitude towards an active lifestyle. For instance, people who start exercising often experience that their families and/or friends view their efforts to "keep themselves going" positively. There are also hints that exercise programmes aimed at sedentary target groups can keep participants engaged over a longer period if the activities are focused on the participation of family members. Studies reporting on exercise in relation to children and young people suggest that the influence through people and groups of people in their close daily environment plays a role in determining the degree of active living. For example, research indicates that children whose parents are inactive often are quite inactive themselves. Studies also show that parental support is important for children's and young people's participation in PA. Thus, links can be found between PA patterns of young people and dimensions of parental support, such as how often parents encourage their children to be physically active, how often children and parents participate in PA together, how often parents see their children engage in PA, as well as how often parents and children discuss the children's PA.

### Environmental determinants

This aspect relates to the environments in which people live their lives. In recent years, there has been growing interest in assessing whether intervening in the surroundings in which we move in connection with work, home, and leisure life can help make more people physically active. The focus is often on how remodelling and planning of urban or public spaces can help to promote activity or hinder sedentarism. The fundamental reason for why these types of environments are at the centre of attention is because of the persistent urbanisation in most, if not all, parts of the world. The planning and design of urban environments can directly or indirectly enable and motivate PA. Directly by establishing and maintaining sports and exercise facilities that are accessible, convenient, safe, and appealing.

Indirectly, the design of residential areas, commercial and public buildings, recreational and green areas, as well as infrastructure make a difference as to whether it is at all possible and desirable to integrate PA into everyday activities. It is also important how well the various elements of an urban area are connected. An interconnected and movement-friendly urban environment is one in which you can go freely, relatively quickly, and safely from one point to another without having to overcome a huge number of obstacles and take several detours. It is also a place where planning of both buildings and infrastructure prioritises non-motorised modes of transport combined with affordable public transport. Much work remains to gain a solid understanding of the environmental influences on healthy behaviour like exercise, but there is little doubt that the physical environment plays an important role in influencing participation in PA.

## A need for a multitude of approaches

We need to generate and identify effective and feasible ways to actively intervene in the social and environmental factors determining health and health behaviour of individuals and populations. The individual approaches have a lot to give, and there is a solid evidence to connect personality and behaviour. Still, such approaches are not always sensitive to how temporal and social issues influence the ability and interest in being physically active. It may be overlooked, or at least undervalued, how, for instance, personal lifestyles are a matter of habit ingrained over many years and may have been learned from the individual's principal role models. Thus, the individual approach can be criticised for failing to consider the contexts within which health behaviour is shaped and enacted. There is certainly a positive role for personal responsibility, perhaps better called personal opportunity, in the choice of lifestyle. Taking the widest possible personal responsibility for our actions are, in the words of John Roemer, American economist and political scientist, "the cost of freedom" (Roemer, 1998). But the bottom line is that determining what constitutes a truly voluntary, free action is extremely difficult.

So, what is needed is not to omit the individual-based methods to promote health enhancing PA but to integrate these with approaches trying to manipulate factors concerning social, physical, and political conditions of life to enable people to lead active lives.

## Complex initiatives with a focus on many factors

In the case of PA as a strategic link in health, there is now strong evidence and political recognition of the fact that there is a need to act on individual, social, and structural levels. PA and health are very much a collective issue requiring joint, coordinated action. This impetus should not be taken in isolation from a specific branch of public administration or a specific commission. Health enhancing PA is a topic that must cut across many sectors and be a consideration in connection with decisions at many levels. Also, effective strategies should be used to systematically increase citizen and community participation in as large parts of the decision-making processes as possible.

Fortunately, the many initiatives focusing on, for instance, innovative sports facilities, the city and wider urban areas as a privileged space for cyclists and pedestrians and holistic initiatives for children and young people indicate that in many countries and regions there is a willingness to act through cross-sectoral collaborations to impact a broad range of determinants for PA.

## Workable solutions to complex challenges – A way forward

There are no quick fixes to curb the problem of physical inactivity. Politicians, researchers, professionals working with health-related issues, and the public are often searching for clear solutions. But what we are dealing with is a complex system shaped by individual, social, and environmental determinants. If our goal is to enable *all* people to influence determinants of health and well-being, like PA, we must install measures directed at influencing both lifestyle and general living conditions of real importance for the individual's and the community's prosperity. The ideal is equal opportunities for individuals to actualise optimal levels of health given their health potential (Chang, 2002). Of course, exactly how and by what standards equal opportunities should be measured and valuated is both an empirical and normative question. Still, when taking an interest in using PA as an effort to promote health for all, regardless of social, economic, ethnic, or gender differentials, the following three points are to be considered:

- To promote active living, settings and conditions should be created that enable the individual to make qualified choices about both short- and long-term engagement in health-enhancing PA. Subsequent efforts are needed to support the transformation of such active choices into concrete daily action.
- For promoting PA and reducing systematic differences in exercise behaviour across the population, best available knowledge on determinants of physical (in)activity with solid evidence on the efficacy, corroboration, and cost effectiveness of possible interventions should be combined. Regarding the determinant issue, special attention should be given to describing which determinants of PA and sedentary living are especially weak or intense in vulnerable sections of the population. A better understanding of the mechanisms related to patterns of active or sedentary behaviour is required to establish what interventions will help the most to reduce observed disparities. Regarding the evidence issue, there is a need to develop a "mixed economy" of knowledge in which context-free information on what works in general is combined with context-sensitive inputs on how a potential successful intervention might be realised in the specific circumstances under consideration (Lomas et al., 2005).

44 Johan de Jong and Thomas Skovgaard

- Interventions and policies on PA are composed of both an individual and structural dimension. Solely focusing on individual determinants may lead to little impact. On the other hand, an exclusive focus on structural factors reduces people to impotent products of life's circumstances without personal drive, responsibilities, desires, and motives. Understanding this tension between individualism and structuralism is crucial for both the scientific and practical political push for active living for all.

## Implications for future education in sport, PA, and health

But what does a complex system approach mean for the future education of sport, PA, and health professionals? What type of "future" professionals in the field of sport, PA, and health do we need? And how should these students, the professionals of the future, be trained so they have the right competences for their challenging task in practice? Finally, what should the education environment look like to, best possible, challenge, support, and train sport, PA, and health students in specific situations that hold comparable complexity as real-life practices?

### T-shaped sport, PA, and health professionals

Stimulating sport and PA for health from a complex system approach means working together with other sectors, being able to combine multiple levels of influence, etc. For that we need dual specialists in the field of sport, PA, and health, so-called T-shaped professionals.

A T-shaped professional combines deep knowledge of core aspects of a given area (e.g., sport, PA, and health) with operational knowledge and understanding of other disciplines (e.g., interdisciplinary work, research, and innovation processes, communication, and management) (Gardner and Estry, 2017) (Figure 3.2).

In our case, the vertical part of the T refers to disciplinary knowledge and competences. For the sport, PA, and health professional this broadly means knowledge and expertise on the interconnections between human movement and health-related issues. Examples are knowledge on exercise physiology, experience in applying behavioural change models and theories to the area of PA, and insights into target groups like children, adolescents, older adults, or people with disabilities. Furthermore, a solid understanding of the various concepts of health that are used these days is necessary.

The horizontal part of the T stands for the skills and abilities that support professionals to interact meaningfully with other professionals possessing disciplinary knowledge essential to producing the outcomes needed in a particular situation, an outlined project, or a more broad-based initiative. Examples of these transversal types of knowledge are communication skills, ability to relate to others and build bridges between different viewpoints, interests, and stakeholders, innovation and understanding of adjacent areas. Also, a strong commitment to

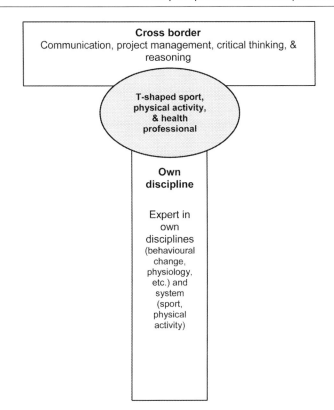

*Figure 3.2* The T-shaped sport, PA, and health professional (adapted from Gardner and Estry, 2017, p. 1).

work together with professionals such as policy makers or (urban) designers is needed when creating physically activating cities, schools, and public spaces.

These "double experts" are required for the complex and multidisciplinary challenges in sport, PA, and health. The T-shaped professional is such a double expert: an expert in their own domain (sport, PA, and health) and a skilled operator in cooperating with other domains and professionals. The practical field of sport, PA, and health urgently needs this new type of professionals who are capable of working at different levels with different sectors as described in the socio-ecological framework.

### *Future educational environment: Living Labs*

For future education in the field of sport, PA, and health, a "from inside the classroom to outside in practice approach" is a more congruent way of experiencing and learning how to deal with complex sport, PA, and health challenges. For that, a shift from primarily "on campus" education to education in the field, where stakeholders (ideally) learn, work, research, and experiment together, should be stimulated. One way to stimulate such a shift is by using so-called "Living Labs" (LL).

LLs are defined as user-centred, open innovation ecosystems based on systematic co-creation approaches and the integration of research and innovation processes in real-life communities and settings focused on a specific topic or shared goal. LLs are practice-driven organisations that facilitate and foster collaborative innovation in real-life environments where both open innovation and user innovation processes can be studied and subjected to experiments to generate new and effective solutions. LLs operate as intermediaries or mixed zone among citizens, research and educational organisations, companies, NGOs, urban and other residential areas for joint value co-creation and rapid prototyping (Enoll, 2020).

LLs, in the context of sport, PA, and health, should be situated in and focused on practice (and the improvement hereof) where different professionals from different disciplines and sectors work, learn, innovate, and research together. A (fictional) example of an LL where students can learn to operate as a T-shaped sport, PA, and health professional might be "An active and healthy primary school".

### Living Lab example "Active and Healthy Primary School"

The goal of this LL is to promote PA in and around school and tackling the issue of sedentariness. Sport, PA, and health students co-create and work together with primary school children and their parents, schoolteachers and management, school health services, researchers, representatives from the municipality, (urban) designers, and architects and combine their effort to develop and implement feasible ideas to positively impact the sport and PA behaviour at school.

Activities and innovations developed and facilitated by sport, PA, and health students could be the following:

- During school time, systematically developing, training, and implementing energisers (moments of PA) during classes; and PA is integrated in math lessons.
- At break time, children must go outdoors or go to the gym to play in an (un)structured way; and after-school-care is offered in cooperation with local sports clubs.
- Public education, and providing opportunities for physical activities in the neighbourhood for free and for all ages, is installed to reduce sedentary behaviour as well as increase PA.
- Stimulating active commuting by bike is promoted for long-distance trips.

Via their engagement in this complex real-life case on "Active and Health school", students learn to communicate and work with other stakeholders and a variety of citizen groups. Furthermore, they experiment and use their own expertise regarding sport and PA in creating energisers and other PA and sport-related initiatives in and outside the school setting.

## Conclusion

Stimulating sport and PA for health is a complex challenge that requires combining a multitude of approaches at multiple levels – as illustrated through the socio-ecological model. Dual specialists, or T-shaped sport, PA, and health professionals, are needed. This type of specialisation can be promoted by learning methods like Living Labs.

## References

Bartholomew, J. B., Morrison, D. and Ciccolo, J. T. (2005) 'Effects of acute exercise on mood and well-being in patients with major depressive disorder', *Medicine and Science in Sports and Exercise*, 37(12), pp. 2032–2037.

Biddle, S. J. H., Mutrie, N. and Gorely, T. (2015) *Psychology of physical activity: Determinants, well-being and interventions*. 3rd edn. Oxon: Routledge.

Blair, S. N. (2009) 'Physical inactivity: The biggest public health problem of the 21st century', *British Journal of Sports Medicine*, 43, pp. 1–2.

Bouchard, C., Blair, S. N. and Katzmarzyk, P. T. (2015) 'Less sitting, more physical activity, or higher fitness?', *Mayo Clinic Proceedings*, 90(11), pp. 1533–1540.

Chang, W. C. (2002) 'The meaning and goals of equity in health', *Journal of Epidemiology and Community Health*, 56, pp. 488–491.

Conn, V. S., Hafdahl, A. R. and Brown, L. M. (2009) 'Meta-analysis of quality-of life outcomes from physical activity interventions', *Nursing Research*, 58(3), pp. 175–183.

Ekelund, U. *et al.* (2016) 'Does physical activity attenuate, or even eliminate, the detrimental association of sitting time with mortality? A harmonised meta-analysis of data from more than1 million men and women', *Lancet*, 388(10051), pp. 1302–1310.

Enoll (2020) *About Us*. Available at: https://enoll.org/about-us/ (Accessed: 13 January 2021).

Fitbit (2020) *The Impact of Coronavirus on Global Activity Retrieved.* Available at: https://blog.fitbit.com/covid-19-global-activity/ (Accessed: 13 January 2021).

Gardner, P. and Estry, D. (2017) *A primer on the T-professional*. East Lansing, MI: Michigan State University. Available at: https://ceri.msu.edu/_assets/pdfs/t-shaped-pdfs/Primer-on-the-T-professional.pdf (Accessed: 13 January 2021).

Henson, J. *et al.* (2016) 'Sedentary behaviour as a new behavioural target in the prevention and treatment of type 2 diabetes', *Diabetes/Metabolism Research and Reviews*, 32, pp. 213–220.

Katzmarzyk, P. T. *et al.* (2009) 'Sitting time and mortality from all causes, cardiovascular disease, and cancer', *Medicine and Science in Sports and Exercise*, 41(5), pp. 998–1005.

Lee, I. M. *et al.* (2012) 'Effect of physical inactivity on major non-communicable diseases worldwide: An analysis of burden of disease and life expectancy', *Lancet*, 380, pp. 219–229.

Lomas, J. *et al.* (2005) *Conceptualizing and combining evidence for health system guidance.* Ottawa: Canadian Health Services Research Foundation.

Martinsen, E. W. (2008) 'Physical activity in the prevention and treatment of anxiety and depression', *Nordic Journal of Psychology*, 62(S47), pp. 25–29.

McLeroy, K. R. *et al.* (1988) 'An ecological perspective on health promotion programs', *Health Education Quarterly*, 15(4), pp. 351–377.

Mead, G. E. *et al.* (2009) 'Exercise for depression', *Cochrane Database of Systematic Reviews*, 3.

Olander, E. K. *et al.* (2013) 'What are the most effective techniques in changing obese individuals' physical activity self-efficacy and behaviour: A systematic review and meta-analysis', *International Journal of Behavioural Nutrition and Physical Activity*, 10(1), p. 29.

Owen, N. *et al.* (2010) 'Too much sitting: The population health science of sedentary behavior', *Exercise and Sport Sciences Reviews*, 38, pp. 105–113.

Puetz, T. W. (2006) 'Physical activity and feelings of energy and fatigue: Epidemiological evidence', *Sports Medicine*, 36(9), pp. 767–780.

Roemer, J. E. (1998) *Equality of opportunity*. Cambridge: Harvard University Press.

Sallis, J. F. *et al.* (2006) 'An ecological approach to creating active living communities', *Annual Review of Public Health*, 27, pp. 297–322.

Sallis, J. F. and Owen, N. (2002) 'Ecological models of health behavior', in Glanz, K., Rimer, B. K. and Viswanath, K. (eds.) *Health behavior and health education: Theory, research, and practice*. San Francisco, CA: Jossey-Bass, pp. 462–484.

Spence, J. C. and Lee, R. E. (2003) 'Towards a comprehensive model of physical activity', *Psychology of Sport and Exercise*, 4, pp. 7–24.

WHO (2018) *Global Action Plan on Physical Activity*. Available at: https://apps.who.int/iris/bitstream/handle/10665/272722/9789241514187-eng.pdf?ua=1 (Accessed: 13 January 2021).

Yau, M. K. (2008) 'Tai chi exercise and the improvement of health and well-being in older adults', *Medicine and Sport Science*, 52, pp. 155–165.

# Chapter 4

# Outdoor education as a deep education for global sustainability and social justice

*Heather Prince and Jean Cory-Wright*

Outdoor education is an Anglocentric approach to describe a range of organised and facilitated activities in the outdoors and includes outdoor activities (sport) as well as physical activity. As a term, it is pervasive in North America, the United Kingdom (UK), Australasia, and parts of Asia with variants such as adventure education, experiential education, and experiential learning. Traditionally separated through terminology from "environmental" education, there is a widespread view that education about, for, and in the environment is an important part of education in the outdoors, with a consequent shift in recent years to incorporate this through "outdoor learning" (the United Kingdom and New Zealand (NZ)) or "outdoor environmental education" (Thomas, Dyment and Prince, 2021).

Education in the outdoors is contextualised in different countries through cultural, regional, and historical influences. The genesis of activities in Europe in the 18th century was influenced by the ideas of Enlightenment and Romanticism (Becker, 2008). Beyond experiential space for outdoor activities, nature was seen as a therapeutic space and led to the emergence of outdoor cultures such as Friluftsliv (literally "open-air life") in Scandinavia (Henderson and Vikander, 2007; Gurholt, 2014), outdoor education in the United Kingdom, variant forms of Erlebnispädagogik (literally "experiential pedagogy") in Austria and Germany (Becker, 2015), Turistika (active movement involving outdoor and cultural activities) in the Czech Republic and Slovakia (Jirásek and Turcova, 2017), the "Center šolskih in obšolskih dejavnosti" (CŠOD) organisation in formal education in Slovenia (Dimec and Kokalj, 2018) and developments in Iceland, Poland, and the Baltic States (Becker, 2018). The differences in approaches to education in the outdoors have been sustained and are important for intra-continental cultural identity and diversity.

In Europe, cultural diversity promotes inclusivity both in individual countries and through international collaborative organisations such as the European Institute of Outdoor Adventure Education and Experiential Learning (EOE[1]). The emphases of different approaches vary (or this is the extrinsic perception) between more focus on outdoor recreation and outdoor sport (e.g., Turistika) to outdoor "living" (e.g., friluftsliv). However, all cultures view outdoor practice as space in nature for people to participate in sport, activities, and/or experiences

DOI: 10.4324/9781003002666-6

towards a broad spectrum of inclusive and pluralistic outcomes, cross-cultural perspectives, environmental and social justice, and trans/inter-disciplinary and formal/non-formal learning contributions (Prince *et al.*, 2018).

In Australasia, there is much debate about the meaning of the concept "outdoor education", and it has been given various terms to broaden it beyond outdoor pursuits. The NZ organisation that caters for teachers in this domain turns the words around to call itself Education Outdoors New Zealand (EONZ). The EONZ interpretation is that in the outdoors, personal attributes, attitudes, and values that help communities flourish are explored. This is framed under the concept "kaitiakitanga", which resonates with guardianship of the environment for future generations.

The question is not just about the benefits or otherwise of different cultural approaches to education in the outdoors but how outdoor education can contribute to societal education in a global context. Deeper perspectives from the United Kingdom and New Zealand are examined here to illustrate current drivers and future directions of outdoor practice, including the training of outdoor professionals, through acknowledged cultural lenses.

## UK perspective

The historical development of outdoor education was influenced by Robert Baden-Powell and the Scouting movement, and Kurt Hahn, founder of Outward Bound. These influences are not without critique in terms of masculinity and "a distinctive form of militarism shap[ing] Anglosphere outdoor education" (Brookes, 2015, p. 13). There is little doubt about the foundations of outdoor education in youth movements with their anxieties about the perceived "declines" in youth in terms of "manliness" and physical fitness. However, the 20th century saw the growth of expeditions contextualised within exploration with components of learning (for young people) and scientific work (Prince and Loynes, 2016).

Thus, many outdoor education programmes were founded on physical activity and traditional outdoor activities (sport) such as climbing, canoeing, mountaineering, sailing, caving, etc., involving technical skills for the development of character, resilience, hardiness, etc., albeit latterly without gendered rhetoric. However, in the last decade of the 20th century, outdoor spaces came to be appreciated for learning and education through a broader conceptualisation. Paradoxically, this might have been influenced by the introduction of the National Curriculum in England in 1989 which, whilst seen as a constraining framework by many educators, included outdoor and adventurous activities in physical education, which through its iterations have been either compulsory or optional at various stages for all children in mainstream schools (Leather, 2018). Some educators pursue this broader notion of outdoor education as an entitlement for all children, supported by such initiatives as the UK government's Learning Outside the Classroom Manifesto in 2006. Therefore, creative and imaginative ways have been developed by many educators in teaching the curriculum outdoors for cognitive, social

Outdoor education as a deep education 51

construct, environmental care and concern as well as health and well-being outcomes (Ager, 2019; Prince, 2019). There are also sector-wide campaigns, for example, to ensure that by 2035 every 18-year-old is an outdoor citizen.[2]

Few would dispute the importance of sport and physical activity for mental well-being as well as individual, social, and community development. The Sport England strategy towards an active nation monitors the activity levels of children and young people, and adults annually and twice per year, respectively, through the Active Lives surveys.[3] Focused on walking, swimming, cycling, and running, it also includes outdoor activities and other sport. In 2019 (Sport England), there was a 3.6% increase in the number of children in England doing an average of 60 minutes or more of physical activity per day, but those from low affluence families and those with a disability or long-term health condition were likely to be less active. Public Health England reported that the use of outdoor space for exercise/health reasons had remained remarkably consistent across all regions (2015–2016) at a mean of 17.9% with initiatives such as "This Girl Can" and parkruns with associated funding maintaining participation rates.

The breadth of contexts for outdoor education is expanding as markets have developed beyond outdoor activities (sport). In their 2015 study of demography, motivation, participation, and provision in outdoor sport and recreation, Sport England identified eight individualised outdoor participant segments from extensive national databases. The majority (51%) of the Active Outdoors market were "Explorers" (people seeking a sense of being part of, and exploring, the natural world) and "Challengers" (people focusing on personal achievement) with a further 17% "keeping fit in nature". The "Thrillseekers" and "Freestylers" comprised only 7% of the market. To facilitate the outdoor experiences of these and future participants requires competent, safe outdoor education professionals.

### Training and development of outdoor educators in the United Kingdom

The role of the adventure sport coach is primarily that of technical sport development (Collins and Collins, 2012). This is distinct from "guides" who lead people in the outdoors and "teachers" who use the outdoors as an environment of practice. However, as outdoor education has broadened its scope, professional training has needed to shift to respond to this. According to R. P. Lemmey (personal communication January 19, 2020) following consultation with 26 stakeholders (organisations, outdoor centres, national governing bodies, government departments, charities, and the community) about the skills and knowledge needed to be an effective outdoor professional, they should be, "autonomous professionals capable of working safely and sustainably in the moment and forming supportive relationships through which to effect change". Employers identified that there need to be cognitive and affective pathways to learning, and the skills to build effective rapport with participants are, in most cases, more important than high-level technical skills. Experiential learning through the first-hand experience of the natural world within outdoor education facilitates the development of motivations, values, and behaviours which, when combined with knowledge, effect change.

Having identified the market, how do we train and develop outdoor educators? Certainly, in the 21st century, there has been an expansion of outdoor studies degrees in the United Kingdom (Collins and Humberstone, 2018). In 2006, Humberstone and Brown edited a collection of papers from higher education lecturers indicating that outdoor education degree programmes reflected a broader curriculum and have become more critical in orientation, perhaps reflecting the growing research culture and evidence-based practice in the discipline. Indeed, Collins and Collins (2019, p. 1) developed the notion of the "pracademic" – people who can understand and exploit "the synergy between theory and practice [lying] at the heart of effective education for outdoor professionals".

Recently, with the influence of neoliberalism, many "outdoor" degree programmes have been cut or amalgamated, including initial teacher education. Those that survive provide a theoretical basis to practice that might not be as integral to other training routes such as instructor trainee/development schemes in outdoor centres or through apprenticeships. Built over the last two years by a wide range of employers, the Outdoor Activity Instructor apprenticeship is a funded training route over 12–18 months for entry-level roles across the breadth of outdoor instructional work in England. Several employers are also proposing further higher-level apprenticeships for more complex roles such as an "Outdoor Programme Leader". In support of existing practitioners, there is currently a debate in the United Kingdom about chartered status for outdoor professionals. At present, the professional body, the Institute for Outdoor Learning, has occupational standards for outdoor professionals and accreditation at three levels: "registered", "associate", and "lead" practitioner of the Institute; although the number of jobs identifying these in person specifications is variable.

## New Zealand perspective

Aotearoa NZ has a human history stretching back about 800 years. Māori narratives talk of Kupe, who, as the first Polynesian to arrive in Aotearoa New Zealand, fished North Island (Te Iti a Maui) out of the Cook Strait (the sea between the two islands of Aotearoa), while on his waka (canoe). We must remember that the Māori of Aotearoa were doing most of their educating outdoors. Learning was passed on by Rangatira (elders/chiefs) in the form of korero (narrative/discourse) and whakatauki (proverbs/wisdoms) and people lived on the land and travelled either by foot (early trekking) or by sea (waka-canoe). Māori originally lived in nature as it was their source of food, water, and shelter (Reti, 2012, p. 148). Like all indigenous people, they have a strong and spiritual connection to the land. They engaged in outdoor recreation as evidenced in whakaheke ngaru (surfing), waka hoe hoe (canoeing), and horua (tobogganing). Aotearoa was then colonised by Great Britain (18th–19th centuries), and The Treaty of Waitangi (TeTiriti o Waitangi, 1840) was written and taken round all Māori tribes to sign. After this, the country experienced

Outdoor education as a deep education 53

British/European colonising influences, and these continue to cause issues and challenges to this day. In terms of indigenous culture, Aotearoa NZ recognises both the indigenous Māori culture and the colonising pakeha culture equally and calls itself a bicultural country. Government departments have Māori names and meld aspects of Māori culture with English. Haka is a symbol of respect and challenge that is performed frequently at many events. It is with this background in mind and with great respect and humility that various Māori concepts are included in this narrative, as these often have richer meaning than the English translation and they have become part of Aotearoa NZ's education and values (Legge, 2012). For pakeha (white New Zealanders), the concept of being an ally to the Maori culture is an acceptable and welcomed way to support the Māori cause.

The Europeans influenced outdoor activities and outdoor education in Aotearoa NZ. Trekking (known as tramping in NZ English) became a very popular activity around the time of World War I. This was followed quickly by the introduction of outdoor sport such as climbing, mountaineering, kayaking, sailing, caving, surfing and, more recently, white-water rafting, mountain biking, kite surfing, windsurfing, adventure racing, orienteering, and rogaining. New Zealand has a strong tourism industry (the second largest earner after agriculture) and a considerable component of this is based on spectacular scenery and outdoors of New Zealand. This ranges from adventure tourism activities such as rafting and bungy jumping to gentler tourism like eco walks and nature studies, and there is a considerable number of cultural activities within the tourism domain.

## Training and development of outdoor educators in New Zealand

### Outdoor education – Tertiary providers

There is a large number of tertiary providers with six to ten polytechnics offering outdoor-related programmes, developed in response to the outdoor tourism industry. From the early 1990s, these proliferated, offering certificates and diplomas – one- to two-year programmes in activity instruction and safety management, each with its separate course and identity. In 2019, the government amalgamated all polytechnics to rationalise funding with a national review of tertiary qualifications including "outdoors". There is now a New Zealand National Certificate (one year) and Diploma (further year) in outdoor adventure education. These programmes are mainly targeted at activity instruction, but they do include an education paper on people development/facilitation, an environmental studies paper including sustainable practice, and a kaupapa Māori paper (total of eight papers in a year). The New Zealand Outdoor Instructors Association is the body that assesses most activity leadership qualifications, and polytechnics sometimes embed these leader awards into their courses. Other activity organisations also grant awards for activity leadership and instruction.

Education outdoors also makes a significant contribution to schools and communities. Some tertiary providers look at education for the future, which includes social and environmental sustainability, health and well-being, and critical thinking. Beyond polytechnics, other tertiary providers are Institutes of Technology offering outdoor courses at various levels, for example as part of a bachelor Sport and Recreation degree (Auckland), in Sustainability and Outdoor Education (Ara Institute of Canterbury), or a post-graduate teacher education programme with outdoor education as one of the many specialist subjects.

At Ara, students are trained to use the activities as a tool to develop people towards a well-rounded set of qualities that is culturally responsive and cares for self, community, society, and environment. Students study a broad range of supporting subjects such as geography, environmental studies, tikanga Māori health, well-being, education, adventure therapy, and safety management alongside a range of outdoor pursuits from the traditional kayaking and rock climbing to other areas such as waka ama paddling, surfing, and rogaining/orienteering. The course also embraces tikanga Māori across the curriculum and develops students' well-being, communication skills, personal attributes, and emotional intelligence, leading to professional capability. At present this is the only outdoor and environmental route into teacher education, so a sizable emphasis is on the school curriculum and how to embed Hauora (Māori view of well-being) and sustainability into it. There are other routes into teacher education in the outdoors through physical education and sports degrees and various postgraduate programmes; all have a close alignment with the NZ education system.

*Outdoor education in schools in New Zealand*

The primary sector caters for five- to 13-year-olds in New Zealand in years zero to eight. Some areas of higher population have intermediate schools which cater for years seven to eight. The curriculum is the same for both types of schools. The background values of the NZ school curriculum include striving for excellence in innovation, equity, community, diversity, integrity, and sustainability with an underlying guideline to respect themselves, others, and human rights (Ministry of Education New Zealand, 2007).

Primary and intermediate schools frequently support their curriculum with education outdoors. This includes activity trips such as surfing, sailing or ski/ snowboard, school camps with visits to outdoor centres, and other outdoor and environmental education trips such as visits to the rocky shore, the local waste management centre, the museum, or the forest. These trips vary across the country depending on the local environment and the ability of parents to pay. An attempt to make this more equitable across socio-economic groups was made by the government when they limited schools from collecting money for out-of-school activities, but this is still work in progress.

Many secondary schools in Aotearoa run outdoor education programmes and have outdoor education teachers. This was aided by the introduction of a new secondary school qualification system from 2002 to 2004, the National Certificate in Educational Achievement (NCEA). It replaced an old norm-referenced system of examinations, which used to leave half of the school leavers failing their school certificate. Although the NCEA had teething problems at its initial inception, it has been developed to be an up to date and relevant qualification. Unlike some other countries, pupils gain small chunks of qualification towards their final result over the course of the year. Students take about 20 credits of learning in each school subject to build a set of 80–120 credits for each of years 11, 12, and 13 (New Zealand Qualifications Authority, 2019). An aspect of the NCEA that saw a growth of outdoor education in secondary schools was the writing of various credits called unit standards. These standards had a vocational focus, and they included many skills in outdoor activities; secondary school pupils were able to take a number of these credits and count them towards their final NCEA. Unfortunately, these credits were quite simple and just included activity skills and covered no broader concepts such as personal growth, community, or the environment, which missed the more holistic and deeper applications of education outdoors. However, some teachers (often graduates of the teacher education programmes above) applied a few of the more academic achievement standard credits to outdoor courses such as sustainability and environmental education.

This demonstrates the link between the tertiary programmes and school courses and how each has influenced the other. Currently, a working group is developing a set of outdoor education achievement standards, which will include personal attributes, interpersonal skills, environment, cultural knowledge, well-being, and activities. Further examples of good practice in education outdoors in Aotearoa NZ schools are illustrated by Education Outdoors New Zealand (2020) with its journal for sharing good practice (Te Whakatia) and book resources.

### Outdoor centres

New Zealand has numerous outdoor centres and camps; this chapter can only give an overview of the most well-known and those seen to be promoting innovative practice. All of them have a common thread which is aptly described using some of Seligman and Csikszentmihalyi's (2000) positive psychology principles: to create thriving people that help communities flourish and nurture and conserve the planet.

Outward Bound established a centre at Anakiwa, Marlborough Sounds in 1962. They have a distinctly Aotearoa NZ flavour, and their vision is "Better people. Better communities. Better world" (Outward Bound, 2019). Following this, Hillary Outdoors (formerly known as Outdoor Pursuits Centre) was established in 1972 by Graeme Dingle with Sir Edmund Hillary of Everest fame as its patron, which now has several centres. Their vision includes experiential learning with participants gaining lifelong impact that helps them connect, create, and shape their learning. Their purpose is "Youth learning through adventure" (Hillary Outdoors, 2019).

Youth development emanates from the outdoor centres into the community with organisations such as "The Graeme Dingle Foundation" (Project K) whose values for young people include Manaaki (caring), Maia (courageous), and Tuhono (collaborative) (Graeme Dingle Foundation, 2019). This overlaps with the concept known as adventure therapy, in which the outdoors is used directly as a personal growth tool for anyone with special needs from disabilities to disaffected youth. YMCA (Known as the "Young Men's Christian Association", but its meaning is much more than this) is renowned around the world for its work in the field of community development and the YMCAs of Aotearoa NZ "are community organisations who aim to develop individuals and families to develop physically, mentally and spiritually and enjoy a healthy quality of life" (YMCA, 2020), many of which include outdoor camps and outdoor activities. The provision extends into environmental and conservation areas in the huge range of Department of Conservation (DOC) and local city council provisions. Most outdoor centres include environmental topics in their agenda, and for some of them, the environment is their main focus. A very recent innovation is an outdoor centre in Raglan, The Institute of Awesome, focusing on the use of technology to solve local, national, and global problems (Education Gazette, 2019). Camps have moved from a traditional entertainment style to a position where schools and camps work together to offer students learning opportunities in the outdoors. Several schools have their own camps or have strong connections with a camp, and courses can be two to three months long. These not only include school study but also cover life lessons like living together, growing food, cooking, and having reduced use of technology.

### Kaupapa Māori

There is a strong link to kaupapa Māori (customs and belief structure) in more recent outdoor education and physical education provision. Hauora is the Māori concept for well-being, and it encompasses much more than the English term. It covers taha tinana (physical), taha hinengaro (mental/emotional), taha whanau (social), and taha wairua (spiritual) well-being. Kaitiakitanga is a frequently applied concept for guardianship. Manaakitanga (respect and generosity) is promoted throughout the outdoor sector. Turangawaewae stands literally for the place where you stand, meaning a connection with land and place, which resonates with whanaungatanga, which is kinship/community. All in all, matatau (proficiency, experience) and observance of whakatauki (proverbs) is what leads to matauranga (wisdom). Aotearoa NZ tries to embed indigenous knowledge in education, it is not just about using the Māori words in place of English (Alsop and Kupenga, 2016).

## Summary

The cultural foundations of much of education outdoors in a global context are as important today as they ever have been in creating identity, teaching, and learning practices, and in the way that people relate and connect to their environment. Outdoor education will continue to enhance learning about place in the future. Whilst there are opportunities for outdoor professionals as adventure sport coaches and activity leadership/instruction, much training and development relates to a wider and more holistic outdoor educational provision that seeks to embed values, social and environmental justice, and citizenship.

Outdoor education globally is an important approach to enhancing physical and mental health and well-being in citizens, and these outcomes will likely be even more valued in the future. The importance of accessibility to green and blue spaces has been heightened in the mindsets of policy makers through a global pandemic, with the valuing of time outdoors for exercise and mental and spiritual well-being, appreciation of local spaces, fresh air, and noticing nature. Future directions for education in the outdoors might concentrate on optimising the benefits of activities and experiences in local spaces including parks and gardens in active and creative ways to provide equitable and inclusive opportunities for a broader demographic. Educators are moving from risk aversion to risk benefit in the management of outdoor experiences for personal and social development. Global future perspectives should see policymakers valuing these opportunities and the environments in which they take place.

Aotearoa NZ may exemplify a bounteous land with rich opportunities for learning in the outdoors but like many other countries, the value of its outdoor education is deeper. If outdoor citizens are to be equipped to address the challenges facing the natural world and their community globally, it follows that outdoor educators need to be similarly equipped to respond to sustainability and social justice issues.

"[…] it feels as though the journey is just beginning […] at last it has begun! We believe that outdoor education can play a critical and crucial role in this process" (Collins and Humberstone, 2018, p. 66). This resonates with the impactful Māori proverb; "He aha te mea nui o te ao, he tangata he tangata he tangata" (proverb uttered by Te Aupouri wāhine rangatira [female chief] Meri Ngaroto in the early 19th century). This is simply translated as: "What is the most important thing in the world? It is the people, it is the people, it is the people". This phrase also uses "tamariki", which is the children who will inherit this world. We need to leave a better world for our children and better children to the world.

Education outdoors is uniquely placed to provide deep education towards a better future, and it must step up with action on this now.

## Acknowledgment

Te Ao Marama Apiata, Ara Institute of Canterbury, Otautahi Christchurch, New Zealand.

## Notes

1. EOE: http://www.eoe-network.eu
2. Outdoor Citizens: https://www.outdoor-learning.org/Members/Current-Projects/IOL-Working-for-You/Outdoor-Citizens
3. Active Lives surveys: https://www.sportengland.org/know-your-audience/data/active-lives

## References

Ager, J. (2019) 'Can I do it outside? How to introduce a CIDIO (can I do it outside?) approach in a primary school', *Horizons*, 84, pp. 33–35.

Alsop, P. and Kupenga, T. R. (2016) *Mauri ora; Wisdom from the Maori world*. Nelson, New Zealand: Potton & Burton.

Becker, P. (2008) 'The European Institute of Outdoor Adventure Education and Experiential Learning', in Becker, P. and Schirp, J. (eds.) *Other ways of learning*. Marburg: Verein zur Förderungsbewegung- und sportorienterter Jugendsozialarbeit e.V.

Becker, P. (2015) 'From 'Erlebnis' to adventure. A view on the German Erlebnispädagogik', in Humberstone, B., Prince, H. and Henderson, K. A. (eds.) *International handbook of outdoor studies*. Oxford, New York, NY: Routledge, pp. 20–29.

Becker, P. (2018) 'Introduction: Dealing with borders, building bridges: How the outdoor movement became European after the fall of the Berlin Wall', in Becker, P. *et al.* (eds.) *The changing world of outdoor learning in Europe*. Oxford, New York, NY: Routledge, pp. 1–10.

Brookes, A. (2015) 'Foundation myths and the roots of adventure education in the anglo-sphere', in Humberstone, B., Prince, H. and Henderson, K. A. (eds.) *International handbook of outdoor studies*. Oxford, New York, NY: Routledge, pp. 11–19.

Collins, D. and Humberstone, B. (2018) 'Outdoor education/studies and eco-feminisms: Reflections on the last 20 years', in Becker P. *et al.* (eds.) *The changing world of outdoor learning in Europe*. Oxford, New York, NY: Routledge, pp. 57–70.

Collins, L. and Collins, D. (2012) 'Conceptualising the adventure sports coach', *Journal of Adventure Education and Outdoor Learning*, 12(1), pp. 81–94. doi: 10.1080/14729679.2011.611283.

Collins, L. and Collins, D. (2019) 'The role of 'pracademics' in education and development of adventure sports professionals', *Journal of Adventure Education and Outdoor Learning*, 19(1), pp. 1–11. doi:10.1080/14729679.2018.1483253.

Dimec, D. S. and Kokalj, I. (2018) 'The development and role of outdoor education and CŠOD in the Slovenian school system', in Becker, P. *et al.* (eds.) *The changing world of outdoor learning in Europe*. Oxford, New York, NY: Routledge.

Education Gazette (2019) 'Institute of awesome; School camp reimagined', *Education Gazette* 98(19).

Education Outdoors New Zealand (2020) *Resources/Publications*. Available at: https://www.eonz.org.nz/resourcespublications/ (Accessed: 1 April 2020).

Graeme Dingle Foundation (2019) *Vision, Purpose and Values*. Available at: https://dinglefoundation.org.nz/about/who-we-are/vision-purpose-values/ (Accessed: 26 November 2019).

Gurholt, K. P. (2014) 'Joy of nature, friluftsliv education and self: Combining narrative and cultural–ecological approaches to environmental sustainability', *Journal of Adventure Education and Outdoor Learning*, 14(3), pp. 233–246. doi:10.1080/14729679.2014.948802.

Henderson, B. and Vikander, N. (2007) *Nature first: Outdoor life the friluftsliv way*. Toronto: Natural Heritage Books.

Hillary Outdoors (2019) *Hillary Outdoors: Our Story*. Available at: http://www.hillaryoutdoors.co.nz/about/ (Accessed: 26 November 2019).

Humberstone, B. and Brown, H. (2006) *Shaping the outdoor profession through higher education. Creative diversity in outdoor studies courses in higher education in the UK*. Penrith: Institute for Outdoor Learning.

Jirásek, I. and Turcova, I. (2017) 'The Czech approach to outdoor adventure and experiential education: The influence of Jaroslav Foglar's work', *Journal of Adventure Education and Outdoor Learning*, 17(4), pp. 321–337. doi:10.1080/14729679.2017.1344557.

Leather, M. (2018) 'Outdoor education in the national curriculum: The shifting sands in formal education', in: Becker, P. *et al.* (eds.) *The changing world of the outdoor learning in Europe*. Oxford, New York, NY: Routledge, pp. 179–193.

Legge, M. (2012) 'A pakeha perspective on biculturalism in education outdoors', in Irwin, D., Straker, J. and Hill, A. (eds.) *Outdoor education in Aotearoa New Zealand*. Christchurch, New Zealand: CPIT, pp. 146–150.

Ministry of Education New Zealand (2007) *The New Zealand Curriculum- Te Marautanga o Aotearoa*. Wellington, New Zealand: Learning Media Ltd.

New Zealand Qualifications Authority (2019) *How NCEA works*. Available at: https://www.nzqa.govt.nz/ncea/understanding-ncea/how-ncea-works/ (Accessed: 26 November 2019).

Outward Bound (2019) *About Outward Bound*. Available at: https://www.outwardbound.co.nz/about-us/about-outward-bound/ (Accessed: 26 November 2019).

Prince, H. E. (2019) 'Changes in outdoor learning in primary schools in England, 1995 and 2017: Lessons for good practice', *Journal of Adventure Education and Outdoor Learning*, 19(4), pp. 329–342. doi: 10.1080/14729679.2018.1548363.

Prince, H. E. and Loynes, C. (2016) 'Adventure, nature, and commodification', in Convery, I. and Davis, P. (eds.) *Changing perceptions of nature*. Newcastle: Boydell & Brewer, pp. 227–233.

Prince, H. E. *et al.* (2018) 'Adventure education and outdoor learning. Examining journal trends since 2000', in: Becker, P. *et al.* (eds.) *The changing world of outdoor learning in Europe*. Oxford, New York, NY: Routledge, pp. 144–159.

Reti, H. (2012) 'Eh tohu: A direction for Maori in the outdoors', in Irwin, D., Straker, J. and Hill, A. (eds.) *Outdoor education in Aotearoa New Zealand*. Christchurch, New Zealand: CPIT, pp. 146–150.

Seligman, M. E. and Csikszentmihalyi, M. (2000) 'Positive psychology: An introduction'. *American Psychologist*, 55(1), pp. 5–14. doi:10.1037//0003-066x.55.1.5.

Sport England (2015) *Getting Active Outdoors: A Study of Demography, Motivation, Participation and Provision in Outdoor Sport and Recreation in England*. Available at: https://sportengland-production-files.s3.eu-west-2.amazonaws.com/s3fs-public/outdoors-participation-report-v2-lr-spreads.pdf (Accessed: 20 March 2020).

Thomas, G., Dyment, J. and Prince, H. (2021) *Outdoor environmental education in higher education: international perspectives*. Cham, Switzerland: SpringerNature.

YMCA (2020) *YMCA New Zealand Impact*. Available at: https://ymca.org.nz/wp-content/uploads/2019/06/YMCA_001025-Impact-Doucment-FINAL-WEB-VERSION.pdf (Accessed: 1 April 2020).

# Part II

# New trends in sport education

Chapter 5

# Sport education from a global perspective

*Richard Bailey and Bettina Callary*

## Introduction

We live in an increasingly connected world. What happens in one part of the world has the potential to significantly impact other areas. For many, globalisation is seen as an inevitability, reflecting immutable changes in the world. Kofi Annan (2002) said: "arguing against globalization is like arguing against the law of gravity" (unpaged). Globalisation is no longer an ambition, but a reality with which policies need to come to terms. This chapter examines globalisation within sport education. It seeks to identify some of the trends through which globalisation has been expressed in practices across the world by assessing the meanings and significance given to this concept in sport and education. It goes on to consider two specific contexts: school physical education and sport coach education. The chapter critically discusses possible opportunities and threats to sport education that may be inherent within globalisation, and how they might change the face of sport education in the future.

## Globalisation

The concept of globalisation comes from 1980s economics and the study of the expansion of international business enterprises, although it quickly became generalised to refer to the idea of people, countries, and economies being inherently interdependent (Tedlow and Abdelal, 2004). In current discourses, globalisation points to the connection of ideas across geographical borders and the impacts this has on individual and cultural identities. In education, the connection of learning resources, environments, and experiences is leading to a global learning ecosystem. Open platforms are providing incomparably greater access to information and new modes of communication. For the first time in history, it is possible to discuss, teach, collaborate knowledge, skills, and values spanning geographical and intellectual boundaries on a near-universal scale.

The forces of globalisation have impacted on educational aspects of sport as they have every other aspect of education. With this change has come an expanding scholar literature exploring causes and effects of increasing connectivity. Much of

DOI: 10.4324/9781003002666-8

this literature has been critical of the political and economic forces behind globalisation and the effects they have on the practice of education and sport. Implicit within this discourse is a conceptualisation of the world into two major, but unequal parts: the Northern Zone, made up of North America, Northern and Western Europe, and the Pacific Rim; and the Southern Zone, consisting of Africa, South American, Caribbean, South Pacific Island nations (Rizvi and Lingard, 2010). The Northern Zone primarily directs its influence through conditional funding for international organisations. The World Bank, for example, provides educational loans to developing countries with the intention of reforming educational ideologies, planning, and institutional structures. Among the numerous changes this funding has brought are a wide-scale embrace of competence-based curricula and assessment models, extensive use of information and communication technologies, and primacy of employability skills. Similarly, the Organisation for Economic Co-operation and Development (OECD) has actively promoted universal educational competences (Voogt and Roblin, 2012). Interestingly, the OECD, with the South Korean Government, has recently led a comprehensive analysis of physical education curricula among its member states (Bailey, 2018a, 2018b) and introduced physical activity within its Program for International Student Assessment (PISA) assessments (OECD, 2018). Other globalising developments have relied more on the subtle power of "soft law", such as non-binding statements, declarations, and charters (Guzman, 2008). Sport education has witnessed many instances of such soft law, including UNESCO's "International Charter of Physical Education, Physical Activity and Sport" (2015a), "Quality Physical Education" guidance, and its support of the "universitisation" of physical education and sport coaching, as well as the World Health Organisation's (WHO) "Global recommendations on physical activity for health" (2010). None of these documents possess legal force, nor do they wield coercive mechanisms, or even typically involve monitoring, yet they can have considerable influence over governments and other agencies. The WHO's recommendation has garnered near-universal acceptance by national governments (Michelini, 2015). Recent years have also witnessed the emergence of business into policy discourses. Nike's "Designed to Move" is, perhaps, the clearest example of this, with its explicit focus on guiding national and international policies in physical activity, physical education, and sport coaching towards a developmental, evidence-based framework (Nike, ACSM and ICSSPE, 2012).

Ennis (2017) frames the rise of globalisation within sport and education in terms of neoliberalism, global uniformity, and knowledge economies, all of which are products of, and in the interests of, the Northern Zone. She partially embeds her argument within postcolonial theory, in which globalisation is an economic and political system that benefits wealthy and rich nations to the detriment of the world's poor countries and individuals. From this perspective, sport education is an economic investment designed to produce skilled and healthy labour to serve the wealthy and powerful. Sport education is also becoming more uniform, as curricula become global, imposing models from the United States, the United Kingdom, France, and others to Southern Zone developing countries (Anderson-Levitt, 2008).

Sport education from a global perspective 65

Not everyone agrees to the premise that globalisation is necessarily harmful, or globalising interests are at the expense of the powerless. Some argue that the spread of globalisation is associated with many benefits. By definition, globalisation assumes the exchange of ideas and practices, and cooperation. In developing countries, globalisation can be transformative, providing opportunities to reconstruct local cultures as knowledge is created and recreated at multiple sites (Stromquist and Monkman, 2014). This coupling, decoupling, and loose coupling of systems with local cultures and communities permits communities to foreground a form of globalisation that values heritage and local knowledge while bringing broad-ranging knowledge and insights into the local conversation.

So, the term globalisation embraces both positive and negative forces from local to international contexts, as each level changes and is changed by informational awareness, economics, and the force of rapidly evolving public opinion. In addition, the complexity and systemic nature of initiatives for reform are necessarily diverse across regions (Anderson-Levitt, 2008).

## The changing state and status of physical education

Compulsory education is in the midst of rapid change around the world. Centralising pressures from international bodies, calling for universal standards and expectations, have coincided with radical rethinking of the relationships between states, non-governmental agencies, and the private sector in many areas of public service. This is the case in physical education and school sport, which have been transformed in recent decades by developments demanding that provision becomes more relevant to the needs of learners and their communities, and more aware of international trends and demands.

All school subjects live within crowded curriculum spaces. Judgements about the time and funds directed to different areas of a curriculum are influenced by a complex suite of factors, of which tradition, social values, and political commitments are among the most significant. Physical education has had to deal with powerful cultural forces related to the body and specifically the legacy in which a sharp distinction is made between the mind and body, with the mind indisputably sovereign (Bailey, 2020). From this perspective, mathematics and the "hard sciences" epitomise universal and stable knowledge, while the body is little more than the mind's unthinking vessel. This vision has been hugely influential, and it helps explain why mathematics has been firmly entrenched at the top of the curriculum hierarchy for more than 2,000 years of educational debates, and physical and vocational subjects have languished at the bottom (Bailey, 2018a). However, physical education's potential contribution to the public health agenda, well as the costs of the "global physical inactivity pandemic" (Kohl *et al.*, 2012), has led some governments to re-evaluate policy commitments. Physical education curricula in Scotland, Australia, and other countries have undergone radical revisions premised on the unique role of the school as a setting for physical activity, with physical education as its hub (Lindsey, 2020). Since UNESCO and the OECD have also called for a greater recognition of societal benefits from quality physical education provision (and with it increased funding and curriculum security) (Bailey, 2018a), the likelihood such changes will spread to other countries significantly increases.

The changing state and status of physical education resulting at least partly from its recruitment to the public health agenda is one of the most visible expressions of the impact of globalisation on the subject area. This claim is supported by a series of international and transnational projects sharing certain guiding presumptions, such as the need to align physical education more closely with health, correct the marginalisation of some groups (most notably girls), and address the relative paucity of a scientific evidence base (Bailey, 2018b).

## Globalised physical education

The International Conferences of Ministers and Senior Officials Responsible for Physical Education and Sport (MINEPS) involve most of the significant players in the field (including the International Olympic Committee, International Paralympic Committee, UN agencies, non-government organisations, and academics). The sixth MINEPS took place in Russia in 2018, and the resultant "Kazan Action Plan" presented an explicitly global and globalising agenda: "to facilitate international and multi-stakeholder policy convergence, ease international cooperation and foster capacity-building efforts of governmental authorities and sport organisations" (UNESCO, 2018, Article 1.2). These developments align with the positive side of globalisation, as they seek to articulate a common vision through collaboration, consensus-building, and global dissemination. However, it has been difficult to deny concomitant negative consequences. Perhaps the most evident of these is that the organisations leading the major developments are all based in Europe. It is difficult to separate even the most well-intentioned ideas from the cultures in which they have grown, so it seems unavoidable that advocacy for global change will carry within globalising (i.e., imperialist) presumptions. An implicit concern in successive MINEPS meetings has been, on the one hand, the inadequate recognition in some countries of what are assumed to be fundamental demands, such as gender equality and teacher education and, on the other hand, the progressive displacement of Indigenous games by sport such as football, cricket, and basketball. Taken together, these developments raise important questions about the scope and limits of the globalising forces in physical education and ambitions to transform its place within education systems.

There have been a number of studies of the place of physical education in schools (Hardman and Marshall, 2009; UNESCO, 2013). These, and evidence reported in international meetings, broadly reinforce several messages:

- There is a near-universal concern about the marginalised position of physical education within the school curriculum.
- Physical education is generally considered to be a low-status subject.

Sport education from a global perspective 67

- Limits to resourcing mean that many schools are unable to deliver a comprehensive, or even coherent, curriculum, and this is especially the case in the Southern Zone.
- There is often a policy-practice gap, so even when the subject is formally a compulsory part of the curriculum, it is sometimes not taught.
- The greatest time allocation to physical education occurs when the children are aged 9–14 and declines with age.
- Inequity, especially in terms of gender and disability, means many children are marginalised from quality physical education experiences or excluded completely.
- Time for physical activities and sport is often extended through extra-curricular activities. In some cases, this was very well developed, in others less so.
- Specialist primary teachers are rare and physical education preparation for generalists is limited.

There have also been doubts about the relationship between physical education and positive outcomes (Bailey *et al.*, 2009). Consensus has emerged about the broad types of objectives attributed to participation in physical education: mainly physical, psychological, and social outcomes (Bailey, 2018a). Research and policy have increasingly recognised that the realisation of intended outcomes does not necessarily follow from participation in physical education activities, since they are dependent on a series of conducive "change mechanisms" (Whitelaw *et al.*, 2010), including effective pedagogy and an appropriate learning environment. These conditions bring with them concomitant implications in terms of the preparation of teachers, investment in facilities, and policy commitments (Hardman and Marshall, 2009). UNESCO's terminological change to "Quality Physical Education" (UNESCO, 2015b), with an emphasis on worthwhile experiences of learners and their long-term commitment to health-enhancing physical activity, is testament to an acknowledgement of this. However, with the greater awareness of the pivotal importance of the teacher's ability to create a positive experience for all learners must also come a proper recognition of the extent of the challenges confronting the profession.

## Competing and shared priorities

There are no internationally agreed methodologies for research or practice in physical education (Bailey and Glibo, in press). However, with the advent of social media, greater access to international conferences, and policy initiatives, strands of consensus have started to emerge. A survey carried out of the content of English language journals (Bailey and Glibo, in press) revealed three dominant themes: "models", "inclusion and diversity", and "instruction". The last of these is perhaps not surprising and research into didactic approaches has a long history. The theme of "models" has emerged more recently, largely due to the recent, rapid growth of research in instructional models in North America (Metzler, 2017). Many of these instructional models were designed to address a second topic emerging from the literature. Physical education has been criticised for being dominated by male, heterosexual norms, limiting movement experiences to an impoverished range of gendered activities (Bailey, Wellard and Dismore, 2004). Similar concerns have been expressed about the imposition of expectations of ability marginalising those whose bodies fall outside the acceptable range of performance (Fitzgerald, 2005). Finally, physical education has long been associated with health outcomes, and this has only increased with rising public health concerns. Physical education curricula in almost every developed country in the world include health-related content, and the promotion of health-enhancing physical activity seems to be the dominant rationale for the subject around the globe (Bailey, 2018a; UNESCO, 2013), despite evidence that it currently has limited positive impact (Farooq *et al.*, 2018).

There remain significant areas of contention surrounding physical education, and these seem to be especially strong when implemented at local levels. At the level of policy development, there is greater consistency. Here, physical education seems to be following the pattern set by mathematics, in which it is becoming increasingly difficult to differentiate formal curricula by country (Bailey, 2018a). Priorities of health and inclusion are inextricably linked to countries' attempts to inculcate best practices whilst maintaining national identities, as, "whatever educators borrow they adapt, wittingly or not, to national culture and local ways of doing school" (Anderson-Levitt, 2008, p. 364).

The next section discusses the field of sport coaching. The relationship between physical education and coaching is a complex one, and many aspects of the two contexts are quite different. However, in some countries, physical education teachers and sport coaches are one person. Perceived deficits in the competence of primary school teachers and changing funding patterns from central government have led physical education in some countries to be "outsourced" to coaches, and some teachers have changed roles to take advantage of this new role (Parnell *et al.*, 2017). Some link this development to the neo-liberal tendencies of globalisation insofar as it reflects prioritising of the market over the state, along with deregulation, and the privatisation of hitherto state-provided services (Macdonald, Johnson and Lingard, 2020). Some seek to stress the common ground in terms of less politically charged aspects (Stodter and Cushion, 2014). Effective pedagogy, of course, is a mutual interest, and there has been an increasing exchange of ideas (Light and Harvey, 2017). Likewise, professional education, mentoring, and other themes related to the preparation and status of practitioners have become the site of bi-directional sharing of ideas. There remain, however, distinctive concerns related to questions of globalisation, and some of those related to coach education are discussed in the next section.

## Globalising sport coaching

While effective pedagogy is a common denominator between physical educators and sport coaches, there is no consensus globally and in many cases, nationally, regarding sport coaching as a profession. Nonetheless, the push for professional standards has led to an increased interest in coach education and development:

> Is it not shocking that much sport coach education is unregulated, haphazard, and informal? Unlike many established professions, the pathway into coaching often omits extensive, rigorous formal education and coaching science researchers have even shown that some coaches criticize the formal coach education programs [sic] they do attend for lacking relevance.
>
> (Callary and Gearity, 2020, p. 1)

Thus, the research and practice into effective coach education has taken an increase in interest during the past two decades.

One expression of this change has been a shift towards international collaboration of coach developers. The International Council for Coaching Excellence (ICCE) has acted to increase reach and dissemination of information to sports governing bodies, institutions of higher education, and thought leaders involved in coach education (ICCE, 2020). For example, it partnered with the Nippon Sport Science University in Tokyo, resulting in the Nittaidai Coach Developer Academy with a vision of "creating coaching cultures that lead to positive experiences for everyone through sport [...] to [...] form a community of coach developers across the world" (NSSU, 2018, p. 2). The programme has now graduated six cohorts from nearly 30 countries. Its structure and content have formed a framework of concepts for coach developers, unifying their abilities to communicate their efforts in working towards a common goal in their respective countries. In addition, the ICCE endorses the *International Sport Coaching Journal* (ISCJ), which publishes research from around the world. Thus, efforts have been made to globalise coach education, which generally create a positive change towards the acceptance of coaching as a profession.

Despite interest in a global coaching agenda, it is important to assess critically the constructs created to spur reflection for further growth. Three themes are presented in the following section regarding the globalisation of coach education: firstly, it has undergone considerable change to become constructivist, learner-centred, and experiential in nature; secondly it has begun to consider the contextual differences of coaching; and thirdly, this is all couched in the understanding that the English language has become the dominant language for international efforts in coach education, thereby providing power and control to English language and Northern Zone cultural beliefs and concepts of "best practices".

## Learner-centred and experiential coach education

One of the patterns of development in coach education is a movement from a top-down delivery of content from experts to a learner-centred approach (Paquette and Trudel, 2018). Previously, coach education used a traditional instructional paradigm that presumed Northern Zone education approaches (Light, 2008). Reduced to a simple hierarchical behaviourist approach, it was relatively easy for organisations to provide coaching courses, tell the coaches what they need to know, check for understanding through multiple choice examinations, and measure impact by the number of coaches certified through the system. However, coaches put little stock in coach education programmes. As Paquette and Trudel (2018, p. 169) noted:

> Thanks to the efforts of coaching scholars to uncover the shortcomings of traditional coach development initiatives and education programs [sic] [...], coupled with the collection of targeted critiques that has accumulated as a result of this discourse [...] our expanded understanding of coach learning has led to both a reconceptualization of coach education and a reconfiguration of programming in many countries around the world.

In 2014, Callary and colleagues explored the high-performance coach education initiatives of seven national governing bodies. In addition to lecture-based instruction-centred approaches, they found coaches also engaged in various forms of workplace learning through ongoing coaching practice, mentorships, and internships in which coaches needed to reflect on their experiences, moving towards constructivist learning approaches. Experiential learning, including reflection on practice, has gained traction in coach education, but is not always effectively delivered. Not all coaches know how to reflect, nor do they do so naturally (Cushion and Nelson, 2013). While Gilbert and Trudel (2006) suggested that programmes teach strategies for coaches to reflect effectively, very few actually do so. Hence, a shortcoming of coach education is in its capacity to teach essential reflective skills for ongoing learning outside of the programme.

Many sports organisations have implemented a "LEARNS" framework (Walters, Rogers and Oldham, 2020). This acronym guides coach developers to facilitate learning that is:

- Learner-centred
- Engaging for learners
- Applicable to coaches' current work to practice implementing knowledge and skills
- Reflective practice oriented
- New knowledge
- Stretching coaches by challenging them

As a practical benefit, this framework provides language for coach developers to share strategies of experiential learning approaches enabling the coach to apply content and reflect on that application, in essence, to construct their knowledge. While this has clear opportunities to drive learning based on what the learner knows, it is important to consider how coaches might develop in areas where they are not aware of what they do not know. Further, this framework's universality may inhibit unique approaches that may work better depending on the context.

## Contextual differences

Coach education has generally moved away from a vertical progression of levels in which the coach moves through educational courses from novice coach learning about working with novice athletes to expert coach working with elite athletes. Instead, it has focused on the coach as a learner (e.g., "newcomer" to "innovator") within the context in which the coach coaches (e.g., "recreational" to "high performance").

Understanding how and what coaches are learning in different contexts has become an important concern in coach education, so coaches learn what they need to know to create quality sports experiences for their athletes. However, could typifying coaches to their perceived abilities and contexts stifle their development? If coach developers put conceptual boxes around learning, guiding coaches towards certification for their context, what happens when coaches move between contexts? Despite preliminary agreement in understanding coach education as different across competitive contexts, there is still a long way to go. For example, coaches may not fit cleanly into these typologies (e.g., they may coach across contexts or they may coach athletes from a variety of contexts within the same training session), and the athlete's competitive level is only one contextual variable. Only recently have national organisations begun to pay attention to these factors.

## "Best practices" in coach education

There has been an increasing shift in borrowing best practices from around the world. This can be seen not only in practice, but also in research. ISCJ and other journals in the field publish research that outlines, appraises, and critiques coaching best practices. These are English-language publications. While the journals have international reach, most publications come from Northern Zone nations, where researchers are often more familiar with the English language. From a practitioners' perspective, the ICCE is run by the United Kingdom and the international leadership group. Though the organisation incorporates people from many different non-English speaking nations, communication takes place mainly in English. In these examples of international efforts in coach education, the English language has become the dominant language. This further distributes power towards Northern Zone cultural beliefs about "best practices". Thus, Northern Zone methods influence as taken-for-granted ways of practicing. This can be seen in popular concepts in the coaching literature, such as athlete centredness, the importance of developing self-directed athletes, and a focus on transference of life skills from sport to everyday life. In contrast, coaching approaches using repetition and rote learning, being instruction-centred and performance-outcome focused, or conformity have progressively been rejected in the North, whilst they remain in many Southern Zone countries.

This is not meant to raise defences in research and practice, but to shine light on existing cultural forces and to enable sport educators to assess critically the ways that ideas of best practices are shaped. When Northern Zone cultures become the dominant "best practice" approaches, the globalisation of coach education becomes a journey towards assimilation that may be difficult for some to follow. At the same time, assimilation has the effect of making coach education across nations indistinguishable from one another, which could limit the scope for growth and innovation.

## Conclusion

There are several ways in which the physical education and coach education professions can move forward in culturally sensitive and growth-oriented directions. In particular, the concept of <u>glocalisation</u> has been advanced for sport educators aiming to become pracademics, familiar with both the research and practice of their trade. Glocalisation is understood here as a process wherein global best practices and ideas are blended with a society's local cultural traditions. To take a glocal approach, sport educators need to balance the demands of national and international frameworks and regulations with the need for local diversity, being global citizens in their local world. This entails an awareness of multiple perspectives, respect for diversity, valuing and protecting the environment, taking responsibility against social injustices, and engaging in non-violent conflict resolution (Ross McClain and Shepard, 2016). Further, while sport and physical activity have the potential to help participants learn important values associated with these practices, positive outcomes are dependent on how sport is presented and led. In this context, coaches and teachers are frontline leaders. Thus, it is beholden on sport educators to be pedagogues in driving positive attributes that move all participants towards global citizenship, while remaining sensitive to local traditions and interests, and this is premised on both practical and theoretical professional learning. In this way, sport educators can become pracademics – a dual role as practitioner and academic.

## References

Anderson-Levitt, K. (2008) 'Globalization and curriculum', in Connelly, F., He, M. and Phillion, J. (eds.) *Sage handbook of curriculum and instruction*. Los Angeles, CA: Sage, pp. 349–368.

Annan, K. (2002) Acceptance Speech for Moscow Award, June 5, 2002.

Bailey, R. (2018a) *Discussion paper on values, aims, and physical education towards 2030*. Paris: OECD.

Bailey, R. (2018b) *Physical education 2030*. Paris: OECD.

Bailey, R. (2020) 'Educating with brain, body and world together', *Interchange*, pp. 1–15.

Bailey, R. *et al.* (2009) 'The educational benefits claimed for physical education & school sport', *Research Papers in Education*, 24(1), pp. 1–27.

Bailey, R. and Glibo, I. (In press) 'Sports didactics in the United Kingdom', in Kleiner, K. and Höger, B. (eds.) *Sports didactics in Europe*. Münster: Waxmann.

Bailey, R., Wellard, I. and Dismore, H. (2004) *Girls' participation in physical activities & sports*. Geneva: World Health Organisation.

Callary, B. and Gearity, B. (2020) 'Introduction', in Callary, B. and Gearity, B. (eds.) *Coach education and development in sport*. London: Routledge, pp. 1–4.

Callary, B. *et al.* (2014) 'An overview of seven national high performance coach education programs', *Sport Coaching Journal*, 1(3), pp. 152–164.

Cushion, C. and Nelson, L. (2013) 'Coach education and learning', in Potrac, P., Gilbert, W. and Denison, J. (eds.) *Routledge handbook of sports coaching*. New York, NY: Routledge, pp. 359–374.

Ennis, C. (2017) 'Globalized curriculum', in Ennis, C. (ed.) *Routledge handbook of physical education pedagogies*. London: Routledge, pp. 112–126.

Farooq, M. *et al.* (2018) 'Timing of the decline in physical activity in childhood and adolescence', *British Journal of Sports Medicine*, 52(15), pp. 1002–1006.

Fitzgerald, H. (2005) 'Still feeling like a spare piece of luggage? Embodied experiences of (dis) ability in physical education and school sport', *Physical Education & Sport Pedagogy*, 10(1), pp. 41–59.

Gilbert, W. and Trudel, P. (2006) 'The coach as a reflective practitioner', in Jones, R. (ed.) *The sports coach as educator*. London: Routledge, pp. 113–127.

Guzman, A. T. (2008) *How international law works*. Oxford: Oxford University Press.

Hardman, K. and Marshall, J. (2009) *Second world-wide survey of school physical education*. Berlin: ICSSPE.

ICCE (2020) *Home Page*. Available at: http://www.icce.ws (Accessed: March 2021).

Kohl, H. *et al.* (2012). 'The pandemic of physical inactivity', *The Lancet*, 380(9838), pp. 294–305.

Light, R. (2008) 'Complex learning theory', *Journal of Teaching in Physical Education*, 27(1), pp. 21–37.

Light, R. and Harvey, S. (2017) 'Positive pedagogy for sport coaching', *Sport, Education and Society*, 22(2), pp. 271–287.

Lindsey, I. (2020) 'Analysing policy change and continuity', *Sport, Education and Society*, 25(1), pp. 27–42.

Macdonald, D., Johnson, R. and Lingard, B. (2020) 'Globalisation, neoliberalisation, and network governance', *Discourse*, pp. 1–18.

Metzler, M. (2017) *Instructional models in physical education*. London: Routledge.

Michelini, E. (2015) 'Disqualification of sport in health-related promotion of physical activity', *European Journal for Sport and Society*, 12(3), pp. 257–280.

Nike, ACSM and ICSSPE (2012) *Designed to move*. Beaverton: Nike.

Nippon Sport Science University (2018) *NCDA welcome booklet 2018–2019*. Tokyo: NSSU Coach Developer Academy.

OECD (2018) *The future of education and skills: Education 2030*. Paris: OECD.

Paquette, K. and Trudel, P. (2018) 'Learner-centered coach education', *International Sport Coaching Journal*, 5, pp. 169–175.

Parnell, D. *et al.* (2017) 'Sport policy and English primary physical education', *Sport in Society*, 20(2), pp. 292–302.

Rizvi, F. and Lingard, B. (2010) *Globalizing education policy*. London: Routledge.

Ross McLain, P. and Shepard, D. (2016) 'Twenty-first century schools, global citizenship, and glocalization', in Sparapani, E. and Ross McClain, P. (eds.) *Teaching in a globally-connected world*. Lanham, MD: Hamilton Books, pp. 109–118.

Stodter, A. and Cushion, C. (2014) 'Coaches' learning and education', *Sports Coaching Review*, 3(1), pp. 63–79.

Stromquist, N. and Monkman, K. (2014) *Globalization and education*. New York, NY: Rowman & Littlefield.

Tedlow, R. and Abdelal, R. (2004) 'Theodore Levitt's "the globalization of markets"', in Quelch, J. and Deshpandé, R. (eds.) *The global market*. San Francisco, CA: Jossey-Bass, pp. 11–30.

UNESCO (2013) *World-wide survey of school physical education*. Paris: UNESCO.

UNESCO (2015a) *International charter of physical education, physical activity and sport*. Paris: UNESCO.

UNESCO (2015b) *Quality physical education*. Paris: UNESCO.

UNESCO (2018) *Kazan Action plan – international conference of ministers and senior officials responsible for physical education and sport, 6th, Kazan, Russian Federation, 2017*. Paris: UNESCO.

Voogt, J. and Roblin, N. P. (2012) 'A comparative analysis of international frameworks for 21st century competences', *Journal of Curriculum Studies*, 44(3), pp. 299–321.

Walters, S., Rogers, A. and Oldham, A. (2020) 'A competency-based approach to coach learning', in Callary, B. and Gearity, B. (eds.) *Coach education and development in sport*. London: Routledge, pp. 154–165.

Whitelaw, S. *et al.* (2010) 'The physical activity–mental wellbeing association in young people', *Mental Health and Physical Activity*, 3(2), pp. 61–66.

World Health Organization (2010) *Global recommendations on physical activity for health*. Geneva: WHO.

Chapter 6

# The utility of new technologies in the future of sport education

*Jonathan Robertson and Margaret Bearman*

## Introduction

Technology is ubiquitous in sport. Globally this is readily apparent: from the golf coach who can simultaneously record a golfer's biomechanics, ball tracking, swing plane, and ball-impact data to the Hawk-Eye technology that can determine whether a ball was a millimetre in or out in a tennis grand slam final. Community sports administrators can upload all results instantaneously so they can be accessed globally whilst a player can do "virtual reps", practicing set plays in virtual reality by using a head-mounted display. As many of these technological "advances" are readily apparent in sport-related performance, our concern is how technology is changing the face of sport-related education within our tertiary education systems generally.

## Technology in higher education

Technology is pervasive in higher education; staff teach, and students learn in what is termed a "post-digital" era. "Post-digital" indicates that almost all social interactions, including those within higher education, are mediated by technology in some form or another (Cramer, 2015). Learning management systems (LMS), student administration systems, and social media all contribute to how students experience and learn within our university systems. The connected and omnipresent nature of our post-digital world has been highlighted as a global pandemic has forced almost all tertiary institutions to shift to online learning.

Increasing computational capacity and our networked and interconnected digital devices have led to a change in higher education. Most of us have access to smartphones, social media, and teleconferencing equipment. These open up exciting new possibilities. We have seen the rise of Massive Open Online Courses (MOOCs), promising a new kind of massification of higher education through open access to a broader market, although recent work suggests these open courses are perhaps more of a niche than a transformation (Reich and Ruipérez-Valiente, 2019). Social media such as Facebook, Pinterest, Instagram, and WhatsApp offer opportunities to support learning through both formal and

DOI: 10.4324/9781003002666-9

informal means (Manca, 2020). From an institutional perspective, big data allows teachers to review how the order of units impacts the students' progress by drawing on their assessment data (Rogaten *et al.*, 2020).

These technological advances do not come without caveats. In any discussion of technology, it is important to counter three commonly held assumptions. Firstly, being a "digital native" is seen as a myth (Bennett and Maton, 2010), and many university students lack the necessary skills to use technology. Therefore, the assumption that just because a demographic grew up in an environment that has been more heavily influenced by technology, it does not automatically follow that they possess the requisite skills to fully utilise varied technological tools, systems, and processes in an educational setting. Secondly, it is not reasonable to expect that all students have adequate access to technology, as the recent Covid-19 pandemic has revealed. Digital equity is an issue and for many students it is difficult to get sufficient access to internet and/or technology to undertake their studies (Selwyn, 2010). Finally, the assumption that students' only form of technology-mediated learning is formal. However, students can also have their own largely technology-mediated lives that may or may not support learning (Aagaard, 2015).

In the following, we highlight three particular trends that illustrate the advances in the uses of technology: audio-visual enhancements, learning analytics, and virtual reality simulations. Those trends range from relying on low-cost, readily accessible technologies to high-level, high-cost technologies.

### Audio-visual enhancements

The availability of easily recorded video on smartphones has turned a high-end technology into a readily accessible tool for university educators. One of the most common uses of video in higher education is to provide feedback information on student work. Rather than typing their comments on the students' work, educators record a few minutes of commentary. Henderson and Phillips (2015) report that students see video messages as "personal, authentic, supportive, stronger and clearer". However, this perception is not universal (Mahoney, Macfarlane and Ajjawi, 2019) and while personalised messages can promote information sharing, further research is needed to investigate how they might be used to enhance feedback dialogues (Pitt and Winstone, 2020). For example, while written feedback is the historical modality in a sport coaching class, a two- or three-minute video record from a tutor showing, pointing, and instructing might have a greater impact (both positive and negative) than written feedback could ever have.

Video can also be used to improve distance learning, particularly regarding content that is enhanced by observation. For example, video can be used to support psychomotor skill learning. Maloney *et al.* (2013) describe how physiotherapy students can share videos of themselves demonstrating complex clinical skills by uploading them to a common repository. The teacher comments on the students' work, and the class asks each student to reflect on the difference between their performance and a selected peer exemplar. A randomised controlled trial indicated that this process led to better performance in subsequent clinical assessments (Maloney *et al.*, 2013). This example illustrates both the ease-of-use of digital video to supplement performance and the necessity for good pedagogical grounding through peer observation, use of exemplars, and teachers designing appropriate feedback processes.

### Learning analytics

Learning analytics or the use of "big data" to enhance learning and teaching plays an increasingly big role in higher education. Analytics entails gathering the "trace data" that students and teachers generate in their daily interactions with technology. For instance, mouse clicks, online access to resources, and even student grades can be collated and analysed to reveal key trends in student behaviours. This information can be used to supplement teachers' and students' capabilities.

Learning analytics can be used for that purpose at an institutional level. For example, the Open University has introduced the use of predictive learning analytics to assist teachers in identifying "at risk" students (Herodotou *et al.*, 2019). Their system Open University Analytics (OUA) uses a traffic light system to indicate if students are likely to miss submission of their next assessment (red), have a moderate possibility of failing or scraping through (yellow), or are likely to succeed (green). A large-scale study of over 14,000 students suggests that teachers who used this system to prompt proactive support had students who did better than prior to the introduction of the OUA (Herodotou *et al.*, 2019). This might simply be a consequence of notifying students of their assignment being due or more complex interventions. Note that, as with any form of predictive work, there are key ethical issues: prediction is merely a correlation and should not be mistaken for an indication of how the student will actually perform. Learning analytics only collect a simple form of data and simple mouse clicks should not be interpreted too deeply. After all, the most significant information provided by learning analytics is a lack of access: if a student fails to log into an LMS and therefore does not have access to key information, it is obvious that they are very likely going to fall behind.

### Extended reality: New forms of simulation-based education

Extended reality (i.e., virtual, and augmented reality) allows students to see, feel, and interact in three dimensions (Fealy *et al.*, 2019). Virtual reality specifically holds great potential in courses that require three-dimensional manipulations or psychomotor skills such as engineering or nursing. These build upon a large empirical and pedagogical foundation underpinning simulation-based education. It is worth noting the emphasis on learning, with simulation being defined as: "[...] a technique, not a technology, to replace or amplify real experiences with guided experiences, often immersive in nature, that evoke or replicate substantial aspects of the real world in a fully interactive fashion" (Gaba, 2004, p. 2).

As immersive virtual reality is expensive to develop, it is important to think about what the modality adds that other modalities cannot supply. For example, in engineering or architecture, immersive virtual reality allows the students to experience spatial immersion (Wang *et al.*, 2018). In nursing or medicine, students can practice haptic (touch-based) skills by, for example, practicing the insertion of a urinary catheter (Butt, Kardong-Edgren and Ellertson, 2018). In line with those applications, different potential uses within sport education unfold. For example to correct alignment in a skill acquisition class using visual cues built into the simulation. As with all simulation-based experiences, the facilitation around the simulation activity itself is a critical factor in promoting learning (Bearman, Greenhill and Nestel, 2019). Practically, this implies that the rationale for using the immersive virtual simulation should be shared as well as the gaps between reality and the simulation outlined. Debriefing processes, whereby the learners make sense of their experiences through interactions with others, are a critical part of simulation-based education (Cheng *et al.*, 2014), and there is no reason to think that immersive virtual reality should be any different.

## Technology adoption in sport and physical activity programmes in universities

Technology adoption in sport-related education faces two main challenges. The first is a rapidly changing technological environment outside of the higher education sector. As indicated before, technological trends have a ripple effect throughout the sport sector. The increases in computational power and number of products have expanded the range and functions of available technology-supported goods and services for physically active consumers whilst lowering the cost. Ubiquitous access to, for example, GPS and accelerometer data via mobile phones and compact accelerometers supports an increased interest in data and the "quantified self" (Lupton, 2016). For instance, Strava, an exercise application that tracks outdoor exercise activities, now has over 50 million users. Widespread adoption of these technologies facilitates the production of gigantic amounts of data. Big data however requires informed analysis to unfold its value. As a result, requirements for graduates, particularly sport science graduates, is shifting to a strong emphasis of statistical analysis to meet the needs of a changing profession.

The second challenge is related to the internal pace of change in sport- and physical education-related studies in the higher education sector. The sector is required to respond to the increasing technological proficiency of students whilst being structured around lecture halls, overheads, and chalkboards in many institutions around the world. Predominant conservatism of many higher education providers slows that process down. Universities need to react: on a pragmatic resource level (e.g., investment in technology, training, and incentivising staff); regarding institutionalised norms and values embedded in higher education (e.g., that higher education should be primarily delivered face-to-face in a classroom relative to other virtual and in person modalities); and facing systemic implementation problems (e.g., the need to implement this across multiple campuses and support many thousands of students to adopt a new approach).

Within this two-speed technological environment, sports and physical activity programmes face the compounding problem that their field touches on most university structures. Sport- and physical activity-related domains range across the social (e.g., management, economics, and psychology), biological (e.g., medical, physiology, nutrition), and physical sciences (e.g., engineering, chemistry). Consequently, there is no one-size-fits-all solution. What can be seen is a range of advances in innovative educational technologies across the university sector. Rather than focus solely on one or few of these innovations here, this section takes a more holistic, future-oriented viewpoint by framing the needs of the sports graduate in 2035.

## A brave new world – Technology-mediated sport and physical education in 2035

From now to the year 2035, it seems to still be a long time. In terms of education it really is not. It is approximately the same period as from when Facebook, Twitter, and Instagram were created up to now, 2021. A student entering high school in 2022 will generally take six years to graduate. During this time, a responsive university must hire staff, develop course content, teach out old content, transition to new structures, and implement a range of technological and pedagogical advances to meet the students' needs for *then*, rather than now. In 2028, the students, having completed their high school degree, will enter programmes responding to the needs of technological trends we are seeing now. Three to four years after their start, assuming they are completing the programme consistently and full-time (i.e., not inclusive of part time, exchange periods, gap years, or degree switching, etc.), they will graduate in 2032. Graduates in 2032 will enter an increasingly globally competitive job market, competing with a growing number of graduates from the same discipline area, to then start their first job. Conservatively, by the time they get a year or two of experience to implement what they have learnt, it is 2035. Our question as sport educators needs to be: what future skills and competencies do we need to think about creating *now* to prepare our students the best we can for *then*?

Coming with many of these changes is a broader employment shift towards automation across several sectors. Thinking about education in these terms has some potential to help sport educators conceptualise technologies' place in education in the years to come. In 2013, a study by Oxford University researchers Frey and Osborne found that routine tasks were more susceptible to computerisation (i.e., automation), those tasks with "well defined procedures that can easily be performed by sophisticated algorithms" (Frey and Osborne, 2013, p. 2). Simultaneously, non-routine tasks such as perception and manipulation (e.g., dexterity involved in movement), creativity and creative intelligence (e.g., coming up with new ideas that are valuable), and social intelligence (e.g., negotiation, persuasion, and care) were all exceedingly difficult skills to build and programme, making automation unlikely. In the sports context, the report found a 98% probability that umpires, referees, and sports officials could become automated given the highly routinised nature of their role – applying a routine procedure called a "rule book" (Frey and Osborne, 2013). The rise of video-enabled technology such as Hawk-Eye technology in tennis and cricket, and goal line/offside technology in soccer, are indicative of this shift. Conversely, athletes and sports competitors only face a 28% chance of automation in the same report (Frey and Osborne, 2013). We adopt this logic to frame the future of sport-related education and technological adoption to argue that routine tasks will increasingly become automated via online content delivery supported by learning analytics. Consequently, the role of sport- and physical activity-related education may combine in the areas of non-routine activities that involve higher order learning outcomes such as critical thinking, problem-solving, and communication.

Knowledge transfer in the form of information and lecture content can be thought of as a fairly routinised process. A lecture in one year may not be substantially different from prior or following years. Additionally, learning analytics regarding automated prompts around engagement and achievement are programmable. Once set, learning analytics require little upkeep year by year. During the global Covid-19 pandemic, universities shifted to online teaching wherever possible. This comes after years of the traditional lecture format slowly disappearing or at least being challenged by new and more effective and efficient forms of teaching in several disciplines. During the period to 2035, we suggest that the classroom, finally, will finish "flipping" to be oriented towards in person skill development (i.e., in class) and digital knowledge transfer online (i.e., digital lectures). Why would students physically attend a lecture if they could watch it online? For sport educators already working in a heavily applied discipline, this means more education is likely to take place out of the class and in the (potential) workplaces of future graduates.

During the past decade we have seen the rise of MOOCs. For sport, this presents both short-term opportunities and substantive long-term challenges. In the short term, universities can position themselves as providing online first options as part of their normal enrolment. Technically, students around the globe could enrol in a subject if they are willing to pay for that subject or degree. Simultaneously, however, a range of courses are offered for free or at low cost. For example, if a student wishes to learn about how to prevent doping, they can take a free anti-doping course via Coursera, provided by the University of Lausanne that has access to guest speakers including the Court of Arbitration for Sport, World Anti-Doping Authority, European football federations (UEFA), and specialists in the doping field. This is just one example of several diverse subject specialisations from marketing to concussion, e-sport to diversity and inclusion. If universities rely on routinised forms of knowledge transmission, then they will be more susceptible to competition from competitors who are able to efficiently automate these routine behaviours.

Coursera are also leading the way in automating learning analytics, with innovative methods to verify users and grade knowledge-based assessments. For example, MOOC providers are increasingly relying on keystroke dynamics to produce "keyprints" (i.e., typing fingerprints based on your typing pattern) to validate users on their platforms (Young *et al.*, 2019). Additionally, pedagogical designs, whilst not perfect, do accommodate levels of feedback information equal to or greater than that of multiple-choice quizzes currently utilised in many LMS at universities. Such feedback information is only possible, at scale, for routinised tasks that are programmable. Non-routine tasks such as creativity and social intelligence require aspects of human judgement and decision-making and thus pose difficulties to extend beyond a basic knowledge at scale.

The automation of routine educational behaviours can drive down the cost of these types of educational opportunities. A MOOC created for doping or digital marketing may need to be updated annually, but the workload to achieve this is arguably no different to what is replicated by academics around the world each year. As such, mass online options may become more legitimate in the market, which poses interesting questions for universities globally. If free, and/or low-cost alternatives to the knowledge provided within your degree programmes are available at the most prestigious universities globally, why would students choose to pay more for local universities? One answer can be to use technology to support the education of non-routine behaviours that require decision-making, critical thinking, communication, and problem-solving.

## Enhancing education or replicating the lecture theatre? The classroom of tomorrow

The job market a sports student is going to enter in the coming years will be substantially different to today. We argue that sport educators should focus on using technology to support the development of non-routine learning outcomes such as critical thinking, problem-solving, and communication – those skills and behaviours that either require physical dexterity (e.g., as is the case with much of the sport sciences) or combinations of creating and social intelligence (e.g., managerial negotiation and decision-making). Sports journalism provides an illustrative example. In recent years, the necessity for sports journalists to produce match reports or highlights packages has substantially been reduced, the skill set has been, and will continue to be, automated by a variety of software solutions that are able to automatically analyse game-related content and package it for consumers (PWC, 2019). Similar at-risk jobs include stadium entry workers, ticketing, umpiring, and video editors. Our argument is therefore that technology innovation should not be seen as "going online", this is a routine behaviour that even the most conservative universities are undertaking in the post-pandemic world. Rather sport educators need to focus on utilising technology to develop non-routine skills and to develop skills and knowledge for professions that are at a low risk of automation. In this way, technology adoption in sport-related education adds value to both educational practice and future job functions.

Extended reality provides examples of how technology can enhance, rather than replicate existing practices. Augmented reality does exactly that, it augments the physical world to provide an enhanced interactive experience with it (e.g., think the Pokémon Go app). This approach has the ability to augment education in the real (i.e., non-virtual) world. Augmented reality could support a sport development student create physical activity solutions for groups who do not have access to traditional forms of exercise. For example, in the same way that Pokémon Go creates virtual "battles", a trainer may be able to create a virtual workout in an open space. Alternatively, immersive virtual environments hold the potential to train social interactions and improve decision-making by immersing students in a virtual environment and following various decision-making scenarios in order to develop an understanding of the implications of various behaviours. An example in the sports domain is decision-making in American Football. In a study by Stanford, the quarterbacks of various college teams utilised virtual reality to simulate plays on the field, read opposition defences, and, via repetition, improve their decision-making under pressure (Bailenson, 2018). Whilst not everyone can be a pro-quarterback, let us translate the analogy to a manager negotiating a contract, a coach explaining a new training drill, or a marketer testing product messaging. If we can develop creative and social intelligence via virtual repetition of decision-making scenarios or similar, the classroom of tomorrow may look substantially different than today.

## Conclusion

Educators are increasingly operating in a post-digital world. Enhancements in computational power and range of products and services mean that students have been progressively reliant on digital and technology-based forms of education. This has led to the increase of audio-visual delivery and feedback, learning analytics, and immersive virtual environments. Looking forward over the next 15 years, we argue that routine educational behaviours will be replicated and digitised, the classroom will be flipped. At the same time, we argue that such advances are not necessarily innovative or improving the educational experience of students. In many cases, simply replicating what has physically been done in universities for more than a century may be more detrimental than positive. Instead, we promote the positioning of technology usage to enhance the education of non-routine behaviours.

## References

Aagaard, J. (2015) 'Drawn to distraction: A qualitative study of off-task use of educational technology', *Computers & Education*, 87, pp. 90–97.

Bailenson, J. (2018) *Experience on demand. What virtual reality is, how it words, and what it can do.* New York, NY: Norton and Company.

Bearman, M., Greenhill, J. and Nestel, D. (2019) 'The power of simulation: A large-scale narrative analysis of learners' experiences', *Medical Education*, 53(4), pp. 369–379.

Bennett, S. and Maton, K. (2010) 'Beyond the 'digital natives' debate: Towards a more nuanced understanding of students' technology experiences', *Journal of Computer Assisted Learning*, 26(5), pp. 321–331.

Butt, A. L., Kardong-Edgren, S. and Ellertson, A. (2018) 'Using game-based virtual reality with haptics for skill acquisition', *Clinical Simulation in Nursing*, 16, pp. 25–32.

Cheng, A. *et al.* (2014) 'Debriefing for technology-enhanced simulation: A systematic review and meta-analysis', *Medical Education*, 48(7), pp. 657–666.

Cramer, F. (2015) 'What is 'post-digital'?', in Berry, D. M. and Dieter, M. (eds.) *Postdigital aesthetics*. London: Palgrave Macmillan, pp. 12–26.

Fealy, S. *et al.* (2019) 'The integration of immersive virtual reality in tertiary nursing and midwifery education: A scoping review', *Nurse Education Today*, 79, pp. 14–19.

Frey, C. B. and Osborne, M. A. (2013) *The future of employment: How susceptible are jobs to computerization? Working paper.* Oxford: Oxford University.

Gaba, D. M. (2004) 'The future vision of simulation in health care', *BMJ Quality & Safety*, 13(1), pp. 2–10.

Henderson, M. and Phillips, M. (2015) 'Video-based feedback on student assessment: Scarily personal', *Australasian Journal of Educational Technology*, 31(1), pp. 51–66.

Herodotou, C. *et al.* (2019) 'Empowering online teachers through predictive learning analytics', *British Journal of Educational Technology*, 50(6), pp. 3064–3079.

Lupton, D. (2016) *The quantified self.* Cambridge: Polity Press.

Mahoney, P., Macfarlane, S. and Ajjawi, R. (2019) 'A qualitative synthesis of video feedback in higher education', *Teaching in Higher Education*, 24(2), pp. 157–179.

Maloney, S. *et al.* (2013) 'The effect of student self-video of performance on clinical skill competency: A randomised controlled trial', *Advances in Health Sciences Education*, 18(1), pp. 81–89.

Manca, S. (2020) 'Snapping, pinning, liking or texting: Investigating social media in higher education beyond Facebook', *The Internet and Higher Education*, 44(100707), pp. 1–13.

Pitt, E. and Winstone, N. (2020) 'Towards technology enhanced dialogic feedback', in Bearman, M. *et al.* (eds.) *Re-imagining university assessment in a digital world.* Berlin: Springer, pp.79-94.

PWC (2019) *Artificial intelligence: Application to the sports industry.* London.

Reich, J. and Ruipérez-Valiente, J. A. (2019) 'The MOOC pivot', *Science*, 363(6423), pp. 130–131.

Rogaten, J. *et al.* (2020) 'Are assessment practices well aligned over time? A big data exploration', in Bearman, M. *et al.* (eds.) *Re-imagining university assessment in a digital world.* Berlin: Springer, pp 147-164..

Selwyn, N. (2010) 'Degrees of digital division: Reconsidering digital inequalities and contemporary higher education', *RUSC. Universities and Knowledge Society Journal*, 7(1), pp. 33–42.

Wang, P. *et al.* (2018) 'A critical review of the use of virtual reality in construction engineering education and training', *International Journal of Environmental Research and Public Health*, 15(6), pp. 1204–1222.

Young, J. R. *et al.* (2019) 'Keystroke dynamics: Establishing keyprints to verify users in online courses', *Computers in Schools*, 36(1), pp. 48–68.

Chapter 7

# Industry alignment

## Fit-for-purpose sport education

*Steven Osborne and Elizabeth Lewis*

## Introduction

The sport and active leisure sector is a labour-intensive sector with a share in the national economies comparable to agriculture, forestry, and fishing combined (European Commission, 2018c). Sport has a positive role in tackling social issues such as unhealthy lifestyles (Council of European Union, 2017). The European Union-funded Europen Sector Skills Alliance for Sport and Physical Activity (ESSA-Sport) project (2020) completed an analysis of the professional sport-specific labour market across Europe, reporting that 1,765,728 paid professionals are working in the European sports labour market, an increase of 19.2% since 2011. This total sectoral employment figure represents 0.79% of the European total employment figures (ESSA-Sport, 2020). The report also concludes that national sports organisational ecosystems (Osborne, 2016) differ in their maturity and scale and that there is evidence of traditional careers, self-employment, gaps in professional skill development, and a requirement for detailed workforce planning to meet sports organisations' future needs across Europe. To realise and protect the socio-economic potential that sport holds, educational leaders, policy leaders, and employers need to focus on workforce planning and strengthen prospective and current employees' employability.

The World Economic Forum (2020) warns that workforce transformation is accelerating globally and having a pervasive impact on all industries with critical drivers such as technology advances, an ageing workforce, and skill instability. Retirement and leadership transition will affect the non-profit sector worldwide with the need to replace every existing senior executive position by the mid-2020s (McIsaac, Park and Toupin, 2013). Deloitte Consulting (2018) point out that workforce transitions and re-skilling pose substantial risks to organisations, which need to explore interventions such as talent development pathways and accelerated management programmes to ensure ongoing success and sustainability. The Organisation for Economic Co-operation and Development (OECD, 2016) suggests that all industries and governments need to focus on developing workers employability by anticipating skill needs, reinforcing the role of training, enhancing the adaptability of workplaces, and promoting labour mobility to be resilient to

DOI: 10.4324/9781003002666-10

these global trends. There is also growing evidence of the specific need to develop sports workforce skills, knowledge, and behaviours. In 2019, the Association of Summer Olympic International Federations (ASOIF) produced an international report on "The Future of Global Sport", highlighting several disruptive trends in the industry, changing the business and operational landscape including demographic, social, and technological changes. The report concludes that international sport federations must maintain and strengthen their coordination and oversight roles and develop more proactive, creative, commercially driven, and collaborative mindsets to ensure long-term survival and success (ASOIF, 2019).

As the professional nature and size of the large, stratified, global sports organisational ecosystem (Osborne, 2016) has developed, the number of sports programmes offered by higher education providers has also grown in epicentres such as the United States, Europe, Canada, and Australia. This rapid development in specialist but relatively immature sports disciplines means that curricular design and research agendas are often open to institutions' interpretation and expertise (Pitchford and Bacon, 2005). Due to this rapid massification of sports courses, higher education is being scrutinised by governments and employers questioning graduates' ability to enter the workplace successfully (CIMSPA, 2020). Tensions are now emerging where academics can be conflicted with maintaining academic autonomy with the pressure of preparing students for roles within the sector (Aldous and Brown, 2020).

This academic versus employer divide must be tackled proactively and not lose sight of individual learners' life and career ambitions. Low infiltration of graduates into the sports industry highlights that both sides need to engage in meaningful discourse to prevent further disconnection and wasted potential (CIMSPA, 2020). Barcelona and Ross (2004) argue that, in order to provide students with the skills and tools necessary to deliver recreational sports services, it is imperative for both employers and higher education institutions to clearly define a framework of competencies, knowledge areas, and skill sets. If graduates can secure a job on graduation, they will also need the knowledge and skills to continue developing their employability to maintain or progress in their career (Akkermans *et al.*, 2013). Engaging with sports organisations is therefore vital in validating and developing sports discipline approaches that ensure the knowledge, skills, and competencies within academic programmes can meet the broader organisational sports ecosystem workforce needs.

## Developing employability

The definitions of employability are contested, but with a growing consensus that it is more than obtaining employment and should also focus on supporting learners to build meaningful careers (Cole and Tibby, 2013). Authors from different disciplinary backgrounds agree that a unified definition and integration of conceptual frameworks are needed (Knight and Yorke, 2004; Peeters et al. 2019). Römgens, Scoupe and Beausaert (2020) offer a recent review combining the fields of employability research in higher education and workplace learning, arguing that they both lean on a competency-based approach to employability. In this sense, a competency-based approach to defining employability suggests it is a time-phased, multi-dimensional process in which individuals develop competencies that help obtain and retain employment (Van der Heijde and Van der Heijden, 2006).

The workplace view offers a body of literature on competence-based approaches to employability in the context of workplace learning. Six frequently cited conceptual frameworks consist of different dimensions, including career competencies (DeFillippi and Arthur, 1994), work-related adaptability (Fugate, Kinicki and Ashforth, 2004), movement capital (Forrier, Sels and Stynen, 2009), anticipation, optimisation, and personal flexibility (Van der Heijde and Van der Heijden, 2006), career development competencies (Akkermans *et al.*, 2013), and employability capital (Peeters *et al.*, 2019). The higher education view often cites four core models to conceptualise employability, including the "Understanding Skills Efficacy Metacognition" model (USEM, Knight and Yorke, 2004), the "Key to Employability model" (Dacre Pool and Sewell, 2007), the "Career management for maximum employability" (Bridgstock, 2009), and the "concept of graduate identity" (Hinchliffe and Jolly, 2011).

In 2016, the European Sectoral Social Dialogue Committee for Sports adopted a joint opinion that aligns with literature on employability. They stated that employability is a holistic concept that stresses an individual's capability to move into and within contextually sensitive labour markets and to realise their potential through sustainable and accessible employment. It is not within this chapter's scope to thoroughly review the higher education and workplace views but instead draw from both to present a new employability framework for sports disciplines to plan curriculum design. The broad principles of seven pedagogical planning dimensions that can be utilised to develop employability can include:

- Core Discipline Knowledge
- Work-Related Learning (WRL)
- Work-Based Learning (WBL)
- Career Development Learning (CDL)
- Graduate Skills and Lifelong Learning
- Entrepreneurship and Enterprise Education
- Developing Professional Identity

### Core Discipline Knowledge

The European Commission defines a profession as regulated if an individual needs to hold a specific degree to access the profession, sit special exams, and register with a professional body. Gardner and Shulman (2005) described six characteristics of a profession as being a commitment to clients and society, a specialised body of knowledge, a specialised and unique set of skills, the ability to make judgments with integrity in environments of uncertainty, growing new bodies of knowledge through experience, and a community of professionals who perform oversight and monitoring of professional practice. Sport has seen a growing number of commentaries exploring theses professional principles and has started to offer professional frameworks in coaching (Galatti *et al.*, 2016), sport psychology (Portenga,

Aoyagi and Cohen, 2017), and sport management (CIMSPA, 2020). Academics need to approach the development of industry-relevant discipline and procedural knowledge within sports degrees in response to this professionalisation of sport. The development of professional standards in sport offers a structured approach to curriculum design and an opportunity to define a sports professional's critical tasks. Parry (2015) identified that a marker of professional orientation of bachelor's degrees is their accreditation by professional, statutory, and regulatory bodies, ensuring the degree programme content aligns with the knowledge and skills that employers value most through a constructive alignment process (Biggs, 2014). McMahon and Thakore (2006) suggest that, at institutional levels, constructive alignment can lead to greater standardisation, greater transparency, more accurate inter-university comparisons, greater coherence in learning programmes, and an increase in the criticality and depth of student work.

### *Work-Related Learning (WRL)*

WRL interventions focus on planned activities that use the context of work to develop knowledge, skills, and understanding. This includes learning about work and working practices and learning the skills for work (Work-related Learning Guide, 2008). It involves learners in activities that mirror authentic professional practices (Edelson and Reiser, 2006). This experiential learning is a set of strategies that structure the acquisition of information, analysis of ideas, and self-reflection in order to pull people into active engagement with their world (Braid, 2008). In establishing this notion of WRL, higher education can use on- or off-campus interventions (O'Shea, 2008) like insight visits, guest lectures, case studies, and the application of simulations through live or technology-enhanced experiences, for example augmented and virtual-reality (Makransky *et al.*, 2020). Shulman (2005) describes learning by immersing students in "real world" activities as signature pedagogies. Established practitioner-focused, academic disciplines such as law and health have coined the term "signature pedagogies" as "the types of teaching that organise the fundamental ways in which future practitioners are educated for their new professions" (p. 52). Sports disciplines have not yet explored this approach but can design engaging signature pedagogies using sport's unique characteristics.

### *Work-Based Learning (WBL)*

WBL blends theory and action (Raelin, 1997). Mumm (2006, p. 74) argues that "students learn best by practising the skills, second-best by having the skills demonstrated for them and the least effective ways are lecture and discussion". In WBL, students engage in a range of experiences and placement types that range in proximity (to a workplace) and authenticity (Kaider, Hains-Wesson and Young, 2017). Work shadowing is a vicarious experience that involves observing a professional in their job to understand the role better, resulting in an experience that has high proximity but low authenticity. Detached and integrated live briefs offer similar examples, involving commissioning projects where students can engage with employers on a specific problem (QAA, 2018). Virtual and in-person work placements can be short or extended periods of work experience where a student works with employers in the workplace or a digitally supported learning environment. These experiences can offer high levels of proximity and authenticity. "Cooperative education" is a further example of alternating academic terms and paid work terms, offering an immersive experience in a workplace setting related to the student's professional study field (Khampirat and McRae, 2016). WBL and WRL can support the development of students' professional identities (Nixon and Murr, 2006). There is evidence that an accumulated learning effect occurs with each placement opportunity a student engages with (Sheepway, Lincoln and McAllister, 2014). O'Brien *et al.* (2019) argue that in this sense, work experiences provide students with multiple opportunities to apply academic theory to practice, to develop discipline-specific and cross-disciplinary skills, to socialise into their chosen profession, and to hone relevant interpersonal skills required by employers.

### *Career Development Learning*

Greenbank (2014) argues that for students to be more rational in their career-building activities, they need appropriate support. CDL develops specific knowledge, skills, and capabilities to secure initial employment and ongoing career management and is typically enhanced by useful career guidance (Watts, 2006). Early differential approaches (Parsons, 1909) to CDL focused on trait-based assessment and guidance, fixated on how individuals differ and how these differences can be measured. Minten and Forsyth (2014) however argue that traditional views of linear and hierarchical career progression should be rejected and instead viewed as fluid and contingent, in line with modern organisational environments. There is a growing evidence that a multi-faceted curricular and extracurricular approach to embedding guidance, coupled with multiple interactions with career advisors, has the most significant impact on student CDL (Christie, 2016). The CDL and guidance field is subsequently evolving into a group of theories, associated interventions, and tools that can facilitate employability and transition from education settings into professional settings. These learning and guidance approaches aim to develop the learners' metacognitive, career management, workplace exploration, and career control competencies (Akkermans *et al.*, 2013).

### *Graduate Skills and Lifelong Learning*

Human capital refers to the general and specific knowledge, skills, and attitudes needed to meet the performance expectations of a given occupation or professional domain (Van der Heijde and Van der Heijden, 2006). The language of "skills" describes the range of personal abilities and features that students and graduates need to possess. Kalfa and Taksa (2015) are critical of the idea that employability should focus on skills or human capital in isolation, arguing that skills are socially constructed and that the focus on development of generic skills may not be sensitive to the contextual occupational or organisation differences that students may face.

However, Rust (2002) offers a centre ground suggesting the synthesis of attributes will only happen if the student is aware of the attributes they have, how they work together and can articulate them. Programme designers can also consider developing learners' self-awareness, self-reliance, independence, academic mindsets and dispositions, self-regulated learning skills, academic behaviours, and commitment to embedding themselves in the professional community (Haynes *et al.*, 2016). Fostering generic academic and lifelong learning competencies enables learners to react and adjust to the demands of ongoing social, cultural, technological, and economic changes and contribute as active citizens to their communities (Otten and Ohana, 2009). Relevant frameworks such as the European Commission DIGIcomp (2018a) and ENTREcomp (2018b) frameworks can provide a key focus for developing innovative teaching, learning, and assessment interventions.

### *Entrepreneurship and Enterprise Education*

ESSA-Sport (2020) has identified that Eurostat data highlights high levels of self-employment within the sports industry across Europe. There are also persistent requirements from industry employers to develop broader entrepreneurial orientation skills such as innovation, creativity, proactiveness, and autonomy, as the sports industry restructures in response to technology and socio-economic disruptions (ASOIF, 2019). It is necessary to support students to develop enterprise and entrepreneurship knowledge, skills, and behaviour as part of a more comprehensive employability strategy. "Enterprise" education is the process of developing students in a manner that provides them with an enhanced capacity to generate ideas, and the behaviours, attributes, and competencies to make them happen (QAA, 2018). Alternatively, "Entrepreneurship" education is the application of the above to create cultural, social, or economic value; this can, but does not exclusively, lead to venture creation (QAA, 2018). Herrmann *et al.* (2008) suggest that developing enterprising and entrepreneurial graduates requires teaching and learning practices including experimentation, discovery, innovative pedagogies, and experiential approaches through entrepreneurial sensitisation, education, and training. Herrmann *et al.* (2008) also imply that universities need to engage stakeholders including academic faculty, student societies, other entrepreneurs, and businesses, indicating that these groups can act as "agents" in creating entrepreneurship activities. Finally, universities need to commit to creating an enabling environment that embeds an entrepreneurial culture to see the full benefit of this approach (Herrmann *et al.*, 2008).

### *Developing Professional Identity*

Jackson (2017) asserts that "Professional Identity" (PI) encompasses an understanding of one's professional goals and commitments, and perceptions of meaningfulness of work and future orientations as professionals. Monrouxe (2010) asserted that external values and formalised ways of carrying out work are internalised and accepted by the learner in this socialisation process. Within sports subjects, the process of identity formation of emerging professionals has attracted little attention but can be explored, as disciplines and occupations in sport establish a formal professional status. Wilkins (2020) suggests "Professional Identity Development" (PID) should focus on a balance of technical components – skill, knowledge, and competencies – and the transmission of the values, morals, rules, and behaviours of a profession. Aside of this it is the role of educators to support and guide students to think, feel, and act as members of the profession they are being trained for, facilitating PID through deliberate pedagogical design (Wilkins, 2020).

Jackson (2017) calls the emerging, less mature version of the PI of students their "pre-professional identity" (PPI). She defines it as "an understanding of and connection with the skills, qualities, conduct, culture, and ideology of a student's intended profession" (Jackson, 2017, p. 836). The definition marks the conception that students are becoming, rather than being, a professional, what De-Weerdt *et al.* (2006) describe as pre-accredited professionals. Many of the PPI components overlap with attributes connected to employability including the ability to reflect on experiences and an understanding of responsibilities involved (Jackson, 2017). Barbara-i-Molinero, Cascón-Pereira and Hernández-Lara (2017) argue that developing a strong PPI in students has been associated with a successful transition to the workplace, higher student motivation, and confidence in their early career roles.

## Conclusion

The sports organisational ecosystem aspires to have a coherent, fit-for-purpose training and education system, supported by a sector-wide professional development culture. This chapter points out that establishing a single unified voice between employers, academics, and learners will ensure that there is a shared ownership to developing and improving sport education. The chapter proposes a shift from the over-reliance on traditional pedagogical strategies to a sports curriculum that creates competent, confident, and resilient graduates. Despite the concerns raised by some academics, Biggs (2014) argues that teaching devolved to the discretion of individual teachers to – in the name of "academic freedom" – teach how and what they want can result in a range in the quality of teaching from the "irresponsibly bad" to the "individually excellent". The move towards the professionalisation of sports occupations presents an opportunity to reimagine how sports curricula can be designed and delivered in partnership with employers and learners. This shift in focus can help students clarify career interests and goals, apply classroom theory to practical experiences, and develop specific and lifelong skills. Embedding employability pedagogies in programmes should ensure students build confidence, maturity, professionalism, and develop opportunities for employment and long-term career success. The seven employability dimensions outlined in this chapter offer a menu of interventions based on the combination of critical theories from the higher education and workplace views of employability. Programme leaders should consider the dimensions and questions outlined in the "professional identity and employability framework" (Table 7.1), utilising them individually or in combination when designing their curricular.

Table 7.1 Professional Identity and Employability Framework

| Foundation Attributes / General Skills | Professional Identity | Work-Based Learning | Knowledge | Work-Related Learning | Career Development Learning | Enterprise Education |
|---|---|---|---|---|---|---|
| Lifelong learning | Knowledge of the profession | Proximity and authenticity | Discipline-specific conceptual knowledge | Engineer learning through deliberate and managed experiences | Develop metacognitive skills that support self-awareness | Develop key human skills including creative and innovative thought |
| General attributes | Knowledge of the industry qualifications | Develop knowledge and skills | Discipline-specific procedural knowledge | Authentic information, tasks, industry contexts, and professionals | Manage transition from novice into career professional | Explore experiences and activities that support self-awareness |
| Ethics Morality | Personal identity formation | Mirroring and vicarious observations of existing professionals | Constructive alignment to professional standards | Develop deep knowledge and provide vicarious observations | Transition into employment, identify the industry and employer expectations | Developing skills that identify and monitor industry trends |
| Digital literacy | Collective identity formation | Authentic rehearsal and practice of skills and behaviours | | Reinforce industry values, provide authentic rehearsal of skills and behaviours | Developing skills to manage ongoing professional development | Developing skills and knowledge to manage new ideas into sustainable action |
| Research literacy | Specific/shared behaviours Codes of practice professional ethics/values | Developing skills to build social and professional capacity | | | Developing skills to enter and progress career | Developing skills to work for others or self |

Moving forward, the challenge for the sport sector is how to establish core knowledge in an ever-changing environment, with the development of new sports activities and global megatrends such as digitisation. To be effective in this dynamic environment it will take a collective and collaborative leadership effort from sports employers and academics to ensure that sport education is "empathetic" to the needs of the sport, "fit-for-purpose", and "future-facing".

## References

Akkermans, J. *et al.* (2013) 'Competencies for the contemporary career: Development and preliminary validation of the career competencies questionnaire', *Journal of Career Development*, 40(3), pp. 245–267.

Aldous, D. and Brown, D. (2020) 'A critical analysis of CIMSPA's transformative aspirations for U.K. Higher education sport and physical activity vocational education and training provision', *Sport, Education and Society*. pp.1–14.

Association of Summer Olympic International Federations (ASOIF) (2019) *The Future of Global Sport Report*. Available at: https://www.asoif.com/sites/default/files/download/future_of_global_sport.pdf (Accessed: December 2020).

Barbarà-i-Molinero, A., Cascón-Pereira, R. and Hernández-Lara, A. (2017) 'Professional identity development in higher education: Influencing factors', *International Journal of Educational Management*, 31(2), pp. 189–203.

Barcelona, B. and Ross, C. M. (2004) 'An analysis of the perceived competencies of recreational sport administrators', *Journal of Park & Recreation Administration*, 22(4).

Biggs, J. (2014) 'Constructive alignment in university teaching', *HERDSA Review of higher education*, 1(1), pp. 5–22.

Braid, B. (2008) 'Majoring in the minor: A closer look at experiential learning', *HIP*, 4, pp. 37–42.

Bridgstock, R. (2009) 'The graduate attributes we've overlooked: Enhancing graduate employability through career management skills', *Higher Education Research & Development*, 28(1), pp. 31–44.

Chartered Institute for the Management of Sport and Physical Activity (CIMSPA, 2020) *Workforce Insight Report (U.K.)*. Available at: https://www.cimspa.co.uk/cimspa-news/workforce-insight (Accessed: December 2020).

Christie, F. (2016) 'Careers guidance and social mobility in U.K. higher education: Practitioner perspectives', *British Journal of Guidance & Counselling*, 44(1), pp. 72–85.

Cole, D. and Tibby, M. (2013) *Defining and developing your approach to employability: A framework for higher education institutions*. Heslington: The Higher Education Academy.

Council of the European Union (2017) *Resolution of the Council and of the Representatives of the Governments of the Member States, Meeting within the Council, on the European Union Work Plan for Sport*. Available at: https://data.consilium.europa.eu/doc/document/ST-9639-2017-INIT/en/pdf (Accessed: February 2019).

Dacre Pool, L. and Sewell, P. (2007) 'The key to employability: Developing a practical model of graduate employability', *Education+ Training*, 49(4), pp. 277–289.

DeFillippi, R. J. and Arthur, M. B. (1994) 'The boundaryless career: A competency-based perspective', *Journal of Organizational Behavior*, 15(4), pp. 307–324.

Deloitte Consulting, L. L. P. (2018) *Global Human Capital Trends 2018: The Rise of the Social Enterprise*. Available at: https://www2.deloitte.com/content/dam/Deloitte/at/Documents/human-capital/at-2018-deloitte-human-capital-trends.pdf (Accessed: February 2019).

De Weerdt, S. *et al.* (2006) 'Identity transformation as an intercontextual process', *Industry and Higher Education*, 20(5), pp. 317–326.

Edelson, D. and Reiser, B. (2006) 'Making authentic practices accessible to learning: Design challenges and strategies', in Sawyer, R. K. (ed.) *The Cambridge handbook of the learning sciences*. New York, NY: Cambridge University Press, pp. 335–354.

ESSA-Sport (2020) *European Report on Skills Need Identification: Situations, Trends, Perspectives and Priorities for the Sport and Physical Activity Sector*. Available at: https://www.essa-sport.eu/library/resources/european_report/ (Accessed: March 2020).

European Commission (2018a) *DigComp into Action – Get Inspired Make It Happen: A User Guide to the European Digital Competence Framework*. Available at: http://publications.jrc.ec.europa.eu/repository/bitstream/JRC110624/dc_guide_may18.pdf (Accessed: February 2019).

European Commission (2018b) *EntreComp into Action – Get Inspired, Make It Happen: A User Guide to the European Entrepreneurship Competence Framework*. Available at: https://ec.europa.eu/jrc/en/publication/eur-scientific-and-technical-research-reports/entrecomp-action-get-inspired-make-it-happen-user-guide-european-entrepreneurship-competence (Accessed: February 2019).

European Commission (2018c) *Study on the Economic Impact of Sport through Sport Satellite Accounts*. Available at: https://publications.europa.eu/en/publication-detail/-/publication/865ef44c-5ca1-11e8-ab41-01aa75ed71a1/language-en/format-PDF/source-71256399 (Accessed: February 2019).

European Sectoral Social Dialogue Committee for sports and active leisure (2016) *Strengthening Employability in the Sport and Active Leisure Sector – A Joint Opinion*. Available at: http://www.uni-europa.org/wp-content/uploads/2016/11/ESD_Sport_opinion.pdf (Accessed: February 2019).

Forrier, A., Sels, L. and Stynen, D. (2009) 'Career mobility at the intersection between agent and structure: A conceptual model', *Journal of Occupational and Organisational Psychology*, 82, pp. 739–759.

Fugate, M., Kinicki, A. J. and Ashforth, B. E. (2004) 'Employability: A psycho-social construct, its dimensions, and applications', *Journal of Vocational Behavior*, 65, pp. 14–38.

Galatti, L. *et al.* (2016) 'Coaching in Brazil sport coaching as a profession in Brazil: An analysis of the coaching literature in Brazil from 2000–2015', *International Sport Coaching Journal*, 3(3), pp. 316–331.

Gardner, H. and Shulman, L. S. (2005) 'The professions in America today: Crucial but fragile', *Daedalus*, 134(3), pp. 13–18.

Greenbank, P. (2014) 'Career decision-making: I don't think twice, but it'll be all right', *Research in Post-Compulsory Education*, 19(2), pp. 177–193.

Haynes, E. *et al.* (2016) *Looking under the hood of competency-based education: The relationships between competency-based education practices and students' learning skills, behaviors, and dispositions*. Washington, DC: Nellie Mae Education Foundation.

Herrmann, K. *et al.* (2008) *Developing entrepreneurial graduates: Putting entrepreneurship at the centre of higher education*. London: NESTA.

Hinchliffe, G. W. and Jolly, A. (2011) 'Graduate identity and employability', *British Educational Research Journal*, 37(4), pp. 563–584.

Jackson, D. (2017) 'Developing pre-professional identity in undergraduates through work-integrated learning', *Higher Education*, 74(5), pp. 833–853.

Kaider, F., Hains-Wesson, R. and Young, K. (2017) 'Typology of authentic WIL activities and assessment', *Asia-Pacific Journal of Cooperative Education*, 18(2), pp. 153–165.

Kalfa, S. and Taksa, L. (2015) 'Cultural capital in business higher education: Reconsidering the graduate attributes movement and the focus on employability', *Studies in Higher Education*, 40(4), pp. 580–595.

Khampirat, B. and McRae, N. (2016) 'Developing global standards framework and quality integrated models for cooperative and work-integrated education programs', *Asia-Pacific Journal of Cooperative Education*, 17(4), pp. 349–362.

Knight, P. and Yorke, M. (2004) *Learning, curriculum and employability in higher education*. London: Routledge.

Makransky, G. *et al.* (2020) 'Investigating the feasibility of using assessment and explanatory feedback in desktop virtual reality simulations', *Educational Technology Research and Development*, 68(1), pp. 293–317.

McIsaac, E., Park, S. and Toupin, L. (2013) *Shaping the Future: Leadership in Ontario's Nonprofit Labour Force*. Available at: http://theonn.ca/wp-content/uploads/2011/06/ONN-Mowat-Shaping-the-Future-Final-Report.October2013.pdf (Accessed: March 2021).

McMahon, T. and Thakore, H. (2006) 'Achieving constructive alignment: Putting outcomes first', *The Quality of Higher Education (Aukštojo mokslo kokyb)*, 3, pp. 10–19.

Monrouxe, L. V. (2010) 'Identity, identification and medical education: Why should we care?', *Medical Education*, 44(1), pp. 40–49.

Minten, S. and Forsyth, J. (2014) 'The careers of sports graduates: Implications for employability strategies in higher education sports courses', *Journal of Hospitality, Leisure, Sport & Tourism Education*, 15, pp. 94–102.

Mumm, A. M. (2006) 'Teaching social work students practice skills', *Journal of Teaching in Social Work*, 26, pp. 71–89.

Nixon, S. and Murr, A. (2006) 'Practice learning and the development of professional practice', *Social Work Education*, 25(8), pp. 798–811.

O'Brien, E. *et al.* (2019) 'Problem-based learning in the Irish SME workplace', *Journal of Workplace Learning*.

OECD (2016) *Enhancing Employability Report Prepared for the G20 Employment Working Group*. Available at: https://www.oecd.org/g20/topics/employment-and-social-policy/Enhancing-Employability-G20-Report-2016.pdf (Accessed: February 2019).

Osborne, S. K. (2016) *Commercialisation of leisure – sports development back to the future conference*. Cardiff : Sports Development Network.

O'Shea, A. (2008) *A developmental approach to work-integrated learning. Unpublished manuscript*. Queensland: University of Southern Queensland.

Otten, H. and Ohana, Y. (2009) *The eight key competences for lifelong learning: An appropriate framework within which to develop the competence of trainers in the field of European youth work*. Bonn: Institute for Applied Communication Research (IKAB).

Parry, G. (2015) 'English higher education and its vocational zones', *Research in Comparative & International Education*, 10(4), pp. 493–509.

Parsons, F. (1909) *Choosing a vocation*. Boston, MA: Houghton Mifflin.

Peeters, E. *et al.* (2019) 'Employability capital: A conceptual framework tested through expert analysis', *Journal of Career Development*, 46(2), pp. 79–93.

Pitchford, A. and Bacon, P. (2005) 'Constructing knowledge: The case of leisure management in the U.K.', *Studies in Higher Education*, 30(3), pp. 311–326.

Portenga, S. T., Aoyagi, M. W. and Cohen, A. B. (2017) 'Helping to build a profession: A working definition of sport and performance psychology', *Journal of Sport Psychology in Action*, 8(1), pp. 47–59.

QAA, Quality Assurance Agency for Higher Education (2018) *Enterprise and Entrepreneurship Education Guidance for U.K. Higher Education Providers*. Available at: https://www.qaa.ac.uk/docs/qaas/enhancement-and-development/enterprise-and-entrpreneurship-education-2018.pdf (Accessed: December 2020).

Raelin, J. A. (1997) 'A model of work-based learning', *Organization Science*, 8(6), pp. 563–578.

Römgens, I., Scoupe, R. and Beausaert, S. (2020) 'Unravelling the concept of employability, bringing together research on employability in higher education and the workplace', *Studies in Higher Education*, 45(12), pp. 2588–2603.

Rust, C. (2002) 'The impact of assessment on student learning: How can the research literature practically help to inform the development of departmental assessment strategies and learner-centred assessment practices?', *Active Learning in Higher Education*, 3, pp. 145–158.

Sheepway, L., Lincoln, M. and McAllister, S. (2014) 'Impact of placement type on the development of clinical competency in speech-language pathology students', *International Journal of Language & Communication Disorders*, 49(2), pp. 189–203.

Shulman, L. S. (2005) 'Signature pedagogies in the professions', *Daedalus*, 134(3), pp. 52–59.

Van der Heijde, C. M. and Van der Heijden, B. I. J. M. (2006) 'A competence-based and multi-dimensional operationalisation and measurement of employability', *Human Resource Management*, 45(3), pp. 449–476.

Watts, A. G. (2006) *Career development learning and employability*. York: Higher Education Academy.

Wilkins, E. B. (2020) 'Facilitating professional identity development in healthcare education', *New Directions for Teaching and Learning*, 162, pp. 57–69.

Work-related Learning Guide (2008) *A guidance document for employers, schools, colleges, students and their parents and carers*. The Department for Children, Schools and Families.

World Economic Forum (2020) *The future of jobs report 2020*. Geneva: World Economic Forum.

# Part III

# Education in sport and physical activity around the globe

Chapter 8

# European perspectives on qualifications in sport

*Stefan Walzel, Ruth Crabtree, and Karen Petry*

## Introduction

According to the European Commission (2018), education is the largest sport-related sector in the European Union (EU) with nearly 1.1 million employees and a monetary volume of 51.2 billion euros. In addition, the sports industry accounts for a large and expanding sector of the European economy, contributing approximately 3% of Europe's total gross domestic product (GDP) and 3.5% of employment in the EU (European Commission, 2016). The European Commission (2018) suggests that, due to the labour-intensive nature of the sports industry, a 1% increase in GDP can result in a 1.35% increase in employment. Hence, from an economic and political perspective, the sport sector is of particular importance and provides many opportunities for both sport education and training providers.

An essential component regarding sport education within the EU is the Europe-wide recognition of qualifications, diplomas, and certificates within education which is considered a central element of the European unification process. On top of that, both in the university and non-university sector, transformation approaches are becoming apparent which pursue the goal of a Europe-wide education and labour market in sport. The European Commission's political management tools are fundamental to the development of an overall strategy for sport-related study and training programmes. The transformation of the education sector in the European countries represents challenges and opportunities for sport, particularly regarding the interactions between the labour market and education. These arise from two questions:

- Are the existing training and higher education systems within EU countries of central importance for the promotion and development of the workforce in the EU?
- Are they properly adapted to social and economic requirements?

In this transformation process, one of the most important tasks is to ensure that sport education is enveloped within the European Qualifications Framework (EQF).

DOI: 10.4324/9781003002666-12

Between 2017 and 2020, the EU Expert Group on Skills and Human Resources and Development in Sport (XG HR) was initiated by the European Commission under the EU Work Plan for Sport. Issues addressed included coach education, development of skills through sport, qualifications in sport, and dual careers of athletes. EU policy in the fields of education and training is designed to support action at the level of member states, which remain responsible for these competence areas, to help address common challenges including ageing societies, skill deficits, technological developments, and competition at the global level. Resulting from the growing importance of education and training within Europe, a variety of European organisations have been established in recent years, focusing on the European dimension of (higher) education in sport, the European labour market, and the internationalisation of sport science disciplines (Tokarski *et al.*, 2009, p. 97 ff.).

The university and non-university education systems in sport differ greatly between European countries according to the respective education and sport system. The following part will provide a status quo of the sport education and training panorama, followed by focusing on the sport management and coaching sectors, including employability.

## The sport education and training panorama in European sport

Over the last few years, around 3.9 million coaches, 3.7 million sport managers, and 1.5 million referees have become qualified in the EU on a yearly basis (European Commission, 2016, p. 8). The qualifications obtained were offered by various institutions, on different levels and with different occupational purposes. Therefore, it is not surprising that the period of time, content, levels of performance, entrance requirements, educational standards, and scope and level of examinations of the individual qualifications vary greatly within and between individual European countries, as well as the qualification providers. This is compounded by the still fragile recognition and acceptance of degrees between different educational institutions and between different countries, acknowledged by the European Commission (2016, p. 6), who stated that the "EU sport education and training panorama is highly fragmented". The mutual recognition of qualifications from different providers within a national qualification framework and at European level (EQF) has not yet been implemented in all EU countries and requires further efforts from all parties involved (European Commission, 2016), particularly to ensure the comparability and recognition of qualifications across national borders. This also entails systematic monitoring for the long-term success.

Europe-wide, three dimensions can be used to systematise the qualification landscape in sport:

- Different job categories, such as coaches, referees, managers, physiotherapists, and sports journalists

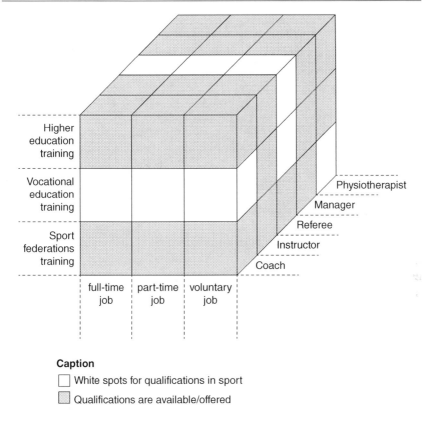

*Figure 8.1* Systematisation approach for qualifications in sport.

- Different occupational levels, such as voluntary work, part-time employment, or full-time employment
- Different qualification providers, such as sports organisations, vocational training providers, and universities (see Figure 8.1)

While the latter two qualification providers offer formal qualifications, sport federations often cannot. However, non-formal qualifications have evolved over time through various sports organisations, mainly due to increased recognition and importance placed on formalised requirements and at the same time the lack of comparable qualification offers within higher education. This is still true today for the training of referees, as, according to the authors' knowledge, there is neither vocational training nor a university programme for this profession due to the high degree of specialisation and only some sport (e.g., football) and a few countries employ full-time referees. As a result, the sports organisations have a monopoly on refereeing, which also applies to a certain extent to coaching.

However, some sports organisations have established formal links with universities to provide formal qualifications, for example the Union of European Football Associations (UEFA) Academy with the University of Lausanne (Switzerland) or the European Handball Federation (EHF) with the German Sport University Cologne. Even in those cases, sport federations still autonomously determine the requirements for obtaining and for renewing a coaching licence. For example, the problematic aspect here is that whilst students may potentially study for years to obtain a bachelor's or master's degree in sport coaching, this does not automatically allow them to work as a coach at a certain sports level (e.g., head coach of a football Bundesliga team), because sport federations require a specific coaching licence (e.g., A-level), issued by the federation itself. Contrarily, sport federations have not yet defined any minimum qualification requirements for sport managers.

Even if sports organisations are not perceived and recognised as formal educational institutions, they play an important role in the further development of sport and the sport-concerned, as well as regarding employment opportunities within European sport. The former is provided above all by the permanent training of referees, instructors, and coaches. In accordance with the hierarchical sport system, the requirements for referees and coaches increase with the level of performance. Similarly to athletes, referees and coaches are developed over several years of training and further education at local, regional, national, and international levels, which is expressed by the hierarchically structured licence levels. Through this systematic qualification, sports organisations make a significant contribution to increase the quality of sports competitions. In addition, the sports organisation's systematic qualification system enables access to a part-time or full-time employment in sport, especially at the upper licence levels. For career changers as well as former elite athletes, the qualification system provided by sports organisations offers a valuable and important pathway to employment in the sport sector.

On closer inspection, two weaknesses in the sports qualification system become apparent:

- While minimum qualification requirements are defined regarding further training and education at regular intervals (usually every one to three years) to renew the licences for volunteer, part-time, and full-time referees and coaches, there is nothing comparable for elected or appointed voluntary board members in sports clubs and federations.
- This also applies almost without exception to the part-time or full-time managers in sports clubs and federations.

Closing these two gaps in the sports qualification system would be an important step towards the long-term, sustainable development of sports organisations in Europe and the mitigation of ethical misconduct in European sport.

## Employability of sport managers and coaches in Europe

Considering the highly fragmented EU sport education and training sector in addition to the increasing number of various sport educational institutions, the sport education and training sector can be characterised as increasingly competitive due to the number of institutions that offer education and training. Hence, employability is one of the key performance indicators for sports qualification providers, as well as an important selection and decision criterion from the individual's perspective (Dinning, 2017).

In this context, employability applies to the individual who wants to obtain a sports qualification and can be defined as "having a set of skills, knowledge, understanding and personal attributes that make a person more likely to choose and secure occupations" (Dacre Pool and Sewell, 2007, p. 280). From an educational and training provider's perspective, employability refers to the ability to adapt qualification programmes to new conditions and forms of work and to implement lifelong learning principles (Cumming, 2010; Wickramasinghe and Perera, 2010; Cole and Tibby, 2013).

According to the European Sectoral Social Dialogue Committee for Sports and Active Leisure (ESSDCSL) (2016, p. 2) in cooperation with various partners, the following barriers to employability, applicable to the entire sport sector, were identified:

- "Short-term employment and high turnover especially in coaching professions;
- Physically and mentally demanding job profiles negatively impacting the health and the longevity of workers;
- Skills gaps and skills mismatches;
- Discrepancies between national skill levels that impede mobility;
- Lack of strategic financial management which hinders sustainable employment. [sic]"

As outlined in Table 8.1, the individual sport sub-sectors hold specific barriers to employability. Education and training providers are not able to reduce and remove these employability barriers completely by themselves because it also requires efforts from employers, sports organisations, and politics.

As has been discussed, the qualification of coaches and managers is critical, hence, the following section will focus on this issue.

### Employability of sport managers

Since the turn of the millennium, the demand for sport managers has risen dramatically, resulting in increased provision of sport management programmes (Pitts, 2001; Petry, Froberg and Madella, 2006; Yiamouyiannis *et al.*, 2013) and

104 Stefan Walzel et al.

*Table 8.1* Specific Barriers to Employability in the Different Sport Sub-Sectors (European Sectoral Social Dialogue Committee for Sports and Active Leisure, 2016, pp. 3–4)

| *Professional sport* | *Not-for-profit sport* | *Active leisure* |
| --- | --- | --- |
| • Contractual instability and lack of employment-related rights<br>• Non-compliance with health and safety requirements and inadequate medical treatment<br>• Lack of equal rights and opportunities<br>• Insufficient support for dual careers | • Contractual instability or absence of contracts<br>• Physical health issues | • Skill shortages and mismatches<br>• Lack of labour market integration |

a subsequent surge in the requirements of sport managers (Wohlfart and Adam, 2019). Due to general social changes, the rising commercialisation and professionalisation in sport, the successful Europeanisation (Radaelli, 2003), globalisation, and digitalisation (Giulianotti and Robertson, 2007; Danylchuk *et al.*, 2008; Mathner and Martin, 2012; Miragaia and Soares, 2017), the requirements for sport managers' employability also changed (see also Chapter 2 in this book). Even though there are differences in quality and scope between the individual European countries due to distinct levels of development (Wohlfart and Adam, 2019), changes and shifts in the competencies of sport managers can be observed.

Research suggests that sport managers need to possess a diverse set of competencies beside the professional competencies, including better soft skills. More specifically, those are personal, socio-communicative, activity and action competencies as outlined in Table 8.2 (Wohlfart and Adam, 2019). "It is interesting

*Table 8.2* Top Five Current, Future, Core, and Special Competencies in Sport Management (Wohlfart and Adam, 2019, pp. 11–14; for Country-Specific Results, Please See Wohlfart and Adam, 2019)

| *Rank* | *Current competencies* | *Future competencies* | *Core competencies* | *Special competencies* |
| --- | --- | --- | --- | --- |
| 1. | Ability to work autonomously | Teamwork | Teamwork | Digital marketing |
| 2. | Teamwork | Decision-making skills | Ability to work autonomously | Use of virtual medial/platforms in work |
| 3. | Desire to succeed | Oral communication | Organisational skills | Use of social media in work |
| 4. | Organisational skills | Planning skills | Capacity to adopt to new situations (flexibility) | Sales management |
| 5. | Capacity to adopt to new situations (flexibility) | Organisational skills | Planning skills | Marketing |

European perspectives on qualifications in sport    105

to observe that the majority of the core competencies include generic skills (e.g., socio-communicative competencies) rather than (or on top of) sport management specific methods and professional competencies" (Wohlfart and Adam, 2019, p. 13). This research also revealed that whilst the first seven core competencies do not differ significantly in the various sub-sectors (managers in sports clubs, sport federations, public sector, and private sector), varying sets of competencies were identified from rank eight and following (for more details please see Wohlfart and Adam, 2019, p. 16). Within the category "special competency", digital marketing emerged as an important skill.

Based on the findings, Wohlfart and Adam (2019) provide 12 key recommendations for curriculum development within sport management education. They suggest to focus more on developing soft skills, digital competencies, the integration of compulsory internships, the development of sales, relationship, and financial management skills, the inclusion of entrepreneurship and innovation management, and the promotion of foreign language courses and international exchange. In addition, they emphasise that the employability of future sport managers will increase if business and education work together to develop their own interests.

### Employability of sport coaches

As discussed, coaches play a central role in the sport system as they have a decisive influence on the quality of sports competitions via their athletes, with ripple effects on the entire sport system. The demand for coaches at different performance levels remains high and, in some cases, the demand cannot be met. Therefore, the recruitment and retention of coaches is a challenge both in high-performance sport and in the leisure sector (Breuer, Wicker and Orlowski, 2017; Breuer and Feiler, 2019). The reasons for this situation are very diverse. For coaches in high-performance sport, fixed-term employment contracts, low remuneration, and high pressure to perform are only some issues (Digel, Burk and Fahrner, 2006; Breuer, Wicker and Orlowski, 2016 and 2017, Wicker, Orlowski, and Breuer, 2018).

Another factor associated with the unmet demand for coaches is the increasing specialisation of coach profiles, such as athletics coach, mental coach, goalkeeping coach, technical and tactical coach, offence, and defence coach. In addition, there are specialised activities and job profiles at the interface of two different disciplines, such as a nutrition coach or a sports director, who are increasingly establishing themselves at the interface of sport science and management (Parnell *et al.*, 2018).

A recent report by the European Commission (2020) identified that in terms of sport coaches' employability across different sports levels and sport, the following skills are the most important ones: sport-specific knowledge and skills, clearly communicating instructions, ensuring health and safety of the participants, planning coaching sessions and programmes, and ability to work in compliance with codes of practice/ethics (p.13). The report also identified five competence weaknesses including: working with people with disabilities, using information/ communication technology (ICT) skills, using the right marketing and selling skills,

## Future developments and challenges

Whilst substantial developments have been fostered with regard to sport education and the training of people who wish to work in the sports industry, there are still challenges that need to be addressed. There has been a huge increase in the number of educational institutions that provide courses within sports programmes across Europe, but the question remains if these programmes provide the right outcomes to ensure that graduates enter the sport sector with the best skills to pursue their dream job (Jiang and Alexakis, 2017). Researchers have acknowledged that many sports programmes fail to identify which skills and competences are needed within the industry, resulting in graduates who cannot fulfil the roles required by employers (Fahrner and Schüttoff, 2020). Other concerns regarding sports programmes relate to their generic outline and the lack of addressing specific needs required for a particular field or geographical area (Tsitskaria et al., 2017; Pereira, Vilas-Boas and Rebelo, 2019). For example, the skills needed for a sport management graduate within Europe may differ from the specific skills required for a sport management graduate within Africa. Often, programmes are compiled of generic modules that do not consider who the students are, what area of sport they wish to pursue a career in, and where that career may take place geographically.

In the process of designing sport education and training programmes, there is a clear evidence that institutions need to be aware of the changes within the industry and how these changes impact the requirements that graduates face in the work environment (Baird and Parayitam, 2019). Often, educational institutions, when designing sports programmes, will work with many stakeholders to determine the optimum programme that benefits the students, institution, community, and industry (Palheta et al., 2021). They may liaise with industry employers, alumni, sports governing bodies, as well as must adhere to government policies depending on which country they operate in. That many stakeholders involved in the process may bring in differing needs which can lead to conflict, depending on who has the most power, control or often finances within the decision-making process.

Linked to this challenge is the dramatic change of the student population within the past decade (Cotton, Nash and Kneale, 2017; Jahn et al., 2017). Educational establishments need to be aware of this to ensure that the sports programmes they are providing take into account the changing needs of the diverse student population. For example, the average student in the past who studied a degree level sports programme was predominantly single, 18- to 21-year-old, and studied full-time without having a job on the side. Today, many students are mature adults who may study part-time, have families, work part-time whilst studying and may study overseas. Education providers need to account for the changing student demographics and react to the subsequently changing needs to ensure that the growing sports industry is provided with a constant stream of graduates who can fulfil the required roles. This may mean that institutions need to be flexible in how they offer sports programmes, whether they offer blended learning, distance learning, or part-time options. They also need to be conscious of cost implications associated with studying and the impact this may have on potential students.

Furthermore, ethical issues, social responsibility, and gender equality are critical subjects that should be further addressed in sport management and coaching education and research. Evidence of gender discrimination is still mentioned significantly in the literature, particularly of women in managerial positions. Analysing these phenomena is crucial because human values may be compromised in several sports contexts, and higher education institutions have an extremely relevant role in promoting cultural change that breaks through stereotypes and unethical behaviours. The impact of explicitly incorporating these issues in sports programmes on students' behaviour during the training process, when they enter the labour market, and even when they are in their employers' charge should be investigated. Miragaia and Soares (2017) also suggest that educational institutes should include international experts when designing curriculum content to ensure that an international overview is provided within the programme, addressing the issues of globalisation and helping to produce graduates with skills transferrable to different countries. They also suggest that "the quality of organizations [sic] that receive students for experiential learning, service learning, and internship should be supervised to guarantee that the students' orientation is properly adjusted. This accreditation process is crucial in evaluating the students' learning outcomes and the results of experiential learning in terms of the positive partnerships formed between universities and companies (local, national, or international)" (Miragaia and Soares, 2017, p. 113).

The challenges identified are difficult but not insurmountable, and it is clear from the discussion outlined within the chapter that working in partnership with key stakeholders is fundamental to success: to fully understand the situation, the required tasks, the stakeholders' individual needs, and the intended goals and outcomes. The effort put in this process will hopefully result in a sports industry that continues to grow and educational providers generating a rich, constant stream of graduates who can serve, enhance, and develop the sector for generations to follow, who are a benefit not only for the individual stakeholders, but also for society as a whole.

## References

Baird, A. and Parayitam, S. (2019) 'Employers' ratings of importance of skills and competencies college graduates need to get hired: Evidence from the New England region of USA', *Education & Training*, 61(5), pp. 622–634.

Breuer, C. and Feiler, S. (2019) *Sportvereine in Deutschland: Organisationen und Personen. Sportentwicklungsbericht für Deutschland 2017/2018 – Teil 1*. Bonn: Bundesinstitut für Sportwissenschaft.

Breuer, C., Wicker, P. and Orlowski, J. (2016) *Standortbedingungen von Trainerinnen und Trainern im deutschen Spitzensport im internationalen Vergleich*. Cologne: German Sport University Cologne.

Breuer, C., Wicker, P. and Orlowski, J. (2017) *Bundes- und mischfinanzierte Trainer im deutschen Spitzensport – Standortbedingungen und Migrationsanalyse*. Cologne: Strauss.

Cole, D. and Tibby, M. (2013) *Defining and developing your approach to employability: A framework for higher education*. Beijing: The Higher Education Press.

Cotton, D., Nash, T. and Kneale, P. (2017) 'Supporting the retention of non-traditional students in higher education using a resilience framework', *European Educational Research Journal*, 16(1), pp. 62–79.

Cumming, J. (2010) 'Contextualised performance: Reframing the skills debate in research education', *Studies in Higher Education*, 35(4), pp. 405–419.

Dacre Pool, L. and Sewell, P. (2007) 'The key to employability: Developing a practical model of graduate employability', *Education & Training*, 49(4), pp. 277–289.

Danylchuk, K. *et al.* (2008) 'International sport management: Creating an international learning and teaching community', *International Journal of Sport Management and Marketing*, 4(2–3), pp. 125–145.

Digel, H., Burk, V. and Fahrner, M. (2006) *High-performance sport – an international comparison*. Weilheim: Braeuer.

Dinning, T. (2017) 'Embedding employability and enterprise skills in sport degrees through focused work-based project; A student and employer viewpoint', *Cogent Education*, 4(1), pp. 1–14.

European Commission (2016) *Study on Sport Qualifications Acquired Through Sport Organisations and (Sport) Educational Institutes*. Available at: https://op.europa.eu/en/publication-detail/-/publication/28026772-9ad0-11e6-868c-01aa75ed71a1 (Accessed: 28 April 2020).

European Commission (2018) *Study on the Economic Impact of Sport Through Sport Satellite Accounts*. Available at: https://op.europa.eu/en/publication-detail/-/publication/865ef44c-5ca1-11e8-ab41-01aa75ed71a1/language-en/format-PDF/source-71256399 (Accessed: 28 April 2020).

European Commission (2020) *Guidelines Regarding the Minimum Requirements in Skills and Competences for Coaches*. Available at: https://op.europa.eu/en/publication-detail/-/publication/8f28e3a0-6f11-11ea-b735-01aa75ed71a1/language-en/format-PDF/source-122543310 (Accessed: 28 April 2020).

European Sectoral Social Dialogue Committee for Sports and Active Leisure (2016) *Strengthening Employability in the Sport and Active Leisure Sector*. Available at: https://www.uni-europa.org/wp-content/uploads/2016/11/ESD_Sport_opinion.pdf. (Accessed: 28 April 2020).

Fahrner, M. and Schüttoff, U. (2020) 'Analysing the context-specific relevance of competencies – Sport management alumni perspectives', *European Sport Management Quarterly*, 20(3), pp. 344–363.

Giulianotti, R. and Robertson, R. (2007) 'Sport and globalization: Transnational dimensions', *Global Networks*, 7(2), pp. 107–112.

Jahn, V. *et al.* (2017) 'Different students – Different ways: Challenges of integrating non-traditional students in higher education and how electronic learning can support inclusion', in Zaphiris, P. and Ioannou, A. (eds.) *Learning and collaboration technologies. Technology in education*. Vancouver: Springer, pp. 158–169.

Jiang, L. and Alexakis, G. (2017) 'Comparing students' and managers' perceptions of essential entry-level management competencies in the hospitality industry: An empirical study', *Journal of Hospitality, Leisure, Sport and Tourism*, 20, pp. 32–46.

Mathner, R. P. and Martin, C. L. (2012) 'Sport management graduate and undergraduate students' perceptions of career expectations in sport management', *Sport Management Education Journal*, 6(1), pp. 21–31.

Miragaia, D. A. M. and Soares, J. A. P. (2017) 'Higher education in sport management: A systematic review of research topics and trends', *Journal of Hospitality, Leisure, Sport & Tourism Education*, 21(A), pp. 101–116.

Palheta, C. *et al.* (2021) 'Between intentionality and reality to promote positive youth development in sport-based programs: A case study in Brazil', *Physical Education and Sport Pedagogy*, 26(2), pp. 197–209.

Parnell, D. *et al.* (2018) 'The emergence of the sporting director role in football and the potential of social network theory in future research', *Managing Sport and Leisure*, 23(4–6), pp. 242–254.

Pereira, E., Vilas-Boas, M. and Rebelo, C. (2019) 'Graduates' skills and employability: The view of students from different European countries', *Higher Education, Skills and Work-Based Learning*, 9(4), pp. 758–774.

Petry, K., Froberg, K. and Madella, A. (2006) *Thematic network project AEHESIS "aligning a European higher education structure in sport science"*. Cologne: German Sport University Cologne on behalf of ENSSEE.

Pitts, B. G. (2001) 'Sport management at the Millennium: A defining moment', *Journal of Sport Management*, 15(1), pp. 1–9.

Radaelli, C. (2003) 'The Europeanization of public policy', in Featherstone, K. and Radaelli, C. (eds.) *The politics of Europeanization*. Oxford: University Press, pp. 27–56.

Tokarski, W. *et al.* (2009) *Perfect match? Sport and the European Union*. Aachen: Meyer & Meyer.

Tsitskaria, E. *et al.* (2017) Employers' expectations of the employability skills needed in the sport and recreation environment. *Journal of Hospitality, Leisure, Sport & Tourism*, 20, pp. 1–9.

Wicker, P., Orlowski, J. and Breuer, C. (2018) 'Coach migration in German high performance sport', *European Sport Management Quarterly*, 18(1), pp. 93–111.

Wickramasinghe, V. and Perera, L. (2010) 'Graduates', university lecturers' and employers' perceptions towards employability skills', *Education and Training*, 52(3), pp. 226–244.

Wohlfart, O. and Adam, S. (2019) *New Age of Sport Management Education in Europe: Research Project under the Erasmus + Programme*. Available at: https://www.ucviden.dk/ws/files/66270980/2019_08_19_NASME_Final_Report.pdf (Accessed: 08 August 2020).

Yiamouyiannis, A. *et al.* (2013) 'Sport management education: Accreditation, accountability, and direct learning outcome assessments', *Sport Management Education Journal*, 7(1), pp. 51–59.

Chapter 9

# Sport development and delivery in Canada, México, and the United States

## Commonalities, differences, and future needs

*Hans van der Mars, Tim Hopper, Gord Inglis,*
*Edtna Jáuregui-Ulloa, Juan Ricardo López-Taylor,*
*Martin Francisco González-Villalobos*

### Introduction

This chapter frames sport as an institutionalised form of play behaviour that has rules and oversight in the form of game officials. By nature, it is competitive and requires physical exertion. Sport should be an experience for all children and youth, across competition levels. We analyse the policy-driven education of institutionalised sport like soccer, tennis, football, and volleyball and their cultural significance in Canada, México, and the United States (US). Table 9.1 highlights the key structures, delivery models, and core programmes promoting the education of sport in the different countries. Using these categories as a general framework, each country will be described to highlight the individual paths for the education of sport and emerging themes that seem to be in common.

### Development and delivery of sport in Canada

#### Defining moments of sport in Canada

The development and growth of sport in Canada has a long, diverse, and rich history. For example, Tom Longboat, an Onondaga First Nations long distance runner from Canada, won the Boston Marathon in 1907 (Kidd and Longboat, 2018). With a historically diverse mixture of Indigenous Peoples, European immigrants, and, more recently, a broader international immigrant population, Canada is truly a multicultural country. Its population of over 37 million people is divided into ten provinces and three territories with each being a part of a national governance system for sport, physical education, and health programming delivery.

Canadian sport has achieved success on the world stage. These sports moments are emblematic of a small nation's systematic approach to sport development through an evolving long-term development framework (Balyi, Way and Higgs, 2013). Some of Canada's most outstanding and memorable sports

DOI: 10.4324/9781003002666-13

*Table 9.1* Comparative Structure and Delivery of Sport in North America

| | Canada | México | The United States |
|---|---|---|---|
| **Development of sport** | Sport in Canada embraces an approach at national and provincial/ territorial levels | A National Commission of Sports (CONADE) is the main organisation that connects with states and municipalities | Schools, community, non-profit, for-profit, US Olympic committee |
| **Delivery of sport** (Organisations that develop and deliver sport) | Three key organisations: 1. The National Coaching Certification Program (NCCP) 2. "Own the Podium" (OTP) 3. Provincial and National Physical and Health Education (PHE) groups | Four key institutions: 1. CONADE sport system 2. Secretary of Education 3. State and municipalities commissions 4. Private organisations | Primarily an exclusionary model focusing on the higher-skilled players with ultimate goal of seeking elite level performance |
| **Relevant programmes promoting sport** | Long-Term Development in Sport and Physical Activity (LTDSPA) (Sport for Life, 2019). Game-based | National Program of Physical Culture and Sports 2020. Key element to promote: Social sport | Sport Education, Game-based approach for sport |

achievements include: Olympic Games, such as Donovan Bailey with the world's fastest 100 metres sprint (Atlanta, 1996), Canadian Men's and Women's Olympic Hockey teams' gold medal wins at the 2006 Salt Lake City Olympic Winter Games with a repeat gold medal win when Canada hosted the 2010 Olympic Winter Games in Vancouver. The Toronto Raptors captured the National Basketball Association (NBA) Championship in 2019, and a notable and remarkable achievement on an individual sports basis was 19-year-old Canadian Bianca Andrescu winning the 2019 US Open Women's Singles Tennis Championship. Sports moments such as these capture the sense of belonging and unification that sports achievement provides in a pluralistic nation like Canada.

### Sport and physical activity: Current state

As noted in the Sport for Life (2019) report, community sport and physical activity participation in Canada have declined over the last three decades, and the vast majority of Canadian adults is physically inactive and spends most of their waking hours sitting. Furthermore, "physical education programs [sic] in schools are marginalised, and the sport and community sports delivery system in Canada remains fragmented" (Sport for Life, 2019, p. 5). At the same time, there has been a rapid growth of "for profit" sports businesses offering ever more specialised "elite" training at ever-younger ages. To address this imbalance, a cross-Canada commitment has developed over the last decade to create an ecosystem to promote sport and physical activity which inspires every Canadian to pursue both excellence and activity for life.

In Canada, The Truth and Reconciliation Report calls for action that addresses the historical colonisation of Indigenous Peoples which led to a cultural genocide over several generations (Truth and Reconciliation Commission of Canada, 2015). The need for this reconciliation identifies sport as a critical element in rebuilding Indigenous cultures and sense of self-worth. This has led to a commitment to recognise the historical contribution of Aboriginal sport (such as the invention of lacrosse) and to strive to support Indigenous communities through barrier-free quality sport and physical activity opportunities. A refocusing of sport development has been called for by Aboriginal Sport Circle (2019), noting that many parts of Canada's mainstream sports pathways do not reflect the needs and cultural priorities of Indigenous Peoples. For example, traditionally for Indigenous People, games were used to teach hunting and other daily skills associated with their life roles. This has now been acknowledged within the Canadian long-term physical activity development framework as a critical contribution to the lifelong and culturally aware perspectives.

Sport for Life (2019) notes that persistent issues within this Canadian ecosystem of sport are the way some groups continue to be marginalised and ignored. In addition to Indigenous Peoples, groups such as "girls and women, individuals with disabilities [...] newcomers to Canada, the LGBTQI2S community, aging adults, and those living in poverty and isolated communities remain underserviced and under-supported" (Sport for Life, 2019, p. 6). This has led Canada to reframe the Long-Term Athlete Development (LTAD) framework (Balyi, Way and Higgs, 2013) to incorporate more diverse perspectives to sports excellence captured by the statement "from the playground to the podium and everywhere in between" (Aboriginal Sport Cycle, 2019, p. 2). The LTAD now has an emerging lifelong perspective that incorporates both elite train-to-win (professional habits of being a high-performance athlete) and recreational train-to-stay-in-sport (how to practice and how to promote competition to sustain the sport) throughout life. Canada's sport development framework has been renamed as Long-Term Development in Sport and Physical Activity (LTDSPA) (Sport for Life, 2019).

### *Canadian sport policy and LTDSPA framework: Development and delivery*

The Canadian Sport Policy for 2012–2022 sets a "roadmap" for the governance structure in Canadian sport development that is inclusive of school, recreational, and high-performance sports programming (Canadian Sport Policy, 2012).

This policy presents a vision for a dynamic and innovative culture that promotes and celebrates both participation and excellence in sport. The stated goals are excellence in sport, enhanced education and skill development, improved health and wellness for all Canadians, increased civic (national) pride, engagement and cohesion, and increased economic development and prosperity through the growth of sport.

The LTDSPA document frames Canada's federal funding process with a commitment that every child, youth, and adult will have the opportunity and guidance for optimal participation in sport and physical activity. It endeavours to educate citizens into sport at different levels in relation to elite, lifelong career, and recreational sport. To guide the development of sport with a common version, an LTDSPA framework has been developed that every sport uses to frame its development programmes (see: https://sportforlife.ca/sport-frameworks/). The intent of the framework is for both elite and recreational to come from the same common roots. Potential participants (children or adults) are introduced to sport through awareness raising in schools and recreational programmes; these promote an active start. Then, qualified instructors (teachers or community leaders) guide participants through the key fundamentals for the sport in an engaging and progressively challenging way. Participants are then guided on how to continue their sports career across one or several sports areas, through personal training processes, as they decide the path into the type of sport they want to maintain throughout their lives.

The LTDSPA document advocates that sports engagement should be a process that takes time and that sport and physical activity should look quite different based on the individual's stage of development. The refocusing of development "in sport and physical activity" signposts a move from a sport-centric notion focused on elite "athlete performance" to inspire participation, to a broader "engagement" focus with people active for life, along with the pursuit of excellence in sport.

A key commitment in this framework is the concept of physical literacy as the "motivation, confidence, physical competence, knowledge and understanding to value and take responsibility for engagement in physical activities for life [...] and knowledge to understand, communicate, apply and analyse different forms of movement" in diverse contexts and against different opponents and challenges (Sport for Life, 2019, p. 12). Though physical literacy as a concept has limited measures to show positive influences on national health outcomes and the take-up of sport, it has become a validating term for quality instruction and has been integrated into numerous national, provincial/territorial, and municipal policies (Giblin, Collins and Button, 2014).

### *Pathways to sport development: A collaborative approach*

Sport in Canada embraces an approach at the national (federal) and provincial/territorial levels with structures and systems for sports delivery and development.

There are three key organisations for sport development and delivery across Canadian provinces.

- The National Coaching Certification Program (NCCP) provides sport education for coaches across 65 different kinds of sport. The Coaching Association of Canada manages and delivers NCCP training through its partner network ational Sport Organizations (NSO) and Provincial/Territorial Sport Organizations (PSO) who are responsible for the development and delivery of coaching certification programmes across Canada.
- The "Own the Podium" (OTP) high-performance programme was launched with a goal of podium success at the 2010 Olympic Games and to carry on into future Olympic Games. The mandate of OTP is to provide technical support to Canada's national sports organisations with the aim of delivering more Olympic and Paralympic medals for Canada.
- Provincial and National Physical and Health Education (PHE) professional organisations promote the practices of physical and health education across the country. The PHE national group for teaching professionals runs an annual conference that circulates around each of the provinces. PHE (2020a) focuses on healthy and active kids "by promoting and advancing quality health and physical education opportunities and healthy learning environments", developing numerous cross-school and community programmes based on recognised and researched practices like "Move Think Learn" series (PHE, 2020b).

Strategic integration between these three key areas and the ability to generate quality instructors across the different populations from elite, college, recreational/community, and school programmes is a key intent of Sport Canada (2012). For example, the sport pedagogy field that has emerged from physical education research and practices advocates game-based approaches informed by manipulation of playing structures that guide player learning along with technical instruction (Mandigo, Butler and Hopper, 2007). This same approach can be seen in the NCCP coaching programmes, the technical instruction of elite athletes, and the curriculum development in the "Move Think Learn" series. Indeed, physical literacy as a process of learning is based on contextual cues to trigger movement responses that parallel the perception-action coupling ideas within a game-based approach to learning to play games (Hopper, 2011).

The Canadian LTDSPA developmental framework offers an integrated and collaborative approach to guide the promotion of sport from school and community to high-level competition and lifelong pursuit of a sport. Though this collaborative approach is promising, issues such as consistent funding streams for sports infrastructure at the local level, the underrepresentation of females as coaches, the lack of Indigenous Peoples' engagement in a range of sport, and the increasing for-profit selling of sport that prices many Canadians out of the sport, are recurring and systemic problems that need to be addressed (Sport for Life, 2019).

## Development and delivery of sport in México

### Introduction

Sport development in México is something that struggles between competing agendas: (a) developing good physical education programmes, (b) creating physical activity and sports programmes for health and general development for all types of population, and (c) promoting sports competition programmes to achieve success internationally. In this section, we will talk about two main issues: organisation and governance of sport and the education and formative process of sports programmes.

### Organisation and governance of sport

In México, the organisation of sport is distributed in two areas: The National Commission of Physical Culture and Sport (CONADE, 2019) and the National Olympic Committee (COM, 2019). This is not only a complex system but also a complicated one, in which the diverse functions, objectives, and projects frequently overlap with proposed goals not clearly articulated or achieved.

#### The National Commission of Physical Culture and Sport

The National Commission of Physical Culture and Sport (CONADE) (The country's National Commission of Physical Culture and Sport) is an organisation similar to a Ministry of Sport, with multiple functions, but without autonomous policy setting authority. Because of austerity, the CONADE budget has decreased by almost 50% in the last seven years from 192,065,029 dollars to 95,866,193 dollars (Government of México, 2014). CONADE's mandate is to work and develop almost everything that has to do with sport, from physical education programmes with the Ministry of Education, development of infrastructure, research projects, accreditation and certification of coaches, physical activities programmes for all the population including people with adaptive abilities, to the organisation and control of national competitions. The Ministry of Education, through CONADE and other departments at the state level, regulates the structure of amateur sport and physical education. The key mandate here is the promotion of sport and the development of physical culture across different levels, such as schools, clubs, organisations, and municipalities. Physical education focuses on the promotion of knowledge, skills, and attitudes to develop the movement culture which tends to focus on the instruction of sport. In the last 30 years, CONADE has popularised the use of the term "Physical Culture" which integrates all types of events that have to do with sport, physical education, massive events, social and recreational sport, high-performance sport, adapted sport, and school sport.

#### National Olympic Committee

The NOC is an independent civil organisation that authorises the participation of athletes and teams in certain competitions, mainly the Olympic Games.

They should have a close relation with the activities of CONADE, because it has the attribution of search and development of elite athletes. México's federal government subsidises the sport federations, so CONADE is responsible for the supervision and control of the different national sport federations through the management of their budget. The financial support is based on the athlete's performance in the Olympic sport (e.g., diving and athletics), although the most played sports are football and basketball. The relationship between this organisation and CONADE has been related to non-convergent projects which influence the effort to have a National Sports Project.

### The formative process of sport education programmes

In México, we can divide the education of sport into two different areas: sport education in the context of school physical education and sport education beyond school physical education.

#### Sport education in the context of the physical education class

The first stream takes place through the subject of Physical Education where basic education (ages 3–15) includes the initiation into sport and school team sport mainly through sport games such as soccer, basketball, and volleyball in order to promote participation, enjoyment, and active lifestyles (Secretaría de Educación, 2017). The physical education programme aims to promote knowledge, skills, and attitudes to develop the culture of movement. Moreover, it promotes sports practice and tournaments during the school year where children learn the basics of sport. Physical educators are the main promoters of different sports at schools based mostly on their own sports skills interest. Unfortunately, as noted by Argumedo et al. (2020) in the National Report Card of Physical Activity, only 36.3% of Mexican children in public schools receive one hour of physical education per week taught by licensed physical education teachers. This severely limits the opportunity for teachers to provide quality sports experiences within that setting.

#### Sport education beyond school physical education

The second stream is related to sports training outside school. It has two options, public and private. The first one depends on the government CONADE's strategies and the school sport counselling board. Some of the sports disciplines that are currently included at the national stage are: soccer (football), athletics, badminton, basketball, handball, baseball, taekwondo, table tennis, and volleyball. The participation in sport depends on human resources available, because not all the schools have a physical education specialist (Rodríguez, Jáuregui and Instituto Nacional de Salud Pública, 2018). This dispersal of expertise across several locations and limitations with equipment at schools has encouraged schools to develop partnerships or collaborations with other institutions (López-Taylor,

Jáuregui-Ulloa and González-Villalobos, 2014). In the last ten years, there have been many alliances between the Ministry of Health, Ministry of Education, and CONADE that have promoted physical activity and sports programmes at schools, which has not been successful because of the lack of evaluation and the evidence of impact (Jauregui et al., 2015). The private services are given by private clubs and sports academies that offer practice and preparation in different sport, such as football/soccer, swimming, dance, taekwondo, karate, gymnastics, and tennis. In these private organisations, it is common to find that those who are responsible for teaching are not necessarily physical educators or professional trainers who have a special certification but are hired based on their professional sports experience.

Sport education in México is mainly offered by the sport federations. There are organisations that accredit sport coaching education programmes usually through the Olympic Mexican Committee. The individual sport federations oversee this, but in many cases the certification courses created lack a real academic structure, besides the fact that this certification is only necessary for coaches who are aiming to compete at the national level. Thus, coaches working with school teams or at any other place do not need a certification.

Finally, we consider important to mention some aspects related to the funding of sport through private entrepreneurs. Unlike the United States and to some degree Canada, México does not have the same level of involvement by companies that donate millions of dollars to sponsor sports programmes. Many national and foreign companies have been committed to develop sports programmes for kids and young people. These companies not only use sport to market their image but also distinguish themselves by helping to develop the sports infrastructure around the country to support child and youth sport.

## Development and delivery of sport in the United States

### Introduction

Except for religion, sport has become the most dominant cultural institution in the United States. Consider the passion for sport across all levels from youth sport to international competition levels. The explosive growth and professionalisation of sport, along with the economic interests and growing passion for sport, are key factors. However, there is the constant tension between investing in sport for the general public (breadth of participation) and for high-performance athletes competing at national and international levels (Farrey, 2008). The search for the next superstar athlete is never-ending. Youngsters showing athletic prowess and talent have ways of working towards ever-better performance with strong support and motivation from parents who can support their search for greatness. Parents may even have genetic tests done to determine their offspring's genetic predispositions for athletic excellence and will spend large sums of money to travel to often-times out-of-state weekend tournaments, so their son or daughter will "be seen" by college scouts. The prospect of getting an athletic scholarship at a college/ university is a significant motivation to make these investments. Yet, the above captures only a small number of the millions of youngsters who start sports participation at a young age. The multiple ways in the United States in which children, youth, and adults can learn to play sport are presented below.

## Child and youth sport

### School physical education

Since the 1990s, school districts have been rolling back time and graduation requirements for physical education in favour of allocating time for improving performance in academic subjects (i.e., mathematics, English language arts). This makes it increasingly difficult for physical educators to accomplish meaningful programme outcomes.

In recent years, two curricular and instructional models have gained prominence. First, Sport Education is perhaps the most widely known and evidence-based curriculum and instruction model (Siedentop, Hastie and van der Mars, 2020). And second, the games-based approach to teaching sports games has gained inroads (Launder and Piltz, 2013; Mitchell, Oslin and Griffin, 2021). In tandem, these models aim to develop competent, informed, and enthusiastic sports participants by emphasising more authentic sports experiences that include a focus on developing both tactical and technical aspects of play.

### After-school sport and physical activity programming

School districts provide after-school programming for many students whose parents work outside of the home. Some are provided through the districts' community education programme, while others are outsourced to private companies. Historically, such programmes have consisted of activities like completing homework, arts and crafts, academic skills, and life skills. Despite after-school time being a prime opportunity for physical activity engagement, little, if any, emphasis was placed on providing physical activity opportunities, until recently.

### Community-based delivery of sport

Communities offer several means through which children and youth can be introduced to sport. They include:

- Non-profit public or community sports programmes. Many of these sports programmes are affiliated with national organisations, such as Little League Baseball. Others include the American Youth Soccer Association (AYSO) and Pop Warner football. Still other programmes are developed and sustained through local recreation departments.

- Fee-based sports specialisation instructional programmes. These target youth as young as 10–12 years of age. Youth from families with the financial means may even have their own personal coach even though they play a "team" sport, who might focus on just one aspect of play (e.g., hitting, catching in baseball). Parents are also known to hire personal conditioning coaches. In addition, there are sport-specific programmes that market themselves as educational and developmental programmes promoting physical development and socialisation with an emphasis on youth having fun.
- Fee-based summer sports camps. Camps like these are also big business. In 2020, in the United States alone, Mysummercamps.com listed almost 20,000 camps in 58 different sports disciplines. Camps for popular high-school sport include basketball (2,532 camps), soccer (983), and American Football (664). Camps are either day camps serving boys and girls in a local community or residential camps where participants stay at the programme site, typically for one week (MySummerCamps, 2020).

### Interscholastic sport

Nowhere in the world is sport as intertwined with post-primary schools as in the United States. Interscholastic sports programmes are offered outside of the school day with practice sessions and games typically scheduled between 3:00 pm and 8:00 pm. For some high schoolers (and their parents), it is a springboard for a potential athletic scholarship at a college/university. Expansive sports facilities, including large-sized weight rooms for strength conditioning, are now standard features on most school campuses. In 2018–2019, almost eight million boys and girls competed in high-school sport, showing a steady increase, notably among girls (NFHS, 2019; Simon and Uddin, 2018).

Sports specialisation has become the norm for many high-school athletes. American Football players use winter and spring for strength training instead of participating in other sports. They commit themselves to year-round participation, with travel to summer camps where their skills can be more fully developed. In part, this again is a consequence of parents and their high-school athlete envisioning a possible university/college athletic scholarship.

### Organisation and governance of sport

Most countries have a national Ministry of Sport (often combined with public health). The US constitution specifically designates education as a state-level function. Neither the federal nor state governments have an agency that funds, oversees, or sets policies to ensure quality sports programming. For example, no national organisation exists that accredits sport coaching education programmes. Thus, sports organisations are left to self-police their programmes and initiatives. And unlike Canada, there is no unifying national governmental agenda or framework to support and promote sports participation through national initiatives.

Despite the absence of any government oversight, there is significant interest nationally to encourage and support broad and inclusive sports participation. The federal government actively promotes better health, with a strong focus on increasing physical activity (including sport). Every decade, the United States Department of Health and Human Services (USDHHS) presents updated national health objectives, along with progress on prior objectives (USDHHS, 2019). It has also developed national physical activity recommendations and guidelines, across all age groups and special populations (USDHHS, 2018).

The non-profit Physical Activity Alliance (PAA) published the National Physical Activity Plan with strategies, specific tactics, and measurable objectives developed by nine societal sectors, aimed at increasing physical activity levels across all age groups (NPAPA, 2016). PAA also publishes the US report card on physical activity for children and youth (NPAPA, 2018). Similarly, the Aspen Institute tracks the "State of Play" nationally, documenting trends and barriers to quality youth sports programming (The Aspen Institute, 2019). Dropout from sport remains a primary concern and is attributed to exclusionary models of sports delivery (i.e., only those who are "good enough to make the team" get to participate), poor coaching, and young athlete burnout.

### Coaches and coach education in the United States

Coaches in child and youth sport in after-school and community settings rely almost solely on volunteers. Required completion of comprehensive coach education programmes is non-existent. And while national standards for sport coaches do exist (Gano-Overway, Thompson and Van Mullem, 2021), because of the heavy dependence on volunteers, actual requirements for coaches are limited to getting cleared through a criminal background check and being certified in first aid and cardio-pulmonary resuscitation (CPR). For certain contact sport (e.g., American Football), coaches are required to complete a module on concussion management.

With some exceptions, coaching in high schools is a part-time position that oftentimes is combined with classroom/physical education teaching duties. Coaches earn a stipend in addition to their regular teaching salary. Depending on the sport and region, coaching stipends range from 1,500 to 5,900 dollars. Varying by state or school district, high-school coaches are required to have an undergraduate university degree, and some states may require coursework in exercise science or physical education.

There is not one single national coach education programme. Coach education programmes do exist, including:

- Those developed by National Governing Bodies (NGBs) of Olympic sport (e.g., USA Volleyball, USA Archery)
- The Human Kinetics Coach Education Centre (www.asep.com, formerly known as the American Sport Education Program)

- National Federation of State High-School Associations' (NFSHSA) online coaching education programme (NFHSLearn.com)
- The National Alliance of Youth Sports' (www.NAYS.org) Coach Training & Membership Programme

Most programmes provide online course offerings and have multi-level certification options.

## Sports programme similarities across the three countries

The above overview of sports delivery and access reflects important similarities across North America. First, there are multiple ways in which people can learn about and participate in a wide variety of sport, across various competitive levels and age groups. Second, school physical education remains a key avenue through which most children and youth are introduced to various sport during their formative years. However, the subject must compete for curricular time with other academic subjects and continues to be marginalised. Second, the tension between supporting elite athletic performance and broad-based participation by the general population exists throughout.

Similarities exist as well in the coach education realm. Of the three countries, Canada has a coherent commitment to coaching education through centrally accredited coaching programmes. The United States has a range of coach education programmes developed by national sports (coaching) organisations committed to supporting quality coaching. México has a centralised funding model but finds it difficult to regulate the education of coaches and work in partnerships with private sports organisations.

In the United States, standards and goals are set across the country from national organisations that try to balance the health benefits with sport for life intent and the goal to promote elite athletes that can compete on the world stage. In Canada, the developmental framework and shared vision is promoted through government funding and supported by corporate sponsorship but like in the United States, this does not necessarily lead to consistently effective instructional practices across the country and across sport, or increased sports participation.

All three countries try to develop a roadmap for success relative to sport. However, a shortfall in funding of sports infrastructure at the local level, the underrepresentation of minority groups, the increasing for-profit selling of sport, and early recruitment of youth into specialised sport confound the desire to use sport as a vehicle to promote community and lifelong health and physical engagement. In summary, Thibault and Harvey (2013) note about Canada, though it could also be said for México and the United States that while, "high performance athletes have continued to strive for medals internationally, overall sports participation […] has been declining, regardless of the type of metrics chosen" (Thibault and Harvey, 2013, p. 407).

The United States has made strides in providing fee-based recreational sports opportunities through municipal parks and recreation departments. Teams can sign up for formal competitions at different levels (e.g., from more social/ recreational to more advanced levels) and different types (single sex and co-educational). In larger urban areas, these programmes may offer a huge range of various sport (e.g., softball, tennis, basketball, volleyball). Similar fee-based recreational sports opportunities exist in México and Canada, with different subsidy levels from local municipalities.

In all three nations, sports opportunities also exist for people with disabilities. The most well-known programme for people with intellectual disabilities are the Special Olympics. However, there are also other organisations that promote engagement in sport by people with various disabilities, including support for Paralympic athletes, though substantially larger in the United States given the size of the population.

Adults and older adults can also continue to compete in their sport of choice through the master's sports programmes, which includes state-level competition. Most state/provincial-level master's games include age-group competition (in five-year increments) in as many as 22 different kinds of sport. Competitors in these programmes can also compete internationally in the World Masters Games held every four years.

The United States has a long tradition of high-school sports programmes tailored for youth elite players. Specialisation in a sport for children and youths is also available through local and national organisations across North America that are linked to publicly funded and private schools that offer scholarships or fee-based programmes to aspiring young athletes. In the United States, this is most fully developed for soccer and basketball. Indeed, for most metropolitan areas, it is now common to have soccer "clubs" offering instruction, age-group competition, and "select teams" that travel to tournaments (oftentimes out-of-state), and often practicing and competing year-round. In México and Canada these types of programmes are more commonly known as sports academies. These programmes hire coaches that typically have extensive playing and coaching experience but lack educational degrees or certification. In México, there is little, if any, professional regulation or oversight on these private sports academies, contrasting with the highly regulated education sector which is overseen by the state. In Canada, in the last decade, there has been a significant growth of sport-specific academies ranging from 20% to 50% of all high schools in each of the three provinces of British Columbia, Alberta, and Québec (Thibault and Harvey, 2013).

In all three countries, these school sports programmes are popular with:

- Parents who see this as a path to university scholarships and professional sports careers
- School administrators, as the academies attract motivated students
- Students who love to engage in their sport

However, as noted by Thibault and Harvey (2013), in these sport-specific academies, there is a tendency to focus too much on the elite level, often leading to young athlete burnout and overuse injuries, rather than pursuing and contributing to experiences that build a sport for life foundation.

### *Looking forward: Towards a more sane and more inclusive sports culture*

Sport in North America will remain firmly entrenched as a dominant cultural institution. However, to develop a saner and more egalitarian sports culture, with access to quality sports experiences for everyone throughout life, requires the following: first, with economic disparities steadily increasing, increased public funding as well as mutually beneficial public-private partnerships are needed to support the development and delivery of quality sports programming. Beyond the government, such partnerships could include private corporations, the health insurance industry, and the professional sports organisations themselves.

Second, proper training of youth sport coaches is essential. The lack of oversight in notably the United States contributes to the deeply concerning dropout rate as youth move into adolescence. Parents should expect that coaches have not only the content knowledge, but also the specialised pedagogical knowledge to design appropriate experiences.

Third, the prevalent trend of youth specialising early on in one sport and playing the sport virtually year-round is counterproductive. Youth who have been playing that much for most of their formative years are more likely to either sustain overuse injuries, and/or experience burnout, and then resort to more sedentary lives.

Last but not least, as part of improving inclusive access/opportunity for all, the excessive focus on supporting elite athletes must be brought into balance with investment in sport for the broader population. National policies are needed to ensure this more balanced funding across participation levels (UNESCO, 2017; USDHHS, 2019). Only then will the goal of "sport for all" become a possibility.

## References

Aboriginal Sport Circle (2019) *Indigenous Sport for Life: Long-Term Participant Development Pathway 1.2.* Available at: https://sportforlife.ca/portfolio-view/indigenous-long-term-participant-development-pathway/ (Accessed: 28 July 2020).

Argumedo, G., Taylor, J. R. L., Gaytán-González. A., González-Casanova. I., Villalobos, M. F. G., Jáuregui, A., et al. (2020) Mexico's 2018 Report Card on Physical Activity for Children and Youth: Full report. *Rev Panam Salud Publica (Pan-American Journal of Public Health*, 44, e26. https://iris.paho.org/bitstream/handle/10665.2/51937/v44e262020.pdf?sequence=1&isAllowed=y

Balyi, I., Way, R. and Higgs, C. (2013) *Long-term athlete development.* Champaign, IL: Human Kinetics.

Canadian Sport Policy (2012) *Canadian Sports Policy*. Available at: https://sirc.ca/wp-content/uploads/files/content/docs/Document/csp2012_en.pdf (Accessed: 28 July 2020).

Farrey, T. (2008) *Game on: The all-American race to make champions of our children.* New York, NY: ESPN Books.

Gano-Overway, L., Thompson, M. and Van Mullem, P. (2021) *National standards for sport coaches: Quality coaches, quality sports.* 3rd edn. Boston, MA: Jones & Bartlett.

Giblin, S., Collins, D. and Button, C. (2014) 'Physical literacy: Importance, assessment and future directions', *Sports Medicine*, 44(9), pp. 1177–1184. doi:10.1007/s40279-014-0205-7.

Government of México (2014) *Diario oficial de la Federación. Programa Nacional de Cultura Física y Deporte 2014-2018.* Available at: http://www.dof.gob.mx/nota_detalle.php?codigo=5342830&fecha=30/04/2014 (Accessed: 27 July 2020).

Hopper, T. (2011). Game-as-teacher: Modification by adaptation in learning through gameplay. *Asia-Pacific Journal of Health, Sport and Physical Education*, 2(2), pp. 3–21. https://doi.org/10.1080/18377122.2011.9730348.

Jauregui, E. *et al.* (2015) 'Using the RE-AIM framework to evaluate physical activity public health programs in México', *BMC Public Health*, 15(162). doi:10.1186/s12889-015-1474-2.

Kidd, B. and Longboat, T. (2018) *In The Canadian Encyclopedia*. Available at: https://www.thecanadianencyclopedia.ca/en/article/tom-longboat (Accessed: 28 July 2020).

Launder, A. G. and Piltz, W. (2013) *Play practice: Engaging and developing skilled players from beginner to elite.* 2nd edn. Champaign, IL: Human Kinetics.

López-Taylor, J., Jáuregui-Ulloa, E., and González-Villalobos, M. (2014). Physical Education in Mexico: Experiences and Trends Related to Physical Activity and Health. In *Physical Education and Health Global Perspectives and Best Practice.* Sagamore Publishing LLC

Mandigo, J., Butler, J. and Hopper, T. (2007) 'What is teaching games for understanding? A Canadian perspective', *Physical and Health Education Journal*, 73(2), pp. 14–20.

Mitchell, S. A., Oslin, J. L. and Griffin, L. L. (2021) *Teaching sport concepts and skills: A tactical games.* 4th edn. Champaign, IL: Human Kinetics.

Mysummercamps (2020) *Sports Camps*. Available at: https://www.mysummercamps.com/camps/Sports_Camps/ (Accessed: 23 June 2020).

National Federation of State High School Associations (NFHS) (2019) *NFHS Annual Report*. Available at: https://www.nfhs.org/ (Accessed: 22 June 2020).

National Physical Activity Plan Alliance (NPAPA) (2016) *The National Physical Activity Plan*. Available at: https://www.physicalactivityplan.org/about/alliance.html (Accessed: 28 July 2020).

National Physical Activity Plan Alliance (NPAPA) (2018) *The 2018 United States Report Card on Physical Activity for Children and Youth*. Available at: https://www.physicalactivityplan.org/projects/reportcard.html (Accessed: 26 July 2020).

PHE (2020a) *Physical and Health Education*. Available at: https://phecanada.ca/ (Accessed: 26 June 2020).

PHE (2020b) *Programs: Move Think Learn*. Available at: https://phecanada.ca/programs/move-think-learn (Accessed: 29 July 2020).

Rodríguez, L., Jáuregui, A. and Instituto Nacional de Salud Pública (2018) *Hacia una estrategia nacional para la prestación de Educación Física de calidad en el nivel básico del Sistema Educativo Mexicano. Cuernavaca, México.* Available at: https://www.insp.mx/produccion-editorial/novedades-editoriales/4974-estrategia-presentar-educacion-fisica-nivel-basico.html (Accessed: 24 July 2020).

Secretaría de Educación Pública (2017) *Aprendizajes Clave para la Educación Integral. Ciudad de México, México. SEP.* Available at: https://www.planyprogramasdestudio. sep.gob.mx/descargables/APRENDIZAJES_CLAVE_PARA_LA_EDUCACION_ INTEGRAL.pdf (Accessed: 27 July 2020).

Siedentop, D., Hastie, P. A. and van der Mars, H. (2020) *Complete guide to Sport Education.* 3rd edn. Champaign, IL: Human Kinetics.

Simon, A. E. and Uddin, S. F. (2018) 'Sports team participation among US high school girls, 1999–2015', *Clinical Pediatrics,* 57(6), pp. 637–644.

Sport Canada (2012) *Canadian Sport Policy 2012.* Available at: https://sirc.ca/app/uploads/ files/content/docs/Document/csp2012_en.pdf (Accessed: 26 July 2020).

Sport for Life (2019) *Long-term Development in Sport and Physical Activity 3.0.* Available at: https://sportforlife.ca/wp-content/uploads/2019/06/Long-Term-Development-in-Sport-and-Physical-Activity-3.0.pdf (Accessed: March 26, 2021).

The Aspen Institute (2019) *2019 State of Play: Trends and Developments in Youth Sport.* Available at: https://www.aspeninstitute.org/publications/state-of-play-2019-trends-and-developments/ (Accessed: July 16, 2020).

Thibault, L. and Harvey, J. (2013) *Sport policy in Canada.* Ottawa: University of Ottawa Press.

Truth and Reconciliation Commission of Canada (TRC) (2015) *Canada's residential schools: The final report of the truth and reconciliation commission of Canada.* Montreal: McGill-Queen's Press-MQUP. Available at: http://nctr.ca/assets/reports/Final%20 Reports/Executive_Summary_English_Web.pdf (Accessed: 26 March, 2021).

UNESCO (2017) *Promoting Physical Education Quality Policy.* Available at https://en. unesco.org/themes/sport-and-anti-doping/sports-education/qpe (Accessed: 28 July 2020).

United States Department of Health and Human Services (USDHHS) (2018) *Physical Activity Guidelines for Americans.* Available at: https://health.gov/sites/default/files/2019-09/Physical_Activity_Guidelines_2nd_edition.pdf (Accessed: 6 June 2020).

United States Department of Health and Human Services (USDHHS) (2019) *National Youth Sports Strategy.* Available at: www.health.gov/our-work/physical-activity/national-youth-sports-strategy (Accessed: 15 July 2020).

Chapter 10

# Education in sport and physical activity across the Pacific

*Dean Dudley, John Cairney, Aue Te Ava, and Jackie Lauff*

## Introduction

Physical activity can be divided into components, including leisure-time, occupational (e.g., physical education participation at school), transport (e.g., walking to and or from different destinations), and domestic (e.g., household chores) related activity, with sport being a subset of leisure-time physical activity.

The health benefits associated with physical activity while participating in organised sport are well established. They include benefits to blood pressure, metabolic syndrome, adiposity, skeletal and mental health, and reduced risk of chronic diseases such as heart disease and Type 2 Diabetes (Khan *et al.*, 2012). Beyond mere physical activity for physiological benefit, organised sports participation is also associated with important psychosocial benefits including increased self-esteem, well-being, social skills, and overall quality of life (Mills *et al.*, 2019).

Educating a population to engage in sport and physical activity across the broader Pacific region requires all countries to embrace multi-strategic policies (Dudley *et al.*, 2017). The experience in the Pacific region highlights phases of innovation and leadership in physical activity and sport policy, as well as periods of stagnation and decline. Several well-received reviews of evidence on good practices in physical activity and public health (Bellew *et al.*, 2008; Heath *et al.*, 2012) have been published, but continuity of leadership within sports organisation peak bodies and consistent delivery of resources are lacking to implement the policies and programmes needed in more in recent years (Diepeveen *et al.*, 2013).

Widespread publicity and increased public and political interest in chronic disease prevention (especially in obesity and Type 2 Diabetes) have dominated the most recent frameworks within the majority of Oceanic policy deliberations, given the prevalence of these conditions. This discourse consequently had a direct influence on education initiatives being undertaken more broadly by all stakeholders invested in physical activity and sport.

DOI: 10.4324/9781003002666-14

# Sport and physical activity in Australia and New Zealand

### *Australia*

The Australian Sport Commission (ASC) is the Australian Government agency responsible for supporting and investing in sport and physical activity at all levels. The ASC unites two entities: Sport Australia – responsible for driving the broader sport sector including participation, physical activity, and industry growth – and the Australian Institute of Sport (AIS) which is responsible for leading the Australian high-performance sport system.

The federated structure of the Australian states and territories means that Sport Australia must invest in a wide range of national sports organisations (NSOs). Each of these NSOs has a state and/or territory federated affiliate known as a state sports organisation (SSOs). Sport Australia therefore focuses on the capacity and capability of NSOs who in turn influence the strategic and operational objectives of their respective SSOs.

The single largest issue confronting Sport Australia, NSOs, and SSOs alike is Australia's marked declines in sport and physical activity participation over recent years. According to the Australian Institute of Health and Welfare (2018), the proportion of children who demonstrate sufficient levels of physical activity declines by the increase of age. This trend is also apparent in adults with the percentage of those meeting the recommendations varying markedly by age group (20.7% of Australians aged 18–24 declining steadily to 11.1% to those aged 55–64).

As noted earlier, sports participation is only one specific component of physical activity. As such, the picture of sport differs from general physical activity. First, sports participation for children and youth occurs in two contexts: in and out of school. Regarding the latter, the best source for tracking participation in the Australian context is the AusPlay Survey conducted by the ASC. The AusPlay Survey is an annual survey which involves 20,000 respondents from across the country. According to this ASC survey, 74% of children (ages 3–14) participate in at least one organised sport outside of school (ASC, 2018). The highest averages for participation outside of school are in the age range 5–11, with over 80% of boys and girls participating in at least one sport. Interestingly, boys outnumbered girls except for the youngest age group (zero to four). The gender gap increases across successively older cohorts reaching its widest point among 12- to 14-year-olds (girls: 75%; boys: 86%).

However, the high prevalence of sports participation among children begins to decline in mid-adolescence, from a high mark of 87% among 9- to 11-year-olds, to 77% among 12- to 14-year-olds, and further down to 68% in 18- to 24-year-olds (ASC, 2018). Sports participation outside of school is characterised by high

## 128 Dean Dudley et al.

rates of participation through middle childhood into pre-adolescence, followed by a decline that persists well into adulthood. Indeed, among adults between the ages of 55 and 64, and those 65 and over, rates of participation decline to 46% and 37%, respectively. The challenge, it seems, is not getting children and youth involved in organised sport, but preventing their departure, especially for girls and young women who start to leave earlier than boys and young men, and at a higher rate in emerging adulthood and beyond.

The high rate of sports participation is defined as those who participate in one sport, perhaps once or twice a week. Even assuming a moderate level of physical activity intensity during games and practice – a benchmark which is often not met (Wickel and Eisenmann, 2007) – this volume falls well below the level of duration, intensity, and volume required to meet the national physical activity guidelines.

### New Zealand

Sport New Zealand by comparison to Sport Australia operates with a similar mandate of improving both sport and physical activity participation and high-performance sport but does so with a much smaller population and absence of a federated government hierarchy. They too operate with a series of NSOs who govern the operations of sport and recreation pursuits. Rather than SSOs being delegated authorities though, New Zealand operates a series of Regional Sport Trusts (RSTs) that are independent, not-for-profit organisations responsible for increasing regional levels of physical activity and strengthening regional sport and physical recreation infrastructures. Sport New Zealand invests not only in its NSOs, but it also invests in RSTs using a population-based formula and provides further investment for targeted initiatives within each region.

Like Australia, New Zealand has experienced ongoing declines in the national physical activity and sports participation profile of its citizens. According to Smith et al. (2018), only 7% of secondary school students meet the current recommendations of 60 minutes of physical activity daily with sharp declines in organised sports participation in older adolescence. That said, organised sports participation remains high in youth from certain ethnic groups within New Zealand, especially European, Maori, and Pacifika peoples.

For adults in New Zealand, around half of all adults (51%) are physically active for at least 30 minutes on five or more days per week but many demographic discrepancies in this data exist. Pacific and Asian adults living in New Zealand, and those aged over 65 years, are less likely to be physically active than other demographics within the New Zealand population.

Like Sport Australia's annual AusPlay survey, Sport New Zealand conducts an annual survey of sports participation. The most recent data from 2018 paints a picture not dissimilar to the results shown for Australia (Sport New Zealand, 2018). First, participation peaks among children ages 12–14, but then declines between the ages of 15 and 17. Participation is highest among 8- to 11-year-olds and 12- to 14-year-olds with weekly sports participation estimates of 95% and 96%, respectively. Among 18- to 24-year-olds, this drops to 73%. The average number of different sports participated in also declines, from a high of 6.4 different kinds of sport played weekly among 12- to 14-year-olds to 2.5 among 18- to 24-year-olds. Compared to 2017, there was a 2% drop in participation among 12- to 14-year-olds. A gender gap was also noted: young males on average spent 90 minutes more per week participating in sport than females. The lowest rates appear among those 75 and older, with only 58% reporting an average participation in 1.3 different kinds of sport per week, spending less than four hours in participation.

## Sport and physical activity across the Pacific region

Participation in sport and physical activity celebrates Pacific nation's cultural heritage, national identity, and regional harmony. The Pacific region encompasses 22 culturally and economically diverse island countries and territories (not including Australia and New Zealand), spanning an exceptionally large geographic area in the Pacific Ocean.

There is a significant gap in the Pacific region when it comes to data collection and analysis as well as regular surveillance at a population level on physical activity and sport. Several surveillance tools are utilised in Pacific Island Countries and Territories (PICTs) to monitor non-communicable diseases (NCDs) risk factors including the World Health Organizations' (WHO) STEPS and STEPS-like surveys for adults, and Global School-based Student Health Survey (GSHS) and other school-based surveys for adolescents.

By 2015, 19 PICTs had completed at least one adult and one adolescent NCD risk factor survey (Tolley et al., 2016). The first progress report in 2017, monitoring progress towards the vision of Healthy Islands in the Pacific, reported insufficient physical activity in adults and inadequate physical activity in adolescents in the Pacific region, with Wallis and Futuna along with Cook Islands stating that more than half of their adult population are insufficiently physically active, followed by Kiribati, the Marshall Islands, and Nauru all with 40% or more (WHO, 2018, p. 14). Nine Pacific countries reported that less than one quarter of their adolescents engage in adequate levels of physical activity on a daily basis (WHO, 2018, p. 30).

NCDs have become the leading cause of premature death and disability in the Pacific region, posing one of the biggest threats to development across the region. Twelve countries with the highest prevalence of diabetes and obesity are PICTs (Tolley et al., 2016). Over the last decade, the prevalence of overweight and obesity in children and adolescents in PICTss has increased dramatically, and a major factor is an insufficient amount of daily moderate-to-vigorous physical activity (MVPA). In the Pacific region, less than 50% of children and adolescents meet the international recommendations of 11,000 steps and 60 min of MVPA per day (Galy, Yacef and Caillaud, 2019).

There are many key stakeholders that play a role in the delivery of sport and physical activity in PICTs, including for example: Government Ministries Responsible for Sport, Statutory Bodies (such as sports commissions and facilities authorities established by legislative acts), National Olympic Committees (NOCs), National Sport Federations, National Disability Sports Organisations (National Paralympic Committees & Special Olympics Accredited Programmes). At the regional level, key organisations include the Oceania National Olympic Committees (ONOC), Pacific Games Council, Organisation of Sport Federations of Oceania (OSFO), Oceania Regional Anti-Doping Organisation, and Oceania University Sports Association, to name a few.

Several organisations and strategic partnerships play a key role in delivering education programmes to encourage Pacific Islanders to engage in sport and physical activity. The Oceania Sport Education Program (OSEP) is one such example of a partnership between the Australian Sports Commission, ONOC, and OSFO that provides a structured regional sport education pathway for coaching and administration (Dorovolomo, 2018).

Recently, scholars across the Pacific region have called for traditional sport and games to be reintroduced into formal curricula and sports programmes to engage Pacific Islanders in physical activity (Te Ava *et al.*, 2013). Of all the traditional ancient sport and games – canoe race, cultural dancing, legends, chants, arts and crafts, and so forth – few remain today with any significant influence. However, there is an enthusiastic revival of interest in promoting cultural traditional workshops to give adults and youngsters the opportunity to learn culture through game implements (Te Ava *et al.*, 2013), creating space for understanding the cultural identity of a whole person (socially, culturally, physically, emotionally, and spiritually) and to show how human movement and culture can tap into the learning potential of Pacific people through culturally responsive pedagogy (Te Ava and Page, 2018;).

While the contribution of sport and physical activity is becoming increasingly recognised as a policy priority in the Pacific, there is a long journey ahead to turn the tide on the NCDs crisis affecting the region at alarming rates.

## Shifting sport and physical activity policy in Australia and New Zealand using an educative approach

In 2015, Sport Australia launched a $240 million initiative designed to help schools increase children's participation in sport and to connect them with community sports opportunities. The "Sporting Schools" initiative is a programme whereby Sport Australia partnered with the majority of its NSOs to run targeted sports programmes for students in primary and lower secondary schools. Whilst over 7,500 schools have received funding for the Sporting School programme since its inception, there is no empirical evidence that the programme has influenced the uptake of community-based sports participation for youth.

In a broader community education strategy, Sport Australia initiated its "Find your 30" campaign. It attempts to promote adults to accumulate between 2.5 and

5 hours of moderate intensity physical activity or 1.25 and 2.5 hours of vigorous activity each week. To do this, the initiative has a strong education focus on physiological, social, and environmental benefits of sport and physical activity. Uniquely though, the "Find your 30" education campaign uses children as the learning change agents in adult physical activity behaviour.

The approach of using children as the medium for instruction has an increasing degree of efficacy in physical activity promotion. The work of scholars from the University of Newcastle explains why this appears to be the case. In a two-arm randomised controlled trial, 115 fathers (29–53 years) and 153 daughters (4– 12 years) undertook an eight-week sport and physical activity educational programme. In a nutshell, the programme involved playful games and sports experiences that fathers could share with their daughters. The results of the study show significant improvements not only in the fundamental movement skill competency and reduced sedentary behaviours of the daughters, but there was also a medium to large effect on the range of physical activity parenting practices undertaken by the fathers (Morgan *et al.*, 2019). The programme is now being rolled out as a sports participation initiative by the New South Wales Government through their Office of Sport.

Sport Australia's most recent sport and physical activity education strategy has been targeted at the population level which targets Australians of all ages and demographics. The Australian Physical Literacy Framework has been developed as a learning intervention to establish a common language across vested stakeholders of sport and physical activity and to support all Australians develop their physical literacy, at every stage of their life. Such an educative approach does not privilege one component of physical activity (e.g., sport) over any other, but rather encourages the development of competencies and attitudes that promote varied movement experiences across different contexts. The goal for Sport Australia is to have the Physical Literacy Framework adopted through systems and policies across health, education, sport, and recreation as a tool that improves individual and societal health and well-being. Policy makers can then target specific aspects of the physical literacy learning domains in their planning and interventions for impact with specific audiences and communities.

Across the Tasman Sea, Sport New Zealand recently launched a revised Community Sport Strategy to ensure that young New Zealanders develop a lifelong love of sport and active recreation. The sector understands that this can only be achieved by improving the physical literacy of their young people through programmes that provide quality opportunities and experiences.

This revised iteration of the Sport New Zealand Community Sport Strategy is broadly aimed at building a more educated population to foster the growth of sport in the community and to better align available resources with regional investors and stakeholders through the RSTs. It also sees more cross-government engagement and collaboration (e.g., Ministry of Education and Ministry of Health) and is focused on a system-led, participant-centred approach. Embedded in the learning-based strategy, there is a strong focus on young people and schools and to work with partners to both sustain and grow traditional sports structures and pathways. Whilst this version of the Sport New Zealand Community Sport Strategy may not be deemed as revolutionary, it does signal Sport New Zealand's determination to play a more decisive leadership role in community sport and physical activity. Using physical literacy as a concept to promote a shared dialogue between agencies and stakeholders also concretely purveys the intent of physical literacy that has been advocated for by scholars in the sector (Dudley et al., 2017; Cairney et al., 2019).

## Emerging sport and physical activity education initiatives across the Pacific region

In recent years, sport has gained some traction on the regional policy agenda with a united call from sports stakeholders for greater regional coordination and targeted action across sport, physical activity, and physical education (ONOC, 2018).

The cross-cutting contribution of sport and physical activity to regional development is further highlighted in a series of regional policy instruments. For example, the inclusion of physical literacy in the Pacific Regional Education Framework (PACREF) 2018–2030, and the Pacific Ending Childhood Obesity Network (ECHO) formed in 2018, which has prioritised physical activity as one of four strategic targets, specifically aiming to increase the proportion of children aged 5–17 years old who meet the WHO recommendations on physical activity.

A Pacific Regional Sports Taskforce was formed in April 2018 to oversee the development of a Pacific Sport, Physical Activity and Physical Education (SPAPE) Action Plan 2018–2030. The initiative will mobilise relevant stakeholders including governments, sports organisations, civil society organisations, regional organisations, United Nations agencies, development partners, university and tertiary institutions, and media organisations to ensure that the contributions of sport, physical activity, and physical education are adequately integrated into the sustainable development agenda in the Pacific and embedded in national and regional policy.

Pacific Governments are beginning to step up to the challenge of harnessing the potential of sport and physical activity with a host of new and revised national sport policies under development and the emergence of innovative multi-sector partnerships to promote physical activity and sport at the community level. For instance, the Government of Samoa introduced a National Sports in Education Policy 2018–2023 for all Samoans who are engaged in formal or non-formal education settings (Government of Samoa, 2019). In Fiji, the Fiji National Sports Commission piloted a village level outreach programme "Vitality through Active Living" in partnership with the Fiji Ministry of Health and the Waikato Institute of Technology to deliver physical activity, health education, and medical screening over 13 weeks, investing in women as agents of change within their families and communities (Longhurst, 2018).

There is a growing body of academic discourse exploring contemporary issues in Pacific sport and physical activity such as national identity and migration, gender, ethnicity, and the inclusion of people with disabilities (Kanemasu and Molnar, 2014; Dorovolomo, 2015; Beckman et al., 2018; Sugden, 2019). Further research is needed to understand the barriers to physical activity across the lifespan and to test solutions that will promote lifelong healthy habits and positive behavioural change to get Pacific Islanders moving and keep them moving for their lifetime.

## Physical literacy – A new shared language of learning sport and physical activity?

The International Charter for Physical Education, Physical Activity, and Sport (UNESCO, 2015) affirms that there are many agencies that must participate in creating strategic policy options enabling the fundamental right for all people to participate in meaningful physical activity and sport across their life course. Dudley et al. (2017) identified that physical literacy is a rapidly evolving concept being used in policy making. That being said, they also identify that much of the incorporation into strategic policy and programmes has been limited by pre-existing and biased interpretations of the construct.

Australia, New Zealand, and now the broader Pacific community are embracing the concept of physical literacy based on work undertaken in the Australian Physical Literacy Framework as a means of uniting stakeholders in sport, public health, and education policy change. This begs the question though of why physical literacy is a concept worth embracing in the pursuit of arresting the declines in physical activity and sports participation.

Cairney et al.'s (2019) evidence-informed conceptual model of physical literacy, physical activity, and health provided some early insight into why this might prove to be a turning point in policy development. Arguing from a pragmatic perspective where learning and knowledge interact with known determinants of physical activity, Cairney and colleagues argued that the interaction of these factors was in fact the driver of physical activity participation.

Their results from confirmatory factor analysis and cluster analysis support the idea that measures related to motor competence, motivation, and positive affect work in an integrative manner to produce learning that results in differences in physical activity and subsequent health outcomes in children. A more recent paper by Brown et al. (2020) further substantiates this claim that physical literacy development may be key to improving physical activity and sports participation.

## Conclusions

Surveillance data, particularly from Australia and New Zealand, shows that most children and adults are not meeting recommended guidelines for physical activity. In Pacific Island nations in particular, high rates of NCDs coupled with high levels of inactivity paint an alarming picture of future health care burden, lost productivity, and lower quality of life. At the same time, sport across the Pacific is popular, evidenced by high rates of participation, especially in children and youth. Even here though, participation declines with age, and gender disparities (among other social determinants) are cause for concern. Sport alone, it would appear, is insufficient as a primary vehicle to increase physical activity to a level that is sufficient to achieve prevention of NCDs. For sport to play a bigger role in achieving physical activity population targets, three things would need to happen. Sports participation would need to be increased in girls and women to levels observed for boys and men; declines would need to be prevented, especially in peri-adolescence, but across the adulthood lifespan; finally, number of hours spent in multiple kinds of sport would need to increase. Even with the popularity of sport, these changes will be difficult to achieve.

Organisations connected to sport are increasingly adopting physical literacy as a vehicle to increase physical activity participation. In doing so, the hope is that richer and more diverse movement behaviours will emerge, increasing physical activity participation to levels needed to achieve health benefits across the whole life course. While there is some evidence that an educative approach – consistent with physical literacy – can have a positive impact on physical activity behaviour (especially when children are the focus), more work is needed to evaluate whether this physical literacy approach offers benefits beyond current health promotion and population health approaches to increasing physical activity.

## References

Australian Institute of Health and Welfare (2018) *Nutrition across the life stages*. Canberra.

Australian Sports Commission (2018) *AusPlay focus children's participation in organised physical activity outside of school hours*. Canberra: Australian Government.

Beckman, E. *et al.* (2018) 'The effectiveness of a cricket programme for engaging people with a disability in physical activity in Fiji', *International Journal of Disability, Development and Education*, 65(2), pp. 199–213.

Bellew, B. *et al.* (2008) 'The rise and fall of Australian physical activity policy 1996–2006: A national review framed in an international context', *Australia and New Zealand Health Policy*, 5(1).

Brown, D. M. *et al.* (2020) 'Physical literacy profiles are associated with differences in children's physical activity participation: A latent profile analysis approach', *Journal of Science and Medicine in Sport*, 23(11), pp. 1062–1067.

Cairney, J. *et al.* (2019) 'Physical literacy, physical activity and health: Toward an evidence-informed conceptual model', *Sports Medicine*, 49(3), pp. 371–383.

Diepeveen, S. *et al.* (2013) 'Public acceptability of government intervention to change health-related behaviours: A systematic review and narrative synthesis', *BMC Public Health*, 13(1), p. 756.

Dorovolomo, J. (2015) 'The inclusion of deaf players into Fiji table tennis activities', *Journal of Pacific Studies*, 35(1), pp. 117–132.

Dorovolomo, J. (2018) 'Evaluation of a sport education program in the Pacific Islands', *Micronesian Educator*, 25, pp. 45–53.

Dudley, D. *et al.* (2017) 'Critical considerations for physical literacy policy in public health, recreation, sport, and education agencies', *Quest*, 69(4), pp. 436–452.

Galy, O., Yacef, K. and Caillaud, C. (2019) 'Improving Pacific Adolescents' physical activity toward international recommendations: Exploratory study of a digital education app coupled with activity trackers', *JMIR mHealth and uHealth*, 7(12), p. e14854.

Government of Samoa (2019) *Pacific sports policy roundtable: Outcome statement, Friday 5 July 2019*. Apia.

Heath, G. W. *et al.* (2012) 'Evidence-based intervention in physical activity: Lessons from around the world', *The Lancet*, 380(9838), pp. 272–281.

Kanemasu, Y. and Molnar, G. (2014) 'Life after rugby: Issues of being an 'ex' in Fiji rugby', *The International Journal of the History of Sport*, 31(11), pp. 1389–1405.

Khan, K. M. *et al.* (2012) 'Sport and exercise as contributors to the health of nations', *The Lancet*, 380(9836), pp. 59–64.

Longhurst, G. (2018). Project ViTAL ViTAL (Vitality Through Active Living) Fijian project.

Mills, K. *et al.* (2019). 'Do the benefits of participation in sport and exercise outweigh the negatives? An academic review', *Best Practice & Research Clinical Rheumatology*, 33(1), pp. 172–187.

Morgan, P. J. *et al.* (2019) 'Engaging fathers to increase physical activity in girls: The "dads and daughters exercising and empowered" (DADEE) randomized controlled trial', *Annals of Behavioral Medicine*, 53(1), pp. 39–52.

Oceania National Olympic Committees (2018) *Sport, sustainable development and public policy in the Pacific. Supporting statement for ONOC's submission for the Framework for Pacific Regionalism prepared by the Pacific Sports Compass Working Group, 28 February 2018.*

Smith, M. *et al.* (2018) *New Zealand's 2018 report card on physical activity for children and youth.* Auckland, New Zealand: The University of Auckland. doi: 10.17608/k6.auckland.7295882.

Sport New Zealand (2018) *Active NZ: Key Findings 2018 Survey Data.* Available at: https://sportnz.org.nz/media/1439/active-nz-key-findings-2018-2.pdf (Accessed: 1 August 2020).

Sugden, J. (2019) 'Sport and ethno-racial formation: Imagined distance in Fiji', *Sport in Society.*

Te Ava, A. *et al.* (2013) 'Akaoraoraia te Peu 'A To 'Ui Tupuna: Implementing Cook Islands core values in culturally responsive pedagogy in Cook Islands physical education classrooms', *The Australian Journal of Indigenous Education*, 42(1), pp. 32–43.

Te Ava, A. *et al.* (2018) 'Atoro'ia te peu 'ā to 'ui tūpuna: A culturally responsive pedagogy for Pasifika peoples', in Te Ava, A. *et al.* (eds.) *Wellbeing in higher education – cultivating a healthy lifestyle among faculty and students.* Oxfordshire: Routledge, pp. 111– 116.

Te Ava, A. and Page, A. (2018). How the Tivaevae Model can be used as an Indigenous methodology in Cook Islands education settings. *The Australian Journal of Indigenous Education*, 1–7.

Tolley, H. *et al.* (2016) 'Monitoring and accountability for the Pacific response to the non-communicable diseases crisis', *BMC Public Health*, 16(1), p. 958.

United Nations Educational, Scientific, and Cultural Organization (2015) *International charter of physical education, physical activity, and sport.* Paris: UNESCO Press.

Wickel, E. E. and Eisenmann, J. C. (2007) 'Contribution of youth sport to total daily physical activity among 6-to 12-yr-old boys', *Medicine and Science in Sports and Exercise*, 39(9), p. 1493.

World Health Organization (2018) *Monitoring Progress towards the Vision of Healthy Islands in the Pacific 2017: First Progress Report.*

Chapter 11

# Education in sport and physical activity

## Current trends, developments, and challenges in Latin America

*Miguel A. Cornejo and Alexander Cárdenas*

### The educational system in Latin America

Latin America is a very heterogeneous region characterised by a multitude of challenges including violence, crime, unemployment, and the lack of education. Latin America is one of the most violent regions in the world. A World Bank Annual Report (2014) concluded that, although Latin America is home to only about nine percent of the global population, it accounts for more than 30% of global homicides. The region ranks first globally in terms of deaths from youth violence. Young people represent 43% of all the unemployed in this part of the world, and only 33% have access to secondary education. Furthermore, Latin America continues to be the most unequal region on the planet.

Among the historical social problems that characterise this part of the world, one of the most pressing challenges it faces is the lack of access to quality education. In recent decades, education in Latin America has been influenced by social and political changes as well as economic trends such as globalisation and the impact of disruptive technologies. However, these processes have only mildly contributed to both expanding the coverage of education and improving its quality across the region. In general terms and with a handful of exceptions, quality education is still concentrated in the upper and upper middle classes, while public education, often of low quality, is delivered to the underprivileged classes.

The educational system in Latin America is structured in four levels of instruction: infant, junior, secondary, and post-secondary education with major differences between countries regarding the duration of the academic cycles and the schemes for their implementation. For instance, compulsory education in Colombia extends to ten years – from age 5 to 15 – which is equivalent to the Organisation for Economic Co-operation and Development (OECD) average. Basic education comprises nine years – five years for junior education and four years for senior education – while secondary education (educación media) lasts two years covering grades 10 and 11 for students aged between 15 and 16 (OLPE, 2014b, p. 24). In Chile, infant education is not compulsory and is offered to children aged zero to five years old. Junior education – known as General Basic Education – is compulsory and lasts eight years. Senior education is divided

DOI: 10.4324/9781003002666-15

into two specialisations, Scientific-Humanistic and Technical-Vocational, and lasts four years. Access to higher education is only possible if senior education credits have been obtained (OLPE, 2013, p. 1). In Argentina, junior and senior educations last 12 years in total. Senior education is divided into two cycles: a basic cycle and an oriented (vocational) cycle that includes various approaches, areas of knowledge, and subjects focused on the social and labour world (OLPE, 2014a, p. 1).

The organisational structure of the education sector varies considerably in terms of administrative bodies and types of institutions that provide educational services in each country of the region. There are public institutions, which are owned and funded by the state, and private institutions, which are owned, funded, and administered by the private sector. Both public and private academic institutions are widespread in the region – excluding Cuba, where the entire educational system is public and freely accessible. There are also mixed models such as the Private Subsidised Institutions in Chile. These are owned and operated by the private sector, but they also receive state funding subsidies for students enrolled in Early Years Foundation Stages (EYFS) – ages zero to six – infant and secondary levels. In the case of higher education, funding is granted through state contributions established within the national budget.

For economically unstable countries, it should be carefully weighed how much is invested and in what. This premise illustrates another characteristic phenomenon in Latin America: education expenditure has neither been stable nor efficient, and, in general terms, it has not been proportional to the increase in each country's gross domestic product (GDP). Whenever the percentage of the GDP attributed to public expenditure has increased, it has been due to an expansion in education. That is, more pupils are accessing the school system, as revealed by the United Nations Educational, Scientific and Cultural Organization [UNESCO] (2015), as opposed to countries increasing the education expenditure per capita. A notable exception to this rule is Cuba, a country where public expenditure on education is one of the highest in the world, with an investment of 12.8% of total GDP in 2010 (World Bank, 2019). The global average of public expenditure on education – taken as a percentage of GDP – was 4.6% in 2010 (Global Economy, 2010).

To consider Latin American countries as a unit carries the risk of falling into generalisations that do not reflect the enormous heterogeneity of situations and experiences existing both between and within countries. Nevertheless, social transformations have been slowly taking place in part due to massive mobilisations of people demanding social, health, and educational reforms. The closing of the social gap as a result of some sectors of the population moving up the social ladder and the decrease in poverty rates in the region have also raised expectations for a more promising future in Latin America. Despite the small progress made, the remaining high levels of inequality, together with the elevated dropout rates of pupils at schools and poor teacher training, remain some of the challenges to overcome in order to build up quality education in the region.

## Physical education in Latin America and health promotion

Physical Education (PE) is an essential component of the academic curriculum of schools and is an integral part of the educational experience of pupils throughout the region. Although there has been a global tendency to reduce the amount of time allocated to PE since 2007, Latin America has increased the weekly time attributed to PE by 17 min for junior education; for secondary levels by seven minutes. Implementation of PE in schools has expanded from 50% in 2000 to 89% in 2013 (Hardman *et al.*, 2014).

The multiple cognitive, emotional, and physical development benefits that PE brings to students have been widely acknowledged across the region. Its promotion is supported by a wide range of programmes and state policies. As defined in Paragraph J, Article 27, Chapter III, Title II of the *Argentinian National Law on Education N° 26.206* (SITEAL, 2006), the role of the state is to "provide opportunities for a physical education that promotes physical and motor training and consolidates the harmonious development of all children". In Venezuela, PE and recreation are part of the personal, social, and communication training learning area, the primary objective of which is to train boys and girls in the acquisition of basic motor skills. PE is a mandatory subject in junior and secondary Mexican education, and although it is not compulsory at the preschool level, 30% of infant educational institutions have a PE instructor (Emiliozzi *et al.*, 2017, pp. 11–12).

Since the early 1990s, it has been emphasised that PE provides an adequate framework for health education. This is based on the belief that PE can play a major role in creating healthy habits with benefits throughout life. Ministries of Education in Chile, Ecuador, and Bolivia have been innovating on this front by incorporating a health education approach into their PE programmes for more than a decade. In the specific case of Chile, different surveys (MDS, 2013, 2015, 2017) have demonstrated increasing levels of physical inactivity in adults as they complete their secondary education, thus validating the importance of educational institutions as centres for early health education.

Nevertheless, as demonstrated by the case of Chile, it seems that although an important focus has been placed on the health benefits of PE in schools, the impact of this approach is yet to be seen. Chile is one of the countries with the lowest rates of physical activity among OECD members. The Physical Activity Habits National Survey states that only 31.8% of the Chilean population, from about 18 years of age or older, participate in sport or physical activity (MINDEP, 2016). In other words, about 70% of the population does not engage in any physical activity.

From a global perspective, these numbers are not very encouraging, especially in comparison with developed countries. For example, sports participation averages 61% for 27 countries of the European Union. This percentage increases considerably when considering highly developed countries such as Finland, where this figure reaches more than 70% (Van Tuyckom and Scheerder, 2010).

Moreover, a test – the National Assessment System "SIMCE" – implemented in 2015 to shed light on the physical condition of pupils of year nine (KS3) in schools found that 45% of pupils were overweight or obese, which implies an increase of four points with respect to previous measurements (Agencia de Calidad de la Educación, 2015).

The results point not only to a prevailing health problem, but they also indicate a lack of effectiveness of existing PE programmes, as they do aim to promote health in schools through education. This situation is the same throughout Latin America wherever physical inactivity in students reaches high levels. A study carried out in 26 countries in the region, for example, concluded that only about 15% of adolescents were physically active with at least 60 min/day of moderate-to-vigorous physical activity (Aguilar-Farias et al., 2018, pp. 976–986). In this context, quality PE programmes that continue to promote healthy habits become increasingly relevant. Those programmes are certainly an item for which ministries of sport, education, and health need to improve future coordination across the region.

### Physical education in schools: Some examples

Regional and national programmes to promote PE and sport in the school setting are popular across Latin America. In general, Latin American countries organise their own national sports competitions. One local competition is the National School Sports Games in Chile, which enable massive and inclusive competitive sport by summoning the entire junior and secondary student body of local-public, private-subsidised, and paid-private schools. Another example comes from Peru, where the National School Sport Games "JDEN" represent an important contribution to the education of children and youth through sport. These Games are intended for the participation of all educational institutions, while at the same time they broaden the scope of school sport and serve as a platform to identify sports talent within the school system.

In Argentina, the National Evita Games are the country's main sports competition. Organised by the Ministry of Sports, Physical Education and Recreation, this event features 39 disciplines in a two-phase competition system. The first phase is a qualifying process in each province in which around 800,000 children, young people, and senior citizens participate, while at the final phase 20,000 competitors take part (Juegos Nacionales Evita, n.d.). In Colombia, the "Supérate Intercolegiados" is a national sport and academic competition programme aimed at children and adolescents aged between 7 and 17, both in and out of school. The programme is present in 100% of the country's municipalities and includes 31 different sports disciplines. Like the Evita Games, competitions are held at the local and state levels, with a national final phase in which the winners of each state compete (MINDEP, 2019). Since its inception in 2013, the "Supérate Intercolegiados" programme has widened its territorial coverage and increased the number of participating students. In 2017, the programme reached almost three million participants while the national finals attracted more than 7,000 school athletes (MINDEP, 2018).

At the South American level, the South American Sports Council "CONSUDE" brings together student-athletes from Argentina, Brazil, Bolivia, Chile, Colombia, Ecuador, Peru, Paraguay, Uruguay, and Venezuela. In addition to contributing to integrating nations and renewing their ties of friendship, these regional games are an initiative to strengthen PE and promote sports participation. The participating athletes are pupils aged between 12 and 14 from both public and private schools who compete in sport such as chess, athletics, para-athletics, handball, basketball, swimming, table tennis, volleyball, beach volleyball, judo, and futsal.

## The role of higher education institutions and sports associations

Latin American universities contribute to the advancement of education in sport and physical activity and the strengthening of the sport sector in various ways, most particularly by:

- Fostering an environment for students and high-performance student-athletes to carry out their sports practice
- Educating and training future sports professionals
- Conducting high impact research in the exercise and sport sciences

Many universities offer physical activity programmes to the university community on a complementary or elective basis. For private universities, sports programmes are oftentimes an important marketing strategy to recruit new students. At the state level, several efforts have been made in the region to facilitate the engagement of university students in both recreational and competitive sports activities. For instance, *Law No. 30476* (Congreso de la República, 2016) was created to regulate "High Competition Sports Programs" in both private and public universities in Peru. This regulation establishes that universities should grant half-tuition scholarships and full scholarships – which include tuition costs in addition to food, health, housing, sports equipment, and education-related expenses – for at least ten student-athletes under this scheme and hold "High Competition Sports Programs" for at least three sports disciplines. Other scholarship schemes provide educational opportunities to highly competitive athletes. In Ecuador, Universidad Internacional de La Rioja in association with Fundación Cofuturo created a scholarship programme geared towards Ecuadorian elite athletes so that they can access tertiary education (UNIR, 2019).

Educating and training future sports professionals is another field where universities can make an impactful contribution to education in sport and physical activity in the region. Latin American Universities offer full academic undergraduate and graduate programmes, as well as individual courses dealing with diverse aspects of PE in areas such as sport management, recreation studies, or sports law, to mention a few, which are incorporated into the curriculum of traditional areas of knowledge including anthropology, health studies, pedagogy, psychology, and sociology, among others. In Argentina, Universidad Nacional de la Plata and Universidad Nacional de Tucumán were the first to incorporate PE programmes in 1953. Currently, 37 institutions – 18 national, 19 private and provincial – offer this university degree (Crisorio *et al.*, 2015). In Brazil, there are more than 1,400 courses dealing with PE according to Guerrero *et al.* (2017, pp. 257–276), while at least 47 higher education institutions offer PE as a subject in Colombia (Carreras Universitarias Colombia, n.d.). Among those, Universidad del Valle and Universidad Pedagógica Nacional also offer academic programmes in recreation, with both universities heavily influencing the training curriculum and practices at the national level (Guerrero *et al.*, 2017, p. 267).

In the Mexican Higher Education system, both Escuelas Normales – educational institutions in charge of training schoolteachers – and universities offer training for PE teachers. To date, there are approximately 20 public higher education institutions that offer programmes related to PE (Emiliozzi *et al.*, 2017, p. 18). In Venezuela, a growing number of universities and institutes train professionals in PE and related areas. Once the PE professional has graduated from the university with the degree of Licenciado (Bachelor) or Profesor (Teacher), he can work at any level and modality of the educational system (Guerrero *et al.*, 2017, p. 271).

Lastly, universities continue to make an important contribution to sport and PE in the Latin American region by promoting research and development activity in those areas. Universidad de Costa Rica and Universidad Nacional de Costa Rica, for instance, contribute to knowledge development through their sports laboratories and research teams. Although these institutions focus on multiple aspects and dimensions of sport, important emphasis has been placed on the health benefits of physical activity. In Chile, Universidad de Concepción has carried out experimental work with children in the school setting to determine the impact that PE classes may have on their eating and health habits. Likewise, the works carried out by the Institute of Sports Intelligence of the Universidade Federal de Paraná provide valuable metadata associated with the Brazilian sport system.

Sports associations also play a pivotal role in the promotion of PE and sport across the region. At its most general level, associations are understood as organisations that unite a group of individuals who pursue similar benefits or interests and constitute an organised expression of civil society (Font, Montero Gibert and Torcal Loriente, 2006). Grassroots sport organisations fulfil at least three functions which help to promote sports participation in the region. The first function is of recreational nature, as these entities offer their members the opportunity to practice sport and to pass their leisure time actively. The second purpose is to foster social interactions, since they also constitute a space for building social networks among participants. The third function is to directly influence sport development and participation in the communities where these associations operate. This entails training athletes, participating in official competitions, and identifying and developing sports talent.

The critical role that sports associations play in Latin America has been validated by Latinobarómetro (2005), an annual public opinion survey which monitors social, economic, and political issues, concluding that sports clubs are the type of organisations with the highest number of members in Argentina, Chile, Ecuador, Uruguay, and Venezuela – despite the strong predominance of religious organisations on the continent. In Chile, article 3, Title I of the *Law on Sports 19712* (Chile, 2001) recognises the contributions of sports associations to the sport system and acknowledges the need of the state to actively work with these actors to promote sports activity throughout the country. Similarly, the protection of sports organisations' autonomy is particularly recognised by the Chilean government, along with the freedom of association based "on the principles of decentralisation and subsidiary action by the state". Furthermore, an important number of sports associations has been positioned as "critical partners" in the development of the national sport system which include sports clubs, sports leagues, local sports councils, regional associations, sport federations, confederations, and the National Olympic Committee (Ministerio del Interior, 2001).

## Challenges

In the past 15 years, countries across the region have taken steps to improve the quality and scope of PE programmes, but major challenges remain. At the broader level, there is limited access to sports programmes within the school system, as well as a generalised lack of awareness persists regarding the importance of PE as a vehicle to support education in Latin America. Successfully addressing both challenges may in part support the achievement of greater social goals including social inclusion and equality. Given that countries of the region feature a diversity of educational systems all of which are essentially based on segregation (OECD, 2018), there is a notable gap in the access to quality education including education in sport and physical activity across the continent. In general terms, sports activities offered in private schools are more comprehensive and of better quality compared to public schools; this difference becomes even more evident when comparing urban to rural schools. Equal access to quality PE programmes for students in public and rural schools is of critical importance in the broader social context. As highlighted by the OECD (2012, p. 3), access to sport may increase equity, while the absence of quality sports activities tends to exacerbate the already existing inequalities among diverse student populations.

An additional challenge is the limited access to quality PE programmes for people with disabilities. People with disabilities are usually excluded from opportunities in education, employment, and community participation which affects their health, social development, and overall quality of life. Despite the fact that international agreement of sport and PE as ideal platforms for inclusion and adaptation goes back several decades, progress on that front has been slow and uneven

## 144 Miguel A. Cornejo and Alexander Cárdenas

in the region. Concrete efforts in Latin America to strengthen inclusion policy in sports programmes for students with disabilities at the school level have only began to materialise in the last ten years. One example comes from Colombia where the National School Sport Programme "Supérate Intercolegiados" has included fencing, underwater sport, and boccia for athletes with disabilities (MINDEP, 2018). In Peru, the para sport has been incorporated in some of the local and national school competitions, thus contributing to the inclusion and participation in sport of pupils with physical, sensory, and intellectual disabilities. In Mexico, the updated General Law on Physical Culture and Sport of 2013 incorporates six sports disciplines for people with disabilities at the municipal and school levels. Although these are small steps, they may open future possibilities for structural changes to allow the inclusion of schoolchildren and adults with disabilities in recreational or training sports programmes.

## Trends and future developments

Current trends in sport education and PE in the region gravitate towards participation in sports activities that are not linked to a federal sport structure, as well as the recent use of sport as a potential vehicle for tackling a range of social phenomena.

The sport sector worldwide is becoming increasingly diversified, specialised, and individualised. Consequently, we have witnessed the emergence of novel and spontaneous practices which adapt to new sports cultures that appear to be less bureaucratic and more ephemeral. In Latin America, more personalised, delocalised, and de-institutionalised practices are developing, generating new forms of social interaction and understanding of what sport is.

Virtual clubs, sports apps, and other sports technologies are heavily shaping the sport and PE landscape in the region. For instance, the sports tech and fitness sector are rapidly growing in Latin America, with Brazil leading regional investments. Between 2012 and 2018, Brazil closed 721 investment deals with sports tech companies, while Mexico ranked second with 235 deals made in the same period (Penkert, 2018). Similarly, the health club industry is dynamic and continues to grow in the region. Nearly 20 million Latin Americans are members of a health club; Brazil alone accounts for more than half of existing health clubs with almost 35,000 facilities (IHRSA, n.d.).

Another visible trend in Latin American, which has aroused expectations for potential future developments across the region, has to do with the growing recognition of sport and PE as viable tools to address a variety of social problems, an approach commonly referred to as Sport for Development and Peace (Cárdenas, 2013). This approach positions sport not only as a platform to promote education and to instil healthy lifestyles among young people, but it also acknowledges the capacity of sport and PE to serve as enablers of wider social goals including social inclusion, school dropout, gender equality, peace building, and the reduction of the social gap, among others. The newly established perception of the potential of sport and physical activity as effective means to tackle social problems in the Latin American context aligns with the growing global acknowledgment of sport as a vehicle to address international development markers, including, most notably, the Sustainable Development Goals (SDGs).

The Evita Games in Argentina, and the "Supérate Intercolegiados" Games in Colombia, are two examples of the recent use of sport and PE within the school context to promote learning while at the same time fostering social inclusion and using sport as a promoter of pro-social values. The Evita Games have become a platform to advance a culture of solidarity, diversity, and inclusion and to strengthen the sense of Argentine cultural and national identity. In Colombia, the "Supérate Intercolegiados" Games have contributed to supporting national peace building efforts by including historically underserved populations in depressed urban and rural communities, which have been disproportionally affected by a five-decade long internal conflict, into sports activities and mainstream education and culture.

## Conclusions

This chapter has examined the role of education in sport and physical activity in Latin America. All throughout the continent, PE is considered an important academic subject in the school system and in higher education institutions. The multiple benefits of PE and sport to support the cognitive, emotional, social, and physical development of pupils have been widely acknowledged by national governments who continue to implement a wide array of sport and education policies and programmes. Nevertheless, still much remains to be done in order to build up quality education in sport and physical activity, while at the same time promoting healthy habits and social cohesion in a region characterised by limited access to education, growing physical inactivity, and high levels of inequality. Enacting concrete sport and PE policies at the national level and implementing dynamic PE curriculum in schools and in higher education institutions is a first step. Added to that, inter-sectorial participation of governmental (e.g., Ministries of Sport, Education and Health), non-governmental institutions (e.g., in the education, development, and social sport sector), and the international community and regional authorities (e.g., UNESCO, Organization of American States [(OAS]) through increased dialogue and cooperative work may boost education in sport and PE in the region.

## References

Agencia de Calidad de la Educación (2015) *Informe técnico SIMCE 2015*. Available at: https://www.agenciaeducacion.cl/evaluaciones/que-es-el-simce/ (Accessed: 1 August 2020).

Aguilar-Farias, N. *et al.* (2018) 'A regional vision of physical activity, sedentary behaviour and physical education in adolescents from Latin America and the Caribbean: Results from 26 countries', *International Journal of Epidemiology*, 47(3), pp. 976–986. doi: 10.1093/ije/dyy033.

Cárdenas, A. (2013) 'Peace building through sport? An introduction to sport for development and peace', *Journal of Conflictology*, 4(1), pp. 24–33, doi: http://dx.doi.org/10.7238/joc.v4i1.1493.

Carreras Universitarias Colombia (n.d.) *Guía de Universidades y Carreras Virtuales de Colombia*. Available at https://carrerasuniversitarias.com.co/carreras/deportes-y-educacion-fisica (Accessed: 12 April 2021).

Congreso de la República (2016) *Law N° 30476*, Available at: https://busquedas.elperuano.pe/normaslegales/ley-que-regula-los-programas-deportivos-de-alta-competencia-ley-n-30476-1398360-4/ (Accessed: 12 August 2020).

Crisorio, R. *et al*. (2015) 'Acerca de la formación en educación física en la república argentina', in Silva, A. M. Molina-Bedoya, V. and Bracht, V. (eds.) *Formação profissional em educação física na América Latina: Encontros, diversidades e desafios*. Jundiaí: Paco Editorial, pp. 19–36.

Emiliozzi, M. V. *et al*. (2017) 'Formación docente y educación física en las escuelas: Foco en Brasil, Argentina, México y Venezuela', in Silva, A. M. and Molina Bedoya, V. (eds.) *Educación física en América Latina: Currículos y horizontes formativos*. Jundiaí: Paco Editorial, pp. 9–36.

Font, J., Montero Gibert, J. R. and Torcal Loriente, M. (2006) 'Perfiles, tendenciase implicaciones de la participación en España', in Montero Gibert, J. R., Font, J. and Torcal Loriente, M. (eds.) *Ciudadanos, Asociaciones y Participación en España*, Centro de Investigaciones Sociológicas CIS España, pp. 325–346.

Global Economy (2010) *Cuba: Education spending, percent of GDP*. Available at: www.theglobaleconomy.com/cuba/education_spending/ (Accessed: 12 July 2020).

Guerrero, G. *et al*. (2017) 'El ocio, la recreación y el tiempo libre en los procesos de formación profesional en América Latina. Los casos de Brasil, Colombia y Venezuela', in Silva, A. M. and Molina Bedoya, V. (eds.) *Educación física en América Latina: Currículos y horizontes formativos*, Jundiaí: Paco Editorial, pp. 257–276.

Hardman, K. *et al*. (2014) *UNESCO-NWCPEA: World-wide survey of school physical education - final report*. Paris: UNESCO.

International Health, Racquet & Sportsclub Association (IHRSA) (n.d.) *IHRSA Latin American Report Segunda Edición*. Available at: https://www.ihrsa.org/publications/ihrsa-latin-american-report-second-edition-spanish-version/ (Accessed: 15 January 2020).

Juegos Nacionales Evita (n.d.) *Los Juegos*. Available at: http://www.juegosevita.gob.ar/los-juegos/jugamostodos/ (Accessed: 30 March 2020).

Latinobarómetro (2005) *Informe 1995–2005, Corporación Latinobarómetro*. Available at: https://www.latinobarometro.org/latContents.jsp (Accessed: 8 February 2020).

Ministerio de Desarrollo Social y Familia (MDS) (2013) *Encuesta CASEN*. Available at: http://observatorio.ministeriodesarrollosocial.gob.cl/encuesta-casen-2013 (Accessed: 12 June 2020).

Ministerio de Desarrollo Social y Familia (MDS) (2015) *Encuesta CASEN*. Available at: http://observatorio.ministeriodesarrollosocial.gob.cl/encuesta-casen-2015 (Accessed: 14 June 2020).

Ministerio de Desarrollo Social y Familia (MDS) (2017) *Encuesta CASEN*. Available at: http://observatorio.ministeriodesarrollosocial.gob.cl/encuesta-casen-2017 (Accessed: 14 June 2020).

Ministerio del Deporte (MINDEP) (2016) *Política nacional de actividad física y deporte 2016–2025*. Santiago de Chile: MINDEP.

Ministerio del Deporte (MINDEP) (2018) *Supérate Intercolegiados, la mayor apuesta al deporte escolar en Colombia*. Available at: https://www.mindeporte.gov.co/92729. (Accessed: 19 August 2020).

Ministerio del Deporte (MINDEP) (2019) *Programa Supérate Intercolegiados*. Available at: https://www.mindeporte.gov.co/coldeportes/eventos_programas_institucionales/programa_superate_intercolegiados (Accessed: 6 July 2020).

Ministerio del Interior (2001) *Law on Sports 19712*. Available at: http://bcn.cl/2fcfz (Accessed: 21 February 2020).

Observatorio Latinoamericano de Políticas Educativas (OLPE) (2013) *Perfil del sistema educativo de Chile*. Available at: https://observatorioeducacion.org/perfiles-por-pais/chile (Accessed: 12 August 2020).

Observatorio Latinoamericano de Políticas Educativas (OLPE) (2014a) *Perfil del sistema educativo de Argentina*. Available at: https://observatorioeducacion.org/perfiles-por-pais/argentina (Accessed: 7 March 2020).

Observatorio Latinoamericano de Políticas Educativas (OLPE) (2014b) *Perfil del sistema educativo de Colombia*. Available at: https://observatorioeducacion.org/perfiles-por-pais/colombia (Accessed: 7 March 2020).

Organisation for Economic Co-operation and Development (OECD) (2012), 'Are students more engaged when schools offer extracurricular activities?', *PISA in Focus*, 18, pp. 1–4. doi:10.1787/5k961l4ccczt-en.

Organisation for Economic Co-operation and Development (OECD) (2018) *Panorama de la educación 2017: Indicadores de la OCDE*. Madrid: Fundación Santillana.

Penkert, B. (2018) 'Overview of the Latin American SportsTech landscape', SportsTechX, 11 September. Available at: https://medium.com/sportstechx/overview-of-the-latin-american-sportstech-landscape-e84be24845ba (Accessed: 6 May 2020).

SITEAL (2016) *Argentina – National Law on Education N⁰ 26.206*, Available at: https://www.siteal.iiep.unesco.org/bdnp/12/ley-26206-ley-educacion-nacional (Accessed: 29 June 2020).

United Nations Educational, Scientific and Cultural Organization (UNESCO) (2015) *Latin America and the Caribbean education for all 2015 regional review*. Available at: https://unesdoc.unesco.org/search/152e6e50-2e2d-42b4-8f75-4fbdafe0e6bd (Accessed: 11 August 2020).

Universidad Internacional de La Rioja (UNIR) (2019) *Deportistas de élite ecuatorianos podrán formarse con becas de UNIR*. Available at: https://www.unir.net/vive-unir/internacional/noticias/deportistas-de-elite-ecuatorianos-podran-formarse-con-becas-de-unir/549204039107/ (Accessed: 4 September 2020).

Van Tuyckom, C. and Scheerder, J. (2010) 'Sport for all? Insight into stratification and compensation mechanisms of sporting activity in the 27 European Union member states', *Sport, Education and Society*, 15(4), pp. 495–512, doi:10.1080/13573322.2010.514746.

World Bank (2014) *The World Bank annual report 2014*. Available at: https://openknowledge.worldbank.org/handle/10986/20093 (Accessed: 9 July 2020).

World Bank (2019) *Government expenditure on education, total (% of GDP)*. Available at: https://data.worldbank.org/indicator/SE.XPD.TOTL.GD.ZS?end=2018&start=2018&view=bar (Accessed: 19 September 2020).

# Chapter 12

# Physical education and school sport in Eastern Asia

*Emi Tsuda, Yoshinori Okade, Takahiro Sato, and Yung-Ju Chen*

This chapter discusses the current systems and trends of physical education (PE) and school sport (extracurricular activities) in three Eastern Asian countries, Japan, South Korea, and Taiwan. The chapter consists of four sections:

- The overall education systems
- The roles and systems of PE and school sport
- The roles of higher education institutions and sport federations
- Current trends, challenges, and future directions in PE and school sport

## Overall education systems in Eastern Asia

Japan, South Korea, and Taiwan employ a centralised education system and require nine years of compulsory education, while nearly all students (above 95%) continue with high school (Organisation for Economic Co-operation and Development [OECD], 2018). The education structure across the three countries is six years of elementary, three years of middle, and three years of high-school education. Table 12.1 illustrates the summary of education systems in Japan, South Korea, and Taiwan.

## The roles and systems of physical education and school sport in Eastern Asia

PE is a compulsory subject in the school curriculum in elementary, middle, and high schools in Japan, South Korea, and Taiwan. Additionally, school sport provides opportunities for students to engage in sport and physical activities outside of PE lessons (Nakazawa, 2011). Table 12.2 summarises the required PE hours, teaching license, PE goals, and systems of the countries. The following sections describe the PE and school sport status, systems, and trends in the three countries.

### Japan

PE is established as an important subject to achieve the overall goal of school education in Japan (Okade, 2005; Tomozoe, Higuchi, and Umegaki, 2014). One of

DOI: 10.4324/9781003002666-16

## PE and school sport in Eastern Asia    149

*Table 12.1* The Education Systems of Japan, South Korea, and Taiwan

|  | *Japan* | *South Korea* | *Taiwan* |
|---|---|---|---|
| Education Governing Body | Ministry of Education, Culture, Sports, Science, and Technology (MEXT) | Ministry of Education (MOE) | Ministry of Education (MOE) |
| National Curriculum | The Course of Study | The Korean National Curriculum | The Curriculum Guidelines of 12-Year Basic Education |
| Curriculum Revision | Approximately every 10 years | 5–7 years | Every 2–3 years (minor revision) |
| Curriculum Last Updated | 2017 and 2018 | 2015 | 2014 |
| Compulsory Education | 9 years | 9 years | 9 years |

Note: The revisions for elementary and middle schools were in 2017, and that of high school was in 2018.

the factors contributing to this PE status includes that every teacher is responsible for promoting students' physical and mental health and lifetime sports engagement indicated in the "Course of Study" (Ministry of Education, Culture, Sports, Science and Technology-Japan [MEXT], 2017). Another factor would be that an *Undokai* (sporting/athletic event), one of the primary school events, is run by the entire school. This event allows everyone in a school and community to share the values of PE, sport, and physical activities.

Middle- and high-school PE are taught by PE licensed teachers, while only ten percent of PE in elementary schools is taught by PE specialised teachers (MEXT, 2019a). Aside of PE, school sport is positioned as a critical educational opportunity which contributes to the overall schools' educational goals and objectives (MEXT, 2017). The data of 2017 shows that 65.2% of middle school students and 41.9% of high-school students participate in school sport teams (Japan Sports Agency [JSA], 2018). In 2019, a total of 28,018 players from 31 different kinds of sport, 8,237 coaches/teachers, and 472,208 spectators participated in high-school sport competitions (All Japan High School Athletic Federation, 2019).

### *South Korea*

In South Korea, PE has a relatively low status in the school curriculum. The emphasis on society's academic achievement has been identified as one of the primary reasons for this situation which is accompanied by a lack of investment in sports facilities (Lee and Cho, 2014; Song *et al.*, 2016). Poorly maintained facilities or simply the lack thereof resulted in approximately 40% of the schools in the country having to regularly cancel their PE classes during poor weather conditions (Lee and Cho, 2014). Because of these limiting factors, less than four percent of elementary, less than eight percent of middle, and just over

Table 12.2 Physical Education Required Hours, Teaching Licensures, and Goals in Japan, South Korea, and Taiwan

| Japan | | | South Korea | | | Taiwan[3] | | |
|---|---|---|---|---|---|---|---|---|
| Elem.[1] | Middle[2] | High[3] | Elem. | Middle | High | Elem.[1] | Middle[2] | High[2] |
| • 1st 102 hrs<br>• 2nd 105 hrs<br>• 3rd 105 hrs<br>• 4th 105 hrs<br>• 5th 90 hrs<br>• 6th 90 hrs | • 7th 105 hrs<br>• 8th 105 hrs<br>• 9th 105 hrs | • 10th–12th<br>7–8[4] credits<br>in total of<br>three years | • 1st 108 hrs[+]<br>• 2nd 204 hrs[1]<br>• 3rd 102 hrs<br>• 4th 102 hrs<br>• 5th 102 hrs<br>• 6th 102 hrs | • 7th 102 hrs<br>• 8th 102 hrs<br>• 9th 68 hrs | • 10th 68 hrs<br>• 11th[2]<br>• 12th[2] | • 1st 80 hrs<br>• 2nd 80 hrs<br>• 3rd 80 hrs<br>• 4th 80 hrs<br>• 5th 80 hrs<br>• 6th 80 hrs | • 7th 102 hrs<br>• 8th 102 hrs<br>• 9th 68 hrs | • 10th 80 hrs<br>• 11th 80 hrs<br>• 12th 80 hrs<br>Plus elective<br>courses for up<br>to 240 lessons<br>(in 3 yrs) |
| Classroom<br>Teacher[5] | HPE | HPE | Classroom<br>Teacher | PE* | PE | PE<br>specialisation[4] | HPE | PE |
| To assist students in engaging in lifelong physical activities and sport to maintain and improve their health and mind and to promote healthy lifestyles (MEXT, 2017) | | | To fulfil one's individual need for movement, to develop fundamental motor skills and physical fitness for successful participation in a diverse range of sport and physical activities, and to understand and apply knowledge to the development of motor skills and health (Kim, 2013) | | | To develop students' physical literacy in order to support their lifelong physical activity participation (MOE, 2014) | | |
| 1. A total of 8 credit hours in 3rd and 4th grades and a total of 16 credit hours in 5th and 6th grades are used for health education (MEXT, 2019a)<br>2. A total of 48 credit hours are used in health education across three years (MEXT, 2019a).<br>3. Two additional credits are required for health education (MEXT, 2019a).<br>4. One credit equal to 35 credit hours (MEXT, 2019a).<br>5. Approximately 10% of elementary PE is taught by PE specialists | | | 1. For 1st and 2nd grades, PE, art, and music are combined as one subject called "pleasant living". The indicated hours are the required hours for "pleasant living" (MOE, 2020)<br>2. PE is elective for 11th and 12th grades (MOE, 2020) | | | 1. One lesson equals 40 min<br>2. One lesson equals 50 min<br>3. Health and PE are combined as one subject area. The ratio of health and PE hours is 1:2 across the grades (NAER, 2018)<br>4. Only 56% of teachers who teach PE in elementary schools have specialisation or endorsements for PE (Sports Administration, 2020) | | |

*PE = physical education; HPE = health and physical education.
1 is elementary schools; 2 is middle schools; 3 is high schools, 4 is PE specialisation; 5 classroom teacher

two percent of high-school students receive the recommended amount of PE (Lee and Cho, 2014). PE at elementary schools is typically taught by classroom teachers while in middle and high schools, PE licensed teachers teach PE lessons Lee and Cho, (2014). The strong focus on academic achievement also keeps the students' participation in extracurricular activities at a low level (Kim, 2013). To increase physical activity opportunities for youth, the government in 2012 decided to mandate weekly after-school sports programmes for students (Sato, Yu, Chen, and Mori, 2015).

### Taiwan

Although there has been an overemphasis on academic achievement, in Taiwan, PE is situated as an essential part of school education to achieve a healthy and balanced life (Hsu, 2013). The focus on a comprehensive education in the new 12-Year Basic Education Curriculum further highlights the importance of PE in schools (Ministry of Education Republic of China [MOE], 2014). Within this curriculum shift, high schools have to adopt exam-free school admission and start evaluating students from multiple perspectives. Many school districts have been using students' health-related fitness scores as part of the admission process since 2016 (MOE, 2017).

While middle- and high-school PE are taught by licensed PE teachers exclusively, in elementary schools the percentage reaches only 54% (Sports Administration, 2020). Beyond PE, schools are encouraged to endorse multiple sports teams for extracurricular school sport provision (School Physical Education Reg., 2008).

One of the unique features in Taiwanese school sport is the early specialisation of student athletes. Schools may have "athletically talented classes" for grades 5–12, grouping high performing student athletes together to customise the academic schedule around their training plans (MOE, 2019). In 2018, approximately 8%, 52%, and 29% of the elementary, middle, and high schools, respectively, provided athletically talented classes (Sports Administration, 2020).

## The roles of higher education and sport federations

To maintain and improve the quality of PE and the school sport environment, the roles of higher education and sport federations are critical. Primarily, higher education institutions serve for the advancement of PE, and sport federations and associations contribute to managing the school sport environment.

### Higher education

Faculty members in higher education institutions contribute to advance the field of PE in various ways. This includes, for instance, providing and contributing to the professional development of teachers and collaborating with professionals at the national and international levels.

## 152   Emi Tsuda et al.

### Teacher professional development

Across the three countries, PE teacher education programmes at universities/ colleges are responsible for training highly qualified PE teachers. In Japan and Taiwan, higher education faculty members are also involved in in-service teacher professional development. For example, teacher educators in Japan are often invited to professional development workshops to provide curriculum/lesson ideas and feedback. In South Korea, recently, teacher-led professional development has been emphasised (National Centre on Education and the Economy [NCEE], n.d.). To implement the most recent version of the national curriculum, the Ministry of Education trained 13,000 teachers to facilitate professional development sessions at the school level in 2017 (NCEE, n.d.).

### National and international collaborations

In Japan, higher education faculty members play a key role in developing national curricula, research, reports (e.g., national fitness assessment data), and government guidelines at the local and regional level. University faculty members also connect with international scholars through research and professional events to share their expertise and experiences in PE and teacher education. To facilitate international networking, scholars in Japan, South Korea, and Taiwan launched the Eastern Asian Alliance of Sport Pedagogy in 2012. The primary goal of the organisation is to promote international collaboration in research and practices in sport pedagogy among the three countries. Multiple cross-cultural research projects and annual conferences have been conducted since the establishment of the alliance.

### Sport federations and associations

Sport federations and associations play a central role in school sport. In Japan, those organisations run school sport competitions and maintain and improve the quality of the school sport environment. For instance, the Nippon Junior High School Physical Culture Association (NJHSPCA) and the All Japan High School Athletic Federation (AJHSAF) are responsible for hosting sports leagues and tournaments for middle- and high-school sport teams. These institutions also provide support for each prefecture's school sport association (e.g., the Tokyo High School Athletic Federation) and research middle- and high-school PE and extracurricular activities (AJHSAF, n.d.; NJHSPCA, n.d.). Both associations are public interest incorporated associations and supported by the Japan Sports Agency, which is positioned under MEXT. The Japan Sport Association (JSPO), a central organisation of Japanese sport, runs a sports instructor certification programme. Within the programme, JSPO provides workshops and endorses certifications for coaches in school sport teams.

Similarly, in South Korea, the Ministry of Education and the Ministry of Culture, Sport and Tourism oversee school sport competitions. In Taiwan, the Sports Administration, under the Ministry of Education, is responsible for promoting school sport and physical activity in school-aged children and adolescents. Moreover, there is a leading association for each sport to govern sport-specific events and certify referees, instructors, and coaches. Both Sports Administration and individual sport-related associations organise competitions for student athletes.

## Current trends, challenges, and future directions in Eastern Asia physical education and school sport

This section addresses the trends, challenges, and future directions of PE and school sport in Eastern Asian countries.

### Current trends and challenges

Four emerging trends and challenges observed in this region, particularly in Japan, include:

- The lack of physical activity engagement in students
- Challenges in providing context-specific quality PE
- Limitations of one-size-fits-all teacher professional development
- The consequence of overemphasis on competition in school sport

#### Lack of physical activity engagement in students

As globally observed, the issue of physical inactivity is prevalent in Japan, South Korea, and Taiwan. In Japan, while 67.5% of eighth-grade female students participate in physical activity more than 420 min per week, 19.7% of the students engage in physical activity less than 60 min per week (MEXT, 2019b). Similarly, in South Korea, only 6.9% of middle- and 4.9% of high-school students participate in more than 60 min of moderate to vigorous physical activity daily (Song et al., 2016). In Taiwan, less than 20% of children and youth meet the recommended 60 min of daily moderate to vigorous physical activity (Wu and Chang, 2019). Keep improving the quality of PE is essential to equip children and adolescents to be physically active across their lifespan. In addition, the use of school sport environments is important because those are critical sites for children and adolescents to engage in sport and physical activity outside of PE lessons.

#### Challenges in providing context-specific quality physical education

While quality PE is central to equip children and adolescents to engage in life-long physical activity, a recent study reported that teachers are struggling to provide context-specific quality PE to them. For instance, the demographic of the three countries has been dramatically changing (e.g., the population decline

[World Population Review, 2020] and the increased foreign-born residents [United Nations, 2019]). A study examining teachers who experienced teaching in a depopulated school in Japan illustrated that elementary school teachers struggle to teach PE with modified class styles (e.g., small class size and teaching two grade levels together) due to their lack of subject-specific training (Tsuda, Sato, Wyant, and Hasegawa, 2019). Regarding increased numbers of foreign-born citizens, teachers need to accommodate lessons with students who have different religious and ethnic backgrounds (MEXT, 2019c). In addition, the most recently updated Course of Study (MEXT, 2017) indicates the need to provide an inclusive learning environment for students with disabilities for the first time. To meet this expectation, teachers are in the process of learning how to make this happen in real life. To help teachers with this ever-changing teaching-learning environment, quality professional development that meets individual teachers' needs is more important than ever.

### Limitations of one-size-fits-all teacher professional development

To provide quality PE, teachers' professional development has been playing a significant role in teachers' growth in Japan. Lesson study is one of the widely known professional development approaches that originate in Japan (Sato, Tsuda, Ellison, and Hodge, 2020). However, potential limitations of lesson study have been discussed recently: they may be shaping instruction approaches into a pattern and resulting in depriving teachers' creativity to their instructions (MEXT, 2016). In other words, through observing each other's lessons and discussing them together, teachers may see the lessons in the same lens and potentially narrowing their perspectives. In addition, the use of the ineffective reflection cycle has been identified as a challenge in lesson study. These limits of lesson study have been discussed not only at the elementary level but also at the middle- and high-school levels. Understanding the needs of teachers to provide quality and individualised professional development is inevitable.

### Consequence of overemphasis on competition in school sport

The challenges in PE and school sport are inseparable. One of the issues tied to school sport in Japan is teachers' overwork who supervise school sport teams. Benesse Corporation (2020) reported that, on average, teachers spend more than 11.5 hours at schools daily across all education levels. In addition, 74.5% of middle-school and 52.4% of high-school teachers claim that they come to school to work almost every weekend. One of the primary reasons for teachers' overwork is supervising/coaching extracurricular activities to train students to win competitions. On top, overemphasis on competition in school sport has been causing a serious problem of physical, verbal, and sexual harassment and abuse in Japan (International Olympic Committee, 2020; MEXT, 2013). This issue is historically grounded in the country, but it still took the incident in 2012 (i.e., a high-school student who was in a basketball team committed suicide due to the physical harassment by a team coach) to finally attract the necessary attention at the government level. The guidelines for teaching/coaching school sport teams were issued and activated in 2013 by MEXT. Cultural shifts in school sport are vital. This could be achievable through providing school sport/physical activity opportunities with different purposes, teachers'/coaches' continuous professional development, and setting the accountability systems to ensure the adoption of the new guidelines.

### Future directions

To address above discussed challenges, the following section proposes three key future directions:

- To continually seek and adopt the best practices to provide quality PE
- To provide context-specific professional development support for teachers and coaches
- To offer school sport opportunities for students in different needs

### Continue to seek and adopt the best practices to provide context-specific quality physical education

The first proposed future direction is to continue to seek and adopt the best practices and to provide quality PE in schools. To achieve this, it is important that for scholars in higher education institutions or other educational organisations/associations keep studying the best practices of PE in school settings. Recently, due to the structural changes in higher education institutions, conducting research in school settings has been becoming more difficult. However, to improve the quality of instruction, research needs to occur in the field. Also, further development of the systems for researchers to share and exchange information and knowledge of best practices in PE at the national and international levels is important. The School Physical Education Research Association (*Gakutairen*) and the Eastern Asian Alliance of Sport Pedagogy are examples that could serve for those purposes.

Additionally, the ministry of education should require schools to hire licensed PE teachers for PE provision at all school levels. To provide developmentally appropriate and effective instruction in PE, teachers need to have specialised knowledge and skills (Rink, 2012). In addition, the national curriculum needs to be updated periodically to meet students' needs and trends of society. For example, Taiwan recently launched its new national curriculum (MOE, 2014), which emphasises the importance of comprehensive education.

## Provide context-specific professional development and support for teachers and coaches

Another key future direction is to provide context-specific professional development support for teachers and coaches. In the higher education institutions, research needs to be continually conducted to understand the status quo of those fields and to explore context-specific problems and solutions using different methodologies in qualitative and quantitative research. In addition, there are still many underdeveloped areas of study such as diversity, inclusion, and adapted PE that need to be explored to improve the quality of PE in all these Eastern Asian countries. In the short term, sharing and learning the knowledge and experiences with researchers in other countries may be valuable. The board of education also should assess teachers' needs regarding professional development. Furthermore, the curriculum of teacher education programmes should regularly be updated to prepare future teachers to meet the needs of society.

## Offer school sport opportunities for all students

The purpose of school sport should not only be winning the competitions but also enjoying moving and exercising with friends. To overcome the overemphasis on competition in school sport, governments of these Eastern Asian countries have proposed guidelines for school sport (MEXT, 2013; MOE, 2019). It is important to examine to what extent the guidelines are implemented and what facilitators and barriers exist to meet those guidelines. The department of education and the board of education should continually put in effort to communicate the guidelines of school sport (MEXT, 2013; MOE, 2019). Along with accountability systems, adopting these guidelines will not only improve the school sport environment for all students but also help teachers and coaches maintain work-life balance. For instance, each sports organisation at the prefecture-level could be responsible for monitoring school teams' practice environments and students' and teachers'/ coaches' experiences. If there is no accountability, the necessary changes are less likely to occur (Japan Olympic Committee, 2020).

Collectively, to improve the quality of PE and school sport environments, exchanging knowledge as well as connecting and collaborating with scholars and educators at different levels are vital.

## Conclusion

This chapter discussed systems and the status quo of PE and school sport in Japan, South Korean, and Taiwan. Overall, to improve school PE and sport, the collective efforts of people from different levels are central. To pursue this process, engaging in national and international exchange and establishing national and global partnerships are vital to the development of the PE and school sport field in Eastern Asian countries.

## Acknowledgement

We would like to acknowledge Gyuil Cho, Jung Hun Han, and Junyong Kim to provide us some insights about information about South Korea PE and school sports.


## References

All Japan High School Athletic Federation (n.d.) *The overview of All Japan High School Athletic Federation*. Available at: https://www.zen-koutairen.com/f_outline.html (Accessed: 5 May 2020).

All Japan High School Athletic Federation (2019) *Zen-koutairen*. Available at: https://www.zen-koutairen.com/pdf/reg-tnop_r01.pdf (Accessed: 5 May 2020).

Benesse Corporation (2020) *Japanese teachers' workhours and perceptions*. Available at: https://berd.benesse.jp/up_images/research/Sido_SYOTYU_05.pdf (Accessed: 27 April 2020).

Hsu, S. H. (2013) 'The role of physical education in Taiwan', in Chepyator-Thomson, J. R. and Hsu, S. H. (eds.) *Global perspectives on physical education and after-school sport programs*. Lanham, MD: University Press of America.

International Olympic Committee (2020) *IOC and JOC discuss measures to eradicate harassment and abuse in Japanese sport*. Available at: https://www.olympic.org/news/ioc-and-joc-discuss-measures-to-eradicate-harassment-and-abuse-in-japanese-sport (Accessed: 16 August 2020).

Japan Olympic Committee (2020) *IOC and JOC discussed measures to eradicate harassment and abuse in Japanese sport*. Available at: https://www.joc.or.jp/english/aboutjoc/statement/pdf/JOC_statement_20200806.pdf (Accessed: 17 August 2020).

Japan Sports Agency (2018) *The status report of school sports teams in 2017*. Available at: https://www.mext.go.jp/sports/b_menu/sports/mcatetop04/list/detail/__icsFiles/afieldfile/2018/06/12/1403173_2.pdf (Accessed: 27 January 2020).

Kim, S. (2013) 'Current issues in physical education and Korean National Standards for physical education', in Chepyator-Thomson J. R. and Hsu, S. H. (eds.) *Global perspectives on physical education and after-school sport programs*. Lanham, MD: University Press of America.

Lee, K. C. and Cho, S. M. (2014) 'The Korean national curriculum for physical education: A shift from edge to central subject', *Physical Education and Sport Pedagogy*, 19(5), pp. 522–532.

Ministry of Education, Culture, Sports, Science and Technology (2013) *The guideline for teaching and coaching school sport teams*. Available at: https://warp.ndl.go.jp/info:ndljp/pid/11050023/www.mext.go.jp/sports/b_menu/sports/mcatetop04/list/1372445.htm (Accessed: 7 May 2020).

Ministry of Education. (2014). Curriculum guidelines of 12-year basic education: General guidelines. Available at: https://www.naer.edu.tw/ezfiles/0/1000/img/52/129488083.pdf (Accessed: 18 February 2020)

Ministry of Education, Culture, Sports, Science and Technology (2016) *The future directions of the Course of Education in elementary, middle, and high schools, and special education*. Available at: http://www.mext.go.jp/b_menu/shingi/chukyo/chukyo0/toushin/1380731.htm (Accessed: 7 May 2020).

Ministry of Education, Culture, Sports, Science and Technology (2017) *The course of study*. Available at: https://www.mext.go.jp/a_menu/shotou/new-cs/youryou/syo/tai.htm (Accessed: 7 May 2020).

Ministry of Education. (2019). The 12-year basic education: Curriculum guidelines for athletically talented classes. Available at: https://www.ylvs.chc.edu.tw/resource/openfid.php?id=29509 (Accessed: 18 February 2020)

Ministry of Education, Culture, Sports, Science and Technology (2019a) *The current status of curriculum implementation in public elementary and middle schools.* Available at: https://www.mext.go.jp/component/a_menu/education/micro_detail/__icsFiles/afieldfile/2019/04/10/1415063_1_1.pdf (Accessed: 10 May 2020).

Ministry of Education, Culture, Sports, Science and Technology (2019b) *The summary of fitness, motor skills, and physical activity engagement of children and adolescents.* Available at: https://www.mext.go.jp/sports/content/20191225-spt_sseisaku02-000003330_1.pdf (Accessed: 15 August 2020).

Ministry of Education, Culture, Sports, Science and Technology (2019c) *Teaching diverse backgrounds of students.* Available at: https://www.mext.go.jp/component/a_menu/education/micro_detail/__icsFiles/afieldfile/2019/04/22/1304738_003.pdf (Accessed: 17 August 2020).

Ministry of Education, Culture, Sports, Science and Technology (2020) *Teaching licensure renewal system.* Available at: https://www.mext.go.jp/a_menu/shotou/koushin/ (Accessed: 7 May 2020).

Nakazawa, A. (2011) 'A comprehensive review of the previous studies regarding extracurricular sports activity: What is known, what needs to be known and what can be known?' [in Japanese] *Hitotsubashi Annual Sport Studies*, 30, pp. 31–41.

National Centre on Education and the Economy (n.d.) *South Korea: Teacher and principal quality.* Available at: https://ncee.org/what-we-do/center-on-international-education-benchmarking/top-performing-countries/south-korea-overview/south-korea-teacher-and-principal-quality/ (Accessed: 20 August 2020).

Nippon Junior High School Physical Culture Association (n.d.) *About Nippon Junior High School Physical Culture Association.* Available at: http://njpa.sakura.ne.jp/ (Accessed: 8 May 2020).

Okade, Y. (2005) 'Japan', in Puhse, U. and Gerber, M. (eds.) *International comparison of physical education. Concepts, problems, perspectives.* Aachen: Meyer & Meyer Sport, pp. 417–439.

Organization for Economic Co-operation and Development (OECD) (2018) *PISA 2018; Insights and interpretations.* Available at: https://www.oecd.org/pisa/PISA%202018%20Insights%20and%20Interpretations%20FINAL%20PDF.pdf (Accessed: 3 May 2020).

Rink, J. E. (2012) *Teaching physical education for learning.* 6th edn.. Boston, MA: McGraw-Hill.

Sato, T. *et al.* (2015) 'Health and physical education symposium – Sharing the crisis of physical education in the world: The changes of national physical education curriculum in Asia and the challenges in Japan', *Annals of Fitness and Sports Sciences*, 51, pp. 53–70.

Sato, T. *et al.* (2020) 'Japanese elementary teachers' professional development experiences in physical education lesson studies', *Physical Education and Sport Pedagogy*, 25(2), pp. 137–153.

School Physical Education Reg (2008) *The implementation of physical education in the first three years of the five-year system of higher secondary schools and junior colleges.* Available at: https://law.moj.gov.tw/LawClass/LawAll.aspx?pcode=H0120007 (Accessed: 15 May 2020).

Song, Y. *et al.* (2016) 'Results from South Korea's 2016 report card on physical activity for children and youth', *Journal of Physical Activity & Health I*, 13(2), pp. S274–S278. doi: 10.1123/jpah.2016-0402. PMID: 27848733.

Sports Administration (2020) *2018-2019 school physical education annual statistical report.* Available at: https://www.sa.gov.tw/ebook/List?id=9&n=170 (Accessed: 15 May 2020).

Tomozoe, H., HIgushi, A. and Umegaki, A. (2014) 'New policy of school physical education and sport in Japan', in Chin, M. K. and Edginton, C. R. (eds.) *Physical education and health global perspectives and best practice.* Champaign, IL: Sagamore Publishing, pp. 243–255.

Tsuda, E. *et al.* (2019) 'Japanese elementary physical education teachers' professional development in depopulated rural school districts', *Curriculum Studies in Health and Physical Education*, 10(3), pp. 262–276.

United Nations (2019) *International migration stuck.* Available at: https://www.un.org/en/development/desa/population/migration/data/estimates2/estimates19.asp (Accessed: 17 August 2020).

World Population Review (2020) *World fertility rate 2020.* Available at: https://worldpopulationreview.com/countries/total-fertility-rate/ (Accessed: 7 May 2020).

Wu, C. L. and Chang, C. K. (2019) 'Results from the Chinese Taipei (Taiwan) 2018 report card on physical activity for children and youth', *Journal of Exercise Science & Fitness*, 17(1), pp. 8–13.

# Part IV

# Education in sport and physical activity in a changing world

Chapter 13

# Sport, physical activity, and health promotion

## Implications for the education of future professionals

*Catherine Woods, Marie Murphy, and Enrique García Bengoechea*

## Introduction

Physical inactivity is one of the leading risk factors for premature mortality worldwide (World Health Organization, [WHO], 2009). To improve public health and prevent non-communicable diseases, the WHO physical activity (PA) guidelines recommend at least 150 min of moderate-to-vigorous intensity PA (MVPA) per week for adults and an average of 60 min of MVPA daily for children (Bull *et al.*, 2020). In addition, muscle-strengthening activities of moderate or greater intensity that involve all major muscle groups should be undertaken on two or more days a week, as these provide additional health benefits. Despite all the evidence of benefits, epidemiological data indicate that 28% of adults and 81% of children and adolescents globally do not meet the PA recommendations (Guthold *et al.*, 2018). Research consistently shows that PA levels decline during adolescence (Dumith *et al.*, 2011), that boys are more physically active than girls (Woods *et al.*, 2018), and that PA habits developed in childhood track into adulthood (Evans *et al.*, 2009; Telama, 2009). Therefore, methods to address such high levels of inactivity, particularly among our youth, are urgently needed. This chapter focuses on the implications for the education of physical education (PE) teachers, sport, PA and health professionals to meet both public health needs and health promotion goals to reduce the inactivity pandemic.

## Implication 1: More emphasis on health promotion

Greater emphasis on health promotion content, philosophy, models, and practices needs to be embedded within the curricula for all PE, PA, and sports professionals. Health promotion has been defined as the process of enabling people to increase control over and improve their health (WHO, 2020a). In line with this definition, empowerment – individual and collective – is a key health promotion strategy that calls for active participation of the community in identifying health problems and solutions (Butler, 2001). In this regard, there is an emphasis in contemporary health promotion on what could be gained by working with individuals

DOI: 10.4324/9781003002666-18

164 Catherine Woods et al.

and communities to make the most of their talents and strengths (Morgan, 2014). Several landmark documents (e.g., the Ottawa Charter for Health Promotion [WHO, 1986]) have contributed to a shift in emphasis from individual lifestyle and behaviour to broader social determinants of health. Furthermore, the Shanghai Declaration (WHO, 2020b) expanded the role of health promotion in achieving the United Nation's Sustainable Development Goals (SDGs). Improving the levels of PA in the population requires multi-level, multi-component interventions guided by systems thinking or approaches (Rutter *et al.*, 2017), as there is no single policy or practice solution. Systems approaches take an ecological perspective to examine the factors involved in a problem (e.g., physical inactivity) by viewing actions as embedded across political, societal, cultural, economic, and scientific domains (Rutter *et al.*, 2019). Consequently, educational curricula for PE, PA, and sports professionals need to be balanced between individual behaviour change and its associated frameworks and theories, e.g., Behaviour Change Wheel (Michie and Atkins, 2014), Self-Determination Theory (Deci and Ryan, 2002), and health promotion models like community empowerment (Laverack, 2000). Beyond that, the curricula need to foster an understanding of the social determinants of health and how they impact on participation levels in sport and PA (Marmot, 2005). Thus, identifying the systemic drivers of inactivity is paramount to help promote PA not only to improve health, but to also address the global syndemic or combined pandemics of obesity, undernutrition, and climate change and their threats to human health and survival (Swinburn *et al.*, 2019).

## Implication 2: Sport is a valuable setting for health promotion

The "Healthy Settings" movement calls for the creation of supportive environments while emphasising the value of settings – such as cities, workplaces, schools, communities, and families – for implementing comprehensive strategies and providing an infrastructure for health promotion (WHO, 2016). Consequently, sport, if considered as a setting, can be used to promote health by becoming a vehicle to reach individuals and provide access to services. The Global Action Plan on Physical Activity (WHO, 2018) highlighted that sport is an under-utilised contributor to PA. The European Commission White Paper on Sport (House of Commons: Culture Media and Sport, 2008) called for the health promotion aspects of sports participation to be further developed. In addition, its potential to promote well-being, improve health behaviours and contribute to the achievement of the SDGs needs to be emphasised more (Eime, Payne and Harvey, 2008). The "health promoting sports clubs" (Johnson *et al.*, 2020) concept, rooted in the settings approach, shows how sport can address a number of contemporary issues, including and beyond PA. Although in adults sport is not a significant contributor to PA (Strain *et al.*, 2016), it can attract hard-to-reach groups who may not engage in the traditional health promotion approaches (Gray *et al.*, 2013). For example, "Football Fans in Training" has been successful in promoting healthy living and weight loss among inactive, overweight men (see https://ffit.org.uk/). Sport is a setting which can provide access to a broad audience, to all ages and to people from a variety of socio-economic backgrounds, and consequently help to address the social determinants of health. The use of the sports club as a vehicle through which to promote broad health concepts needs to be included in contemporary curricula of PE, PA, and sports professionals.

## Implication 3: Use broad pedagogical approaches for teaching PE, PA, and sport

For children, PA occurs across four domains: at home, at school (within the curriculum and in extra-curricular activity), in personal transport, and during leisure/recreational time (Strain *et al.*, 2016). Sport is a significant contributor to PA for children; it has been shown to be an important component of their daily PA (Woods *et al.*, 2018). Moreover, unlike activities undertaken for personal transport (walking to school) or activities in the home, sport is more likely to be of moderate to vigorous intensity. Much sport, particularly that involving running and jumping, also helps children meet the requirements for muscle strength and bone health. These benefits are stimulated by weight bearing and high impact activity, and so are the associated higher levels of muscle force and greater bone loading than can be achieved through less vigorous activity.

Other outcomes of sports participation include enhanced self-efficacy, social skills, and fewer depressive symptoms (Eime *et al.*, 2013). Sport also provides opportunities for leadership and peer mentoring (Hulteen, 2019). Arguably, these benefits may be easier to target within organised sport, where an intentional focus can be placed on achieving them, rather than activities of daily living. Furthermore, children's sport often involves learning new skills and patterns of movement through games (individual and team), aquatics, athletics, or aesthetic activities expanding a child's movement vocabulary (throwing, catching, kicking, hopping, skipping, striking, rolling, balance, body management), providing the building blocks for further lifelong involvement in PA. The implication for education is that approaches to teaching and coaching sport should focus on the development of these fundamental movement skills, hoping that they can allow children to enjoy a variety of sport as they move through childhood, into adulthood, and across the life course (Hulteen *et al.*, 2018).

## Implication 4: Consider the long-term effects of sports participation and its determinants

Youth sports participation is a predictor for future PA (Telama *et al.*, 2006; Basterfield *et al.*, 2015). Sport has been found to track more strongly from childhood to adulthood than other types of PA behaviour. Telama and colleagues suggest a "carry-over hypothesis" (Telama, 2009), proposing that sport participated in at a young age has an increased participation probability in adulthood.

A five-year longitudinal study (n = 873, baseline age 10–18 years), the Children's Sport Participation and Physical Activity plus study (CSPPA+) (Murphy, Rowe and Woods, 2016; Murphy, Rowe and Woods, 2017), showed that baseline sports participation frequency, level (elite = large effect size, competitive = medium-to-large effect size), and type (club = large, extracurricular = medium) were all associated with higher levels of future PA, and results were similar for both genders. It is not surprising that children who choose to allocate a part of their free time to regular sports participation, independently of the school setting, may have an increased likelihood of continuing to allocate their time in that manner in the future (Cleland, Dwyer and Venn, 2012). However, longitudinal research tracking sport and PA participation from childhood to adulthood is limited. The curricula for professionals in PE, sport, and PA need to cover evidence-based and evidence-informed strategies known to encourage regular habitual participation in sport and methods to make organised sport more appealing and accessible to the majority of children. In addition, the previous considerations highlight the need for more longitudinal research in sport to isolate the impacts of participation over time. Professionals in the area need to be trained to understand and be able to carry out this type of research.

## Implication 5: Prevention of youth sports dropout is a key priority

Youth sports dropout is the prolonged absence of systematic practice and competition, either in one sport (sport-specific dropout) or in all sport (sport-general dropout) (Balish *et al.*, 2014). Evidence suggests that sports participation peaks at around 11–13 years before declining through adolescence (Zimmermann-Sloutskis *et al.*, 2010). The statistics on dropout are equivocal, but it is estimated that up to 35% of youth participants drop out of sport every year, and this decline in participation is consistently reported across most sport (Brooke *et al.*, 2014). In the CSPPA+ study (Murphy *et al.*, 2016; Murphy *et al.*, 2017), dropout from sport was influenced by psycho-social (e.g., lack of interest, perceived competence, self-efficacy) and social reasons (e.g., friends no longer participating and coaches being unfriendly). School (or work) commitments were also a highly reported attrition factor. Considering the health benefits associated with sports participation, prevention of dropout should be a key priority. More innovative solutions for assessing and measuring this phenomenon are needed in sport and PA education.

## Implication 6: Global perspectives on youth sports migration are needed

For youth there is a considerable movement into and out of sports participation (Richards *et al.*, 2007). When tracked over a five-year period, the relative amount of youth who reported "dropping out" of a sport is similar with the amount "taking up" a new sport during that time, albeit at a different level of engagement, e.g., changing from competitive to recreational participation (Murphy *et al.*, 2016; Murphy *et al.*, 2017). Respondents listed multiple motives for participation including fitness (19.9% of males; 25.8% of females), enjoyment (~11%), and socialising or spending time with friends (~8%), indicating that a number of factors collectively contribute to the uptake of a new sport. In addition, interests change due to biological, demographic, social, psychological, environmental, or behavioural factors. By understanding this "to and from" movement, sometimes referred to as "sports migration" as opposed to dropout, professionals can understand the factors that foster migration from one sport to another. Sports disciplines with the highest participation rates tend to have the most migration, as youth may tend to try out popular sport. The popularity of sport can be influenced by cultural factors and, therefore, differ from country to country (*Brooke et al.*, 2014). As the popularity of sport differs by country, the promotion of sport should be carried out within the context of that country. As participation in specific sport is dependent on opportunities and access, increased policy and programme efforts to broaden opportunities are needed. Educational approaches and curricula need to teach about migration and dropout from sports participation and the impact of these activities on the lives of children and their families.

## Implication 7: Inequities in participation in youth sport are prevalent and need to be addressed globally

Despite the many potential benefits of sports participation, substantial disparities exist, particularly among some groups of young people. For example, higher sports participation rates among young people from more affluent socio-economic backgrounds have been observed in studies using representative samples from the United States (Hyde *et al.*, 2020), Ireland (Woods *et al.*, 2018), Canada (Bengoechea *et al.*, 2010), and the Otago region in New Zealand (Mandic *et al.*, 2012). In addition, greater rates of PA and sports participation have been reported among young people without disabilities (Woods *et al.*, 2018; Ng, Sainio and Sit, 2019), while continued barriers to participation, particularly in organised sport, for racial/ethnic and sexual minority youth have been documented (Doull *et al.*, 2018; Hyde *et al.*, 2020).

Gender differences in PA and sports participation are also well established (Guthold *et al.*, 2020). Likewise, some of the factors affecting participation differ for boys and girls (Bengoechea, Ruiz-Juan and Bush, 2013). On a positive note, reductions in the gender gap in sports participation have been reported in countries such as Ireland (2010–2018), although only in primary schoolchildren (Woods *et al.*, 2018), and Iceland (1992–2006) (Eithsdottir *et al.*, 2008). Mirroring some of the previous gaps noted, at a global scale, disparity in participation in youth sport exists also between countries according to their level of resources, as reflected in indicators such as the Human Development Index (HDI) (Aubert *et al.*, 2018). This suggests that access to quality, equitable opportunities for children and youth to participate in sport is a concern worldwide. Education curricula need to ensure that PE, PA, and sports professionals are aware of the global issues in relation to inequities and offer students an opportunity to discuss and pose solutions to these challenges.

## Model of effective practices – One case study

### The Walking In ScHools (WISH) study

School-based interventions have the potential to overcome some of the factors leading to unintended health inequalities, as all adolescents can participate irrespective of socio-economic status (Vander Ploeg *et al.*, 2014). Schools are an excellent setting for PA promotion, as young people spend 40% of their waking time at school (Fox, Cooper and McKenna, 2004). Peers and role-models are dominant influences in adolescence (MacDonald-Wallis, Jago and Sterne, 2012). Therefore, a walking intervention delivered by peers in a school setting has the potential to increase PA in a low-cost and sustainable way, while addressing a reported lack of interest in the activities offered in school (Yungblut, Schinke and McGannon, 2012) and a need to provide PA opportunities for those discouraged by the competitive selection process (Humbert *et al.*, 2008). Walking is the most natural form of PA and has been recommended for the promotion of public health (Thompson, 2008), as it is a form of activity that overcomes many of the reported barriers to PA, such as lack of time or money (Townsend *et al.*, 2012).

The Walking In ScHools (WISH) Study is a school-based, low-cost, peer-led, clustered randomised controlled trial. Following a pilot feasibility trial (Carlin *et al.*, 2018), this study is evaluating the effectiveness of a walking intervention on PA levels of adolescent girls (12–14 years) (O'Kane *et al.*, 2020). Following baseline data collection, schools (n = 18) were randomly allocated to intervention or control group. In intervention schools, female pupils aged 15–18 years are trained as walk leaders and will lead younger pupils in 10–15 min walks before school, during the break and at lunch. All walks take place on school grounds and pupils are encouraged to participate in as many walks as possible each week. The intervention is delivered for the whole school year (minimum 20–22 weeks), and the primary outcome measure is accelerometer-measured total PA.

## Recommendations for future education and training

Addressing the public health challenge of physical inactivity requires sustained good practice across multiple sectors. Several implications follow for the future education and training of PE, PA, and sports professionals. Embedding health promotion at the core of these professions is one strategy to enhance lifelong participation in PA. Specific recommendations are listed below:

- PA and sports initiatives should foster frequent, habitual participation for all and incorporate health promotion principles, theory, and practice. They should be multi-component, target multiple levels, and be based on systems approaches. Interventions should take account of participants' circumstances, both limiting and enabling, capitalising on their insights, and involving them in co-design of sports participation and PA programmes when making decisions about designing, implementing, and evaluating actions directed to them.

- Benchmark countries based on their national policy approaches to the promotion of PA, and on how they encourage the efforts of multiple sectors to address physical inactivity in a systems approach.
- Value sport and sports clubs for their potential to deliver health benefits and recognise sport as a "health promoting setting". This broad focus on the role of sport in health would increase awareness of the potential of this popular, underutilised activity to contribute to the health and broader SDGs agenda.
- Promote forms of PA likely to be sustained into adulthood (walking, cycling, active commuting, running, exercise classes, fitness/gym activity, individual sport) in addition to participation in team sport and vigorous activity in which participation declines more steeply with age.
- Challenge coaches, teachers, and other practitioners to know what children will find enjoyable and be aware that what is enjoyable for one (e.g., competition) might be off-putting for another (even if same age, gender, and group). Emphasise enjoyment, whatever this means for the child, youth, adult.
- Teach future PE, PA, and sports professionals how to harness the potential of peers and role models, as positive peer influence is vital in health behaviour.
- Broaden the types of research methodologies taught to PE, PA, and sports professionals to include training in both qualitative and quantitative approaches. Within quantitative approaches, prioritise research collecting longitudinal data, where possible, as information on the determinants, as opposed to the correlates, of PA behaviour is needed.
- More research on effective programmes that increase PA and sports participation, particularly in low- and middle-income countries, is needed to further develop the evidence to inform national policies and action plans.
- Raise awareness of country-wide policies that facilitate access to opportunities for sports participation and PA. Foster a culture of evaluation to improve PA and sports programmes as well as initiatives with a health promotion focus and to better allocate limited resources.

## References

Aubert, S. *et al.* (2018) 'Global matrix 3.0 physical activity report card grades for children and youth: Results and analysis from 49 countries', *Journal of Physical Activity and Health*, 15(s2), pp. 251–273. doi: 10.1123/jpah.2018-0472.

Balish, S. M. *et al.* (2014) 'Correlates of youth sport attrition: A review and future directions', *Psychology of Sport and Exercise*, 15(4), pp. 429–439. doi: 10.1016/j.psychsport.2014.04.003.

Basterfield, L. *et al.* (2015) 'Longitudinal associations between sports participation, body composition and physical activity from childhood to adolescence', *Journal of Science and Medicine in Sport*. 18(2), pp. 178–182. doi: 10.1016/j.jsams.2014.03.005.

Bengoechea, E. G. *et al.* (2010) 'Exploring links to unorganized and organized physical activity during adolescence', *Research Quarterly for Exercise and Sport*, 81(1), pp. 7–16. doi: 10.1080/02701367.2010.10599623.

Bengoechea, E. G., Ruiz-Juan, F. R. and Bush, P. L. (2013) 'Delving into the social ecology of leisure-time physical activity among adolescents from south eastern Spain', *Journal of Physical Activity and Health*, 10(8), pp. 1136–1144. doi: 10.1123/jpah.10.8.1136.

Brooke, H. L. *et al.* (2014) 'Physical activity maintenance in the transition to adolescence: A longitudinal study of the roles of sport and lifestyle activities in British youth', *PLoS ONE*, 9(2). doi: 10.1371/journal.pone.0089028.

Bull, F.C., Al-Ansari, S.S., Biddle, S. *et al.* (2020) World Health Organization 2020 guidelines on physical activity and sedentary behavior, *British Journal of Sports Medicine*, 54, pp. 1451–1462.

Butler, J. (2001) *Principles of health education and health promotion.* Belmont, CA: Wadsworth.

Carlin, A. *et al.* (2018) 'Effects of a peer-led Walking In ScHools intervention (the WISH study) on physical activity levels of adolescent girls: A cluster randomised pilot study', *Trials*, 19(1), pp. 1–12. doi: 10.1186/s13063-017-2415-4.

Cleland, V., Dwyer, T. and Venn, A. (2012) 'Which domains of childhood physical activity predict physical activity in adulthood? A 20-year prospective tracking study', *British Journal of Sports Medicine*, 46(8), pp. 595–602. doi: 10.1136/bjsports-2011-090508.

Deci, E. and Ryan, R. (2002) *Handbook of self-determination research.* 1st edn. Rochester, NY: University of Rochester Press.

Doull, M. *et al.* (2018) 'Are we leveling the playing field? Trends and disparities in sports participation among sexual minority youth in Canada', *Journal of Sport and Health Science*, 7(2), pp. 218–226. doi: 10.1016/j.jshs.2016.10.006.

Dumith, S. C. *et al.* (2011) 'Physical activity change during adolescence: A systematic review and a pooled analysis', *International Journal of Epidemiology*, 40(3), pp. 685–698. doi: 10.1093/ije/dyq272.

Eime, R. M. *et al.* (2013) 'A systematic review of the psychological and social benefits of participation in sport for adults: Informing development of a conceptual model of health through sport', *International Journal of Behavioral Nutrition and Physical Activity*, 10. doi: 10.1186/1479-5868-10-135.

Eime, R. M., Payne, W. R. and Harvey, J. T. (2008) 'Making sporting clubs healthy and welcoming environments: A strategy to increase participation', *Journal of Science and Medicine in Sport*, 11(2), pp. 146–154. doi: 10.1016/j.jsams.2006.12.121.

Eithsdottir, S. T. *et al.* (2008) 'Trends in physical activity and participation in sports clubs among Icelandic adolescents', *The European Journal of Public Health*, 18(3), pp. 289–293. doi: 10.1093/eurpub/ckn004.

Evans, J. M. M. *et al.* (2009) 'Tracking of physical activity behaviours during childhood, adolescence and young adulthood: A systematic review.', *Journal of Epidemiology and Community Health*, 63(Suppl II), p. A$.

Fox, K. R., Cooper, A. and McKenna, J. (2004) 'The school and promotion of children's health-enhancing physical activity: Perspectives from the United Kingdom', *Journal of Teaching in Physical Education*, 23(4), pp. 338–358. doi: 10.1123/jtpe.23.4.338.

Gray, C. M. *et al.* (2013) 'Football fans in training: The development and optimization of an intervention delivered through professional sports clubs to help men lose weight, become more active and adopt healthier eating habits', *BMC Public Health*, 13(1), pp. 1–17. doi: 10.1186/1471-2458-13-232.

Guthold, R. *et al.* (2018) 'Worldwide trends in insufficient physical activity from 2001 to 2016: A pooled analysis of 358 population-based surveys with 1·9 million participants', *The Lancet Global Health*, 6(10), pp. e1077–e1086. doi: 10.1016/S2214-109X (18)30357-7.

Guthold, R. *et al.* (2020) 'Global trends in insufficient physical activity among adolescents: A pooled analysis of 298 population-based surveys with 1·6 million participants', *The Lancet Child and Adolescent Health*. World Health Organization, 4(1), pp. 23–35. doi: 10.1016/S2352-4642(19)30323-2.

House of Commons: Culture Media and Sport (2008) *European Commission White Paper on Sport, Seventh Report of Session 2007–08*. Available at: http://www.parliament.uk/parliamentary_committees/culture__media_and_sport.cfm (Accessed: 24 June 2020).

Hulteen, R. M. (2019) 'Promoting health-enhancing physical activity: A state-of-the-art review of peer-delivered interventions'. *Current Obesity Reports*, 8, pp. 341–353.

Hulteen, R. M. *et al.* (2018) 'Development of foundational movement skills: A conceptual model for physical activity across the lifespan', *Sports Medicine*, 48(7), pp. 1533–1540. doi: 10.1007/s40279-018-0892-6.

Humbert, M. L. *et al.* (2008) 'Using a naturalistic ecological approach to examine the factors influencing youth physical activity across grades 7 to 12', *Health Education and Behavior*, 35(2), pp. 158–173. doi: 10.1177/1090198106287451.

Hyde, E. T. *et al.* (2020) 'Disparities in youth sports participation in the U.S., 2017–2018', *American Journal of Preventive Medicine*, 59(5), pp. 3–6. doi: 10.1016/j.amepre.2020.05.011.

Johnson, S. *et al.* (2020) 'Measuring health promotion in sports club settings: A modified Delphi study', *Health Education & Behavior*, 47(1), pp. 78–90. doi: 10.1177/1090198119889098.

Laverack, G. (2000) 'A planning framework for community empowerment goals within health promotion', *Health Policy and Planning*, 15(3), pp. 255–262. doi: 10.1093/heapol/15.3.255.

MacDonald-Wallis, K., Jago, R. and Sterne, J. A. C. (2012) 'Social network analysis of childhood and youth physical activity: A systematic review', *American Journal of Preventive Medicine*, 43(6), pp. 636–642. doi: 10.1016/j.amepre.2012.08.021.

Mandic, S. *et al.* (2012) 'Getting kids active by participating in sport and doing it more often: Focusing on what matters', *International Journal of Behavioral Nutrition and Physical Activity*, 9, pp. 1–9. doi: 10.1186/1479-5868-9-86.

Marmot, M. (2005) 'Social determinants of health inequalities', *The Lancet*, 365(9464), pp. 1099–1104. doi: 10.1016/S0140-6736(05)71146-6.

Michie, S. and Atkins, L. W. R. (2014) *The behaviour change wheel: A guide to developing interventions*. London: Silverback Publishing.

Morgan, A. (2014) 'Revisiting the asset model: A clarification of ideas and terms', *Global Health Promotion*, 21(2), pp. 3–6. doi: 10.1177/1757975914536849.

Murphy, M. H., Rowe, D. A. and Woods, C. B. (2016) 'Sports participation in youth as a predictor of physical activity: A 5-year longitudinal study', *Journal of Physical Activity and Health*, 13(7), pp. 704–711. doi: 10.1123/jpah.2015-0526.

Murphy, M. H., Rowe, D. A. and Woods, C. B. (2017) 'Impact of physical activity domains on subsequent physical activity in youth: A 5-year longitudinal study', *Journal of Sports Sciences*, 35(3), pp. 262–268. doi: 10.1080/02640414.2016.1161219.

Ng, K., Sainio, P. and Sit, C. (2019) 'Physical activity of adolescents with and without disabilities from a complete enumeration study (N = 128,803): School health promotion study 2017', *International Journal of Environmental Research and Public Health*, 16(17), pp. 1–13. doi: 10.3390/ijerph16173156.

O'Kane, S. M. *et al.* (2020) 'A study protocol for a clustered randomised controlled trial to evaluate the effectiveness of a peer-led school-based walking intervention on adolescent girls' physical activity: The Walking In ScHools (WISH) study', *BMC Public Health*, 20(1), pp. 1–12. doi: 10.1186/s12889-020-08600-0.

Richards, R. *et al.* (2007) 'Tracking club sport participation from childhood to early adulthood', *Research Quarterly for Exercise and Sport*, 78(5), pp. 413–419. doi: 10.1080/02701367.2007.10599441.

Rutter, H. *et al.* (2017) 'The need for a complex systems model of evidence for public health', *The Lancet*, 390(10112), pp. 2602–2604. doi: 10.1016/S0140-6736(17)31267-9.

Rutter, H. *et al.* (2019) 'Systems approaches to global and national physical activity plans', *Bulletin of the World Health Organization*, 97(2), pp. 162–165. doi: 10.2471/BLT.18.220533.

Strain, T. *et al.* (2016) 'Age-related comparisons by sex in the domains of aerobic physical activity for adults in Scotland', *Preventive Medicine Reports*, 3, pp. 90–97. doi: 10.1016/j.pmedr.2015.12.013.

Swinburn, B. A. *et al.* (2019) 'The global syndemic of obesity, undernutrition, and climate change: The Lancet Commission report', *The Lancet*, 393(10173), pp. 791–846. doi: 10.1016/S0140-6736(18)32822-8.

Telama, R. (2009) 'Tracking of physical activity from childhood to adulthood: A review', *Obesity Facts*, 2(3), pp. 187–195. doi: 10.1159/000222244.

Telama, R. *et al.* (2006) 'Participation in organized youth sport as a predictor of adult physical activity: A 21-year longitudinal study', *Pediatric Exercise Science*, 18(1), pp. 76–88. doi: 10.1123/pes.18.1.76.

Thompson, D. L. (2008) 'Walking Works', *Southern Medical Journal*, 101(2), pp. 114–115. doi: 10.1097/SMJ.0b013e3181583a09.

Townsend, N. *et al.* (2012) *Physical activity statistics 2012.* London.

Vander Ploeg, K. A. *et al.* (2014) 'Do school-based physical activity interventions increase or reduce inequalities in health?', *Social Science and Medicine*, 112, pp. 80–87. doi: 10.1016/j.socscimed.2014.04.032.

Woods, C. B. *et al.* (2018) 'The children's sport participation and physical activity study 2018 (CSPPA 2018)', pp. 1–108.

WHO (1986) *Ottawa Charter for Health Promotion: First International Conference on Health Promotion.* Available at: https://www.healthpromotion.org.au/images/ottawa_charter_hp.pdf (Accessed: 26 July 2020).

WHO (2009) *Global Health Risks.* Available at: http://www.who.int/healthinfo/global_burden_disease/GlobalHealthRisks_report_full.pdf (Accessed: 24 June 2020).

WHO (2016) 'Promoting health in the SDGs', *Report on the 9th Global Conference on Health Promotion: All for Health, Health for All* (21–24 November), pp. 1–37.

WHO (2018) *Global action plan on physical activity 2018–2030: More active people for a healthier world.* Geneva, Switzerland.

WHO (no date a) *Creating Health Promoting Settings.* Available at: https://www.who.int/westernpacific/activities/creating-health-promoting-settings (Accessed: 26 July 2020).

WHO (no date b) *World Health Organization: Health Promotion.* Available at: https://www.who.int/health-topics/health-promotion#tab=tab_1 (Accessed: 26 July 2020).

Yungblut, H. E., Schinke, R. J. and McGannon, K. R. (2012) 'Views of adolescent female youth on physical activity during early adolescence', *Journal of Sports Science and Medicine*, 11(1), pp. 39–50.

Zimmermann-Sloutskis, D. *et al.* (2010) 'Physical activity levels and determinants of change in young adults: A longitudinal panel study', *International Journal of Behavioral Nutrition and Physical Activity*, 7, pp. 1–13. doi: 10.1186/1479-5868-7-2.

Chapter 14

# Being active as a sports or PA student in an era of wearable technology

*Charlotte van Tuyckom and Steven Vos*

## Different roles of wearable technology in sport and physical activity

Not only in top-level sport but also in recreational sport and physical activity (PA), the use of wearable (sensor) technology is growing rapidly. Unfortunately, current curricula in higher sport and PA education pay limited attention to this topic. Profound knowledge about this technology should however be a core component of the curriculum of sports and PA students. Therefore, we will elaborate on different roles of wearable technology and the adapting role (and skills) of sports and PA professionals in the current digital era.

In general, the wearable technology market is organised according to the following four roles (see Figure 14.1):

- *Quantified self*: monitoring and improving performance, e.g., sensor systems to monitor physiological and biomechanical data, etc.
- *Gamification and social networking*: enhancing enjoyment and motivation, e.g., interactive playgrounds, gamified sports apps, online sports communities, virtual reality sports experiences, etc.
- *Coaching*: assisting (coaches and referees in their) decision-making, e.g., video assistant referee (VAR)-technology, goal-line technology, video-feedback, online coaching systems, automated distance or time measurement systems, etc.
- *Smart policy planning*: encouraging and enabling participation, e.g., citizen shared information on social networks, air pollution sensors, traffic, and surveillance cameras, etc.

We will elaborate on these four roles with respect to consumer-available sport- and PA-related wearable devices such as activity trackers, fitness trackers, and sports watches (provided by companies such as Nike, Fitbit, Polar, Garmin, Apple, Samsung, etc.), smartphone or smartwatch applications (apps), and even smart clothing, eyewear, headphones, and others (Vos, 2016). These devices and mobile applications are already being used by millions of people during workouts;

DOI: 10.4324/9781003002666-19

*Figure 14.1* Four key roles of wearable technology in sport and PA.

various sensors are assembled into the appliances (e.g., GPS, accelerometers, altimeters, temperature, heart rate monitors, or other sensors to track the wearer's movement and/or biometric data). This exponential increase in the availability and use of consumer-available wearable devices and apps is in line with the progress towards more unorganised sports participation and the increased importance of an active and healthy lifestyle (e.g., Middelweerd *et al*., 2014; Vos *et al*., 2016; Janssen *et al*., 2017; Dallinga *et al*., 2018; Janssen *et al*., 2020). The annual survey on fitness trends by the American College of Sports Medicine (ACSM) shows that wearable technology has been the number one trend since 2016, outperforming previous trends like body weight training or high-intensity interval training (Thompsom, 2019). The total number of connected wearable devices worldwide has more than doubled in the period of three years, increasing from 325 million in 2016 to 722 million in 2019. The number of devices is forecast to reach more than one billion by 2022 (Statista, 2019). Market projections in 2016 stated that in 2020, the health and fitness wearable tech market would be worth 34 billion dollars (Forbes, 2016).

The ability of sport- and PA-related apps and wearable devices to track behaviour over time (in the daily environment) provides opportunities at different levels. For instance, individual users of a running/cycling app such as Strava can measure and monitor their performance and share it on the platform. Coaches and trainers can use the same platform to monitor and adjust the performance of groups of athletes. User-generated (big) data (cfr. Strava's heat map, a record of activities in a given area) also holds value for sport policy makers and urban planners. Through data analytics and data visualisation, interesting patterns can be discovered, and sport and PA policy interventions can be designed, monitored, evaluated, and improved.

Sports and PA professionals should consequently have a thorough knowledge of opportunities created using wearable devices for training, coaching, and policy making. Therefore, we also elaborate on the implications for the sports and PA profession in the context of the four roles. This will then lead us to discussing some of the opportunities and challenges inherent to wearable technology in sport and PA. The chapter as a result concludes by stressing the importance of interdisciplinary collaboration between sport, humanities, and technology.

### Role 1: Monitoring and improving performance – Quantified self

Ever since "physical fitness" became something to be concerned about, people have been looking for ways to quantify the amount of PA they perform (Hoy, 2016). Runners and cyclists track distances and times, swimmers count laps; everybody is counting something. Until a couple of years ago, much of this counting was done manually or with simple tools like a pedometer or spreadsheet software, and sports and PA professionals had an active "expert role". Recent advances in sensor technology have created a new class of wearable devices, allowing users to automatically track information about their PA and physical fitness, from steps taken to vertical distance travelled, from heart rate to calories burned, and sleep (and even menstruation) cycles. Most quantified self-designs in apps and wearables are centred around features that facilitate self-regulatory behaviour in the domain of PA, sleep, stress, nutrition, etc., as they aim to inform and assist their users while attempting to reach their goals (Stragier *et al.*, 2016). In many activity trackers, users can closely self-monitor their exercise data and view their progress over a certain period in detailed longitudinal single subject performance graphs (Janssen *et al.*, 2020). In these apps, users can also set goals to test their competence (such as completing a five-kilometre running event within a given time frame). Besides data generation, digital technology implements behaviour change elements: the availability of interactive displays in activity trackers provides many opportunities for different types of feedback (e.g., habit-disrupting feedback cues such as buzzes, beeps, and push messages or rewards such as medals, stickers, etc.) (Hermsen *et al.*, 2016; Schwartz and Baca, 2016; Hamari, Hassan and Dias, 2018). These innovations have created possibilities for people to become "experts" in self-monitoring of health parameters and PA on a 24/7 basis (Vos, 2016). The desire to attach personal numeric data to everyday activities such as exercising has been named the "quantified self" movement. By observing and recording details of their PA, individuals are enabled to analyse data to self-modify their (sports) behaviour and enhance their health or send vital parameters to sport/health coaches (Fotopoulou and O'Riordan, 2017; Lupton, 2017; Smith and Vonthethoff, 2017; Didziokaite, Saukko and Greiffenhagen, 2018). Yet, sports and PA professionals have not become obsolete but should integrate the available data into their training and coaching and become "quantified self coaches". Curricula should reflect the role-shift from "sports and PA expert" to "coach", and students should have profound knowledge of how wearable devices collect data as well as how accurate and reliable (or not) they are.

### Role 2: Enhancing enjoyment and motivation – Gamification and social networking

Quantified self-solutions such as wearable devices use some form of persuasive design to motivate users to increase their levels of sport and PA (Hamari *et al.*, 2018). They do this by "gamifying" the workout experiences. Gamification can be defined as the use of game design elements in non-game contexts (Deterding *et al.*, 2011). It is a key feature in many sports applications to change the user's behaviour (Toth and Logo, 2018). Gamification involves different game mechanisms such as gaining points, acquiring badges or trophies, and the position on leader boards. These mechanisms help the users to track their progress, compare themselves with others, and collect achievement symbols for excellence. They also serve the purpose of motivating the users to continue their activity (Michie *et al.*, 2009; Mekler *et al.*, 2017; Hamari *et al.*, 2018; Toth and Logo, 2018). Gamification contributes to self-improvement through the visualisation of the users' progress (Hamari *et al.*, 2018). However, it is the after-workout feedbacks and reward mechanisms (e.g., fastest lap, personal record, longest ride, …) that have the strongest effects on the users in many of these applications (Toth and Logo, 2018). As gamification taps into the users' basic desires and needs revolving around the idea of status and achievement (Fogg, 2003), it improves awareness, attitude, and enjoyment towards exercise and PA (Goh and Razikin, 2015; Kari *et al.*, 2016; Villalobos-Zuniga and Cherubini, 2020).

Wearable devices and their associated platforms are also designed to change sports and PA attitudes or behaviours through social influence (Fogg, 2003). The essential goal of any platform is to make you use it again. One step beyond that is community: the key is to embed a platform into someone's life, including their friends and wider circle of acquaintances and fellow athletes they have not even met. Individuals form online sports communities, which provide social support and connection with others (Wright, 2016; Lupton, 2017; Hamari *et al.*, 2018). Some examples of social networking features are messaging, virtual cheers in the form of likes, kudos, and comments, friending, and discussion forums. People receive feedback, social support, and encouragement from these social network services to stay motivated, whilst communities and social groups are important factors in fulfilling this motivation (Hamari and Koivisto, 2015). Engaging in online sports or fitness communities has proven to positively influence engagement and commitment to PA and healthy lifestyles (Stragier *et al.*, 2016). Communities have the potential to provide informational support (such as guidance and advice about PA and how to best engage in it) and emotional support (in which users provide encouragement, care, empathy, and motivation). Social interaction among people in social networks also results in social support, of which research (among others with Pokémon Go and Fitocracy) has demonstrated that it is an important determinant of motivation and PA adherence (Springer, Kelder and Hoelscher, 2006; Cavallo *et al.*, 2014; Hamari and Koivisto, 2015; Althoff, White and Horvitz, 2016). Although these sports communities can support PA in different ways, a prerequisite to benefiting from their potential is that users integrate them into their PA routines (Stragier *et al.*, 2016). After all, it is only when a user regularly logs his/her activities that s/he will be able to understand patterns, to see progress, and to have content around which s/he can interact with other users.

Currently, sports and PA professionals do not have sufficient knowledge of the mechanisms behind persuasive design, gamification, and online sports communities. Sports and PA curricula should therefore address the topics of behavioural change, motivation, social psychology, and behavioural sciences in relation to wearable technology.

### Role 3: Assisting decision-making – Coaching

Wearable technology is also transforming how sports and PA professionals make decisions, how sport is played, and the performance, health, and safety of sports players themselves. The technologies assisting decision-making are moving rapidly from the professional sports arena into lower-level and recreational sport. Wearable devices are measuring overall player workload during games, allowing sport coaches real-time monitoring of the player's biometrics for signs of exhaustion or injury while on the field. Sports and PA curricula should acknowledge the potential of these developments in this rapidly expanding technological niche as they are letting team administrators, coaches, trainers, and players excel in their sport and gain competitive advantage while reducing injury and sport-related illness at the same time (Seshadri *et al.*, 2017; Luczak *et al.*, 2020). In addition, sports and PA professionals should be aware that wearable devices assisting decision-making are being seamlessly incorporated into the fabric of sports apparel, built into sports equipment like balls and rackets, and worn by players as small devices attached to the body in a waistband or skin patch. The devices then link by Bluetooth and GPS technology, providing real-time data to coaches with laptops or other electronic devices for analysing, recording, and responding to the information. Also, consumer-oriented wearable devices and apps such as Strava, Garmin Connect, Polar, etc. allow training data to be shared with sports professionals through coaching software (e.g., Training Peaks or similar programmes). Next to the raw training parameters (e.g., average speed, heart rate, ...), these apps/devices often provide more colour and context to the coaches regarding the workout of their coachee. Even simple things like how a run is titled gives insight into how the training went, how the coachee is feeling, if something memorable happened, etc.

### Role 4: Encouraging and enabling participation – Smart policy planning

Data from wearable technology is also a powerful tool to obtain knowledge about a region or city and contribute to smart policy planning. Citizens share information on social networks about new routes or places where they choose to carry out their daily sports activities. For instance, millions of people upload their rides, runs, and walks on Strava every week via their smartphone or GPS device. Strava Metro aggregates and de-identifies this data and then partners with departments of transportation and city planning groups to improve infrastructure for bicyclists and pedestrians. Different studies have shown how Strava (and other social networking) data can be exploited to make better and more active cities (Romanillos *et al.*, 2016; van Renswouw, Bogers and Vos, 2016; Vos, 2016; Mora *et al.*, 2018). Information on and visualisation of the real uses of public space, the needs and preferences of citizens, popular or avoided routes, intersection waiting times, etc. help planners to design better infrastructure based on where, why, and when citizens use it and ultimately contribute to the decision-making process on the actions to be taken (Alvarez, Borsi and Rodrigues, 2017; Wu *et al.*, 2017; Hamstead *et al.*, 2018).

In the last decades, the image of (sports) planning has gone from static to a reality where the environment and citizens themselves are continuously "in motion" and thus important sources of data, providing relevant information for better (sports) planning which is adapted to the real changing needs of the city and the actual requirements and preferences of citizens. Sports and PA curricula do not yet include courses on big data, data analytics, and Internet of Things. Basic knowledge of these topics would however be an asset for future sports and PA professionals entering the smart policy planning debate.

## Integration of technology in sports and PA curricula

The scale and pace of technological developments such as wearable devices offer tremendous potential for the world of sport-, PA-, and lifestyle-related behaviour change. One of the game changers coming from wearable devices is their ability to track behaviours in daily life situations over time and across many users. The capturing of temporal, behavioural, and ecological data allows better understanding of the correlations and associations between individual, social, and environmental factors. Hence, these wearable devices, for instance, can adapt towards their users and their context and can provide new ways of interaction (Vos *et al.*, 2016).

With these opportunities, new dangers and responsibilities emerge. Not only the accuracy and reliability of the data is a cause of concern (Lee and Finkelstein, 2014; Hoy, 2016), there are also ethical and privacy issues surrounding activity data. Users may not be aware of all the data their device is gathering. For instance, in 2018, Strava's global heat map – a record of one billion activities worldwide – accidentally revealed the location of secret US military bases because personnel had uploaded their activities to Strava and failed to opt out of heat maps. Another problem is the often-commercial use of the data for purposes the users do not know about. Not only sports and PA professionals use wearable data for decision-making, but also employers and insurance companies have an interest in activity tracking data of employees or citizens (Norman *et al.*, 2015). In addition, whilst gamification can promote enjoyment and motivation, it can also lead to negative consequences. There are even fears that apps such as Strava could create hyperaware cyclists, driven by obsession rather than enjoyment, resulting in problems relating to overtraining, overexertion, risk taking, and even cheating because of the social pressure caused by other members in the sports community (Barratt, 2017).

All this implies that innovators need to consider the personal, physical, and social context. Yet, research has shown that in the process of developing consumer-available wearables, only limited non-technological expertise is consulted. Unfortunately, the specific knowledge of various experts, such as behavioural scientists and sport and health scientists, is often not mutually incorporated (Epstein *et al.*, 2016; Vos *et al.*, 2016; Arts, Kromkamp and Vos, 2020).

Although interdisciplinary collaboration is not always easy as scientists and researchers from different disciplines use different ways of communicating, distinct definitions for the same terms and various mental models and paradigms (Arts, Kromkamp and Vos, 2019), educational institutions and students in sport and PA, behavioural sciences, and more technological domains (such as product design, gaming, Internet of Things, big data, data analytics, etc.) should be encouraged to build partnerships and work on interdisciplinary projects together. Cone, Werner, and Cone (2008) define interdisciplinary education as a process in which two or more subject areas (here sport and technology) are combined with the goal of fostering enhanced learning in each subject area. Implementing an interdisciplinary programme would bring educators from the different domains together to create exciting learning experiences for students and to discover new ways of delivering the curriculum. The concept of interdisciplinary education acknowledges the integrity of each subject area, but at the same time recognises the interrelationships among them. Educators should organise their curriculum around common themes, concepts, and skills across both disciplines to facilitate learning. This approach, in contrast to the current discipline-based approach to learning in the sports and PA domain (as well as in other domains), seeks to connect all disciplines. It proposes to foster a holistic understanding by organising skills and knowledge along lines of connection and convergence rather than along lines of divergence and differentiation (as is currently often the case). Finding connections among various knowledge domains leads to a deeper conceptual understanding of the features, dimensions, and characteristics common between them (as elaborated upon through the four different roles of wearable technology). Through interdisciplinary education, both educators and students will experience a wide spectrum of relationships between the subject areas of sport, behavioural sciences, and technology. The experiences educators offer their students will influence the skills and knowledge they develop. Making those learning experiences relevant, meaningful, and transferable to future learning is the ultimate goal of interdisciplinary teaching (Cone *et al.*, 2008). Therefore, we firmly belief that much more attention should be paid to interdisciplinary education that brings together technological experts, behavioural scientists, and sports and PA professionals in a way in which all disciplines learn together, each inspiring and depending on the others. To quote Steve Jobs: "[…] Technology alone is not enough – it's technology married with liberal arts, married with the humanities, that yields us the results that make our heart sing".

## References

Althoff, T., White, R. and Horvitz, E. (2016) 'Influence of Pokemon Go on physical activity: Study and implications', *Journal of Medical Internet Research*, 18(12), e315. doi:10.2196/jmir.6759.

Alvarez, L., Borsi, K. and Rodrigues, L. (2017) 'The role of social network analysis on participation and placemaking', *Sustainable Cities and Society*, 28, pp. 118–126. doi:10.1016/j.scs.2016.06.017.

Arts, D., Kromkamp, L. and Vos, S. (2019) 'COMMONS: A board game for enhancing interdisciplinary collaboration when developing health and activity-related wearable devices', in Lamas, D. *et al.* (eds.) *Human-computer interaction – INTERACT 2019 – 17th IFIP TC 13 international conference, proceedings. Lecture notes in computer science.* vol. 11749. LNCS, Springer, pp. 461–470. doi:10.1007/978-3-030-29390-1_25.

Arts, D., Kromkamp, L. and Vos, S. B. (2020) 'Designing for an active lifestyle: Facilitating interdisciplinary collaboration', in Christer, K., Craig, C. and Chamberlain, P. (eds.) *Proceedings of the 6th international conference on Design4Health.* Amsterdam, pp. 38–45.

Barratt, P. (2017) 'Healthy competition: A qualitative study investigating persuasive technologies and the gamification of cycling', *Health & Place*, 46, pp. 328–336. doi:10.1016/j.healthplace.2016.09.009.

Cavallo, D. *et al.* (2014) 'Social support for physical activity. Role of Facebook with and without structured intervention', *Translational Behavioral Medicine*, 4(4), pp. 346–354. doi: 10.1007/s13142-014-0269-9.

Cone, T., Werner, P. and Cone, S. (2008) *Interdisciplinary elementary physical education.* Champaign, IL: Human Kinetics.

Dallinga, J. *et al.* (2018) 'Analysis of the features important for the effectiveness of physical activity–related apps for recreational sports: Expert panel approach', *JMIR Mhealth and Uhealth*, 6(6), e143. doi:10.2196/mhealth.9459.

Deterding, S. *et al.* (2011) 'From game design elements to gamefulness: Defining gamification', in *Proceedings of the 15th international academic mindrek conference: Envisioning future media environments*, pp. 9–15.

Didziokaite, G., Saukko, P. and Greiffenhagen, C. (2018) 'The mundane experience of everyday calorie trackers: Beyond the metaphor of quantified self', *New Media & Society*, 20(4), pp. 1470–1487. doi:10.1177/1461444817698478.

Epstein, D. A. *et al.* (2016) 'Reconsidering the device in the drawer: Lapses as a design opportunity in personal informatics', in *Proceedings of the 2016 ACM international joint conference on pervasive and ubiquitous computing*, pp. 829–840.

Fogg, B. (2003) *Persuasive technology: Using computers to change what we think and do.* Boston, MA: Morgan Kaufmann Publishers.

Forbes (2016) *Wearable tech market to be worth $34 Billion by 2020.* Available at: https://www.forbes.com/sites/paullamkin/2016/02/17/wearable-tech-market-to-be-worth-34-billion-by-2020/#6cca7b3c3cb5 (Accessed: May 2020).

Fotopoulou, A. and O'Riordan, K. (2017) 'Training to self-care: Fitness tracking, biopedagogy and the healthy consumer', *Health Sociology Review*, 26(1), pp. 54–68. doi:10.1080/14461242.2016.1184582.

Goh, D. and Razikin, K. (2015) 'Is gamification effective in motivating exercise?', in *International conference on human-computer interaction*, pp. 608–617. doi:10.1007/978-3-319-20916-6_56.

Hamari, J. and Koivisto, J. (2015) "Working out for likes': An empirical study on social influence in exercise gamification', *Computers in Human Behavior*, 50, pp. 333–347. doi:10.1016/j.chb.2015.04.018.

Hamari, J., Hassan, L., and Dias, A. (2018) 'Gamification, quantified-self or social networking? Matching users' goals with motivational technology', *User Modeling and User-Adapted Interaction*, 28(1), pp. 35–74. doi:10.1007/s11257-018-9200-2.

Hamstead, Z. *et al.* (2018) 'Geolocated social media as a rapid indicator of park visitation and equitable park access', *Computers, Environment and Urban Systems*, 72, pp. 38–50. doi:10.1016/j.compenvurbsys.2018.01.007.

Hermsen, S. *et al.* (2016) 'Using feedback through digital technology to disrupt and change habitual behavior: A critical review of current literature', *Computers in Human Behavior*, 57, pp. 61–74. doi:10.1016/j.chb.2015.12.023.

Hoy, M. (2016) Personal activity trackers and the quantified self. *Medical Reference Services Quarterly*, 35(1), pp. 94–100. doi:10.1080/02763869.2016.1117300.

Janssen, M. *et al.* (2017) 'Who uses running apps and sports watches? Determinants and consumer profiles of event runners' usage of running-related smartphone applications and sports watches', *PLoS ONE*, 12(7), p. e0181167. doi: 10.1371/journal.pone.0181167.

Janssen, M. *et al.* (2020) 'Understanding different types of recreational runners and how they use running-related technology', *International Journal of Environmental Research and Public Health*, 17, 2276. doi:10.3390/ijerph17072276.

Kari, T. *et al.* (2016) 'To gamify or not to gamify? Gamification in exercise applications and its role in impacting exercise motivation', in *Proceedings of the 29th eConference digital economy*.

Lee, J. and Finkelstein, J. (2014) 'Activity trackers: A critical review', *Studies in Health Technology and Informatics*, 205, pp. 558–562. doi:10.3233/978-1-61499-432-9-558.

Luczak, T. *et al.* (2020) 'State-of-the-art review of athletic wearable technology: What 113 strength and conditioning coaches and athletic trainers from the USA said about technology in sports', *International Journal of Sports Science & Coaching*, 15 (1). doi:10.1177/1747954119885244.

Lupton, D. (2017) 'Lively data, social fitness and biovalue: The intersections of health and fitness self-tracking and social media', in Burgess, J., Marwick, A. and Poell, T. (eds.) *The SAGE handbook of social media*. London: Sage, pp. 562–578. doi:10.4135/9781473984066.n32.

Mekler, E. *et al.* (2017) 'Towards understanding the effects of individual gamification elements on intrinsic motivation and performance', *Computers in Human Behavior*, 71, pp. 525–534. doi:10.1016/j.chb.2015.08.048.

Michie, S. *et al.* (2009) 'Effective techniques in healthy eating and physical activity interventions: A meta-regression', *Health Psychology*, 28, pp. 690–701. doi:10.1037/a0016136.

Middelweerd, A. *et al.* (2014) 'Apps to promote physical activity among adults: A review and content analysis', *International Journal of Behavioral Nutrition and Physical Activity*, 11(97). doi:10.1186/s12966-014-0097-9.

Mora, H. *et al.* (2018) 'Analysis of social networking service data for smart urban planning', *Sustainability*, 10, 4732. doi:10.3390/su10124732.

Norman, G. *et al.* (2015) 'Employee use of a wireless physical activity tracker within two incentive designs at one company', *Population Health Management*. doi:10.1089/pop.2015.0030.

Romanillos, G. *et al.* (2016) 'Big data and cycling', *Transport Reviews*, 36(1). doi:10.1080/01441647.2015.1084067.

Schwartz, B. and Baca, A. (2016) 'Wearables and apps. Modern diagnostic frameworks for health promotion through sport', *Deutsche Zeitschrift für Sportmedizin*, 67(6), pp. 131–136. doi:10.5960/dzsm.2016.237.

Seshadri, D. *et al.* (2017) 'Wearable devices for sports: New integrated technologies allow coaches, physicians, and trainers to better understand the physical demands of athletes in real time', *IEEE Pulse*, 8(1). doi:10.1109/MPUL.2016.2627240.

Smith, G. and Vonthethoff, B. (2017) 'Health by numbers? Exploring the practice and experience of datafied health', *Health Sociology Review*, 26(1), pp. 6–21. doi:10.1080/14461242.2016.1196600.

Springer, A., Kelder, S. and Hoelscher, D. (2006) 'Social support, physical activity and sedentary behavior among 6th-grade girls: A cross-sectional study', *International Journal of Behavioral Nutrition and Physical Activity*, 3(8). doi:10.1186/1479-5868-3-8.

Statista (2019) *Fitness & activity tracker – Statistics & Facts*. Available at: https://www.statista.com/topics/4393/fitness-and-activity-tracker/ (Accessed: May 2020).

Stragier, J. *et al.* (2016) 'Understanding persistence in the use of online fitness communities: Comparing novice and experienced users', *Computers in Human Behavior*, pp. 34–42. doi:10.1016/j.chb.2016.06.013.

Toth, A. and Logo, E. (2018). *The effect of gamification in sport applications. 9th IEEE international conference on cognitive infocommunications*. doi: 10.1109/COGINFOCOM.2018.8639934.

Thompsom, W. (2019) 'Worldwide survey of fitness trends for 2020', *ACSM's Health & Fitness Journal*, 23(6), pp. 10–18. doi:10.1249/FIT.0000000000000526.

van Renswouw, L., Bogers, S. and Vos, S. (2016) *Urban planning for active and healthy public spaces with user-generated big data. Paper presented at data for policy 2016 – Frontiers of data science for government: Ideas, practices and projections*, Cambridge, United Kingdom, 15/09/16–16/09/16. doi:10.5281/zenodo.570550.

Villalobos-Zuniga, G. and Cherubini, M. (2020) 'Apps that motivate: A taxonomy of app features based on self-determination theory', *International Journal of Human-Computer Studies*. doi:10.1016/j.ijhcs.2020.102449.

Vos, S. B. (2016) *Designerly solutions for vital people*. Eindhoven: Technische Universität Eindhoven.

Vos, S. B. *et al.* (2016) 'From problem to solution: Developing a personalized smartphone application for recreational runners following a three-step design approach', *Procedia Engineering*, 147, pp. 799–805. doi:10.1016/j.proeng.2016.06.311.

Wright, K. (2016) 'Social networks, interpersonal social support, and health outcomes: A health communication perspective', *Frontiers in Communication*, 1(10). doi:10.3389/fcomm.2016.00010.

Wu, F. *et al.* (2017) 'Spatial-temporal visualization of city-wide crowd movement', *Journal of Visualization*, 20, pp. 183–194. doi:10.1007/s12650-016-0368-4.

# Chapter 15

# Sport, diversity, and inequality

## Intersecting challenges and solutions

*Karen Petry, Marianne Meier, and Louis Moustakas*

## Introduction

Over the past decade, societies around the globe have undergone developments that have led to greater diversity and heterogeneity. Structural changes, the dissolution of boundaries in media and communication, the individualisation of lifestyles, and increased mobility in a globalised world have led to more diversity in all areas of society. This has been accompanied by fundamental changes in social structures that have privileged market-based approaches and reduced government provision of social services, leading to growing inequality both within and between countries. At the same time, increased diversity has often been – mostly unfairly – blamed for contributing to greater social inequality. Indeed, though we will not expand on this further, research shows that diversity can bread greater creativity, understanding, and innovation (Doherty *et al.*, 2010; Roberge and van Dick, 2010). Thus, managing diversifying societies and fostering greater equality have become two irrevocably related concepts.

Notions of diversity include both internal and external aspects such as gender identity and sexual orientation, social origin, education, socio-economic background, ethnicity, religious affiliation, and physical or intellectual disabilities. These distinctions are supplemented by a variety of attitudes and value orientations. Such a comprehensive understanding, as well as the intersectionality of the different aspects, are essential characteristics of diversity in contemporary societies.

Regarding sport and physical activity, research focuses on existing mechanisms of differentiation, exclusion, and inclusion. It aims to reveal the essential underlying processes such as the deconstruction of stereotypes, removal of deficit and power attributions. Spaaij, Magee, and Jeanes (2014) plead that sport is embedded in gender, racial, and national hierarchies and is neither "a level-playing field" nor "a site for social mobility" (p. 400). Instead, they argue that "sport reflects and reinforces broader hierarchical structures; sport is a site for both inclusion and exclusion, but the way this works is uneven, and sport is ultimately a site for social reproduction of hierarchy and social stratification" (p. 407). Thus, the dominance of Whiteness, wealth, heteronormativity, and masculinity at all levels of sport

DOI: 10.4324/9781003002666-20

must be part of any reflection on diversity and inequality in sport. Keeping this and the inherently intersectional nature of diversity in mind, we wish to reflect on three crucial issues:

- How does inequality manifest itself within sport and physical activity?
- How can sport be (re)oriented to combat social inequality?
- How can sport educational settings tackle these challenges?

Before we proceed, however, an important distinction is necessary between the term equality and equity, which are often used interchangeably. In this chapter, we mainly refer to the term equality, which means we focus on socially valued goods and resources, including education, equal chances, or opportunities. Equity, on the other hand, strives for fairness and consideration of individuals' different needs to enable life choices and achieve equality in the end.

## Inequality and power structures in a global context

The relation between diversity and inequality can most readily be seen through the emergence of power structures, which relate to routines of behaviour, language as well as thinking, and provide information about placement in the hierarchical structure of a society. The corresponding logic here is simple: to clarify the dominant relationships among a group of people, individuals subordinate to a largely invisible logic. Man or woman, young or old, native or immigrant, these differences are organised hierarchically, and some affiliations are privileged over others – especially the affiliation to the "we" over the "others". Homogenisation and stigmatised ascriptions can result in emphasising otherness instead of dismissing differences to the so-called norm.

While the sociopolitical discourse at a societal level is primarily concerned with central questions of how to consider diversified life backgrounds (access to opportunities, discrimination, gender mainstreaming), the international and development policy perspective opens up further dimensions. Here, the diversity of social and economic living conditions of people in different countries and the simultaneous transnational interdependence of societies are relevant.

Globally, societies have done an uneven job of managing diversity and ensuring equal opportunities for all. According to the 2019 United Nations (UN) Human Development Report, income inequality within countries as well as between countries are currently at some of their highest levels since measurement began (Conceição, 2019). In turn, higher inequality generally correlates with higher crime rates, higher mortality rates, poorer health, lower social mobility, lower social trust, and lower political involvement. Thus, reducing global inequality is an important – if not the most important – global goal of the present.

The United Nations' Agenda 2030 for Sustainable Development, which was adopted by 189 UN member states in September 2015, explicitly addresses this goal. Seventeen Sustainable Development Goals (SDGs) and 169 sub-objectives form the core of the Agenda. The SDGs take all three dimensions of sustainability (social, environmental, and economic) equally into account. Specifically, SDG ten aims to reduce "inequality in and among countries" and calls on states to take measures that will enhance the empowerment of "all people regardless of age, gender, disability, race, ethnicity, origin, religion or economic or other status" (United Nations General Assembly, 2015). Even though the UN Agenda 2030 explicitly claims to "leave no one behind", not all aspects of diversity are equally considered. Compromises were made, for example, in SDG five regarding gender equality, where the wording focuses on "girls and women" and formally excludes other gender issues such as sexual orientation or gender identity.

## (In)equality in sport and physical activity

Sport and its associated institutions frequently position themselves as beacons of diversity, tolerance, and equality. Indeed, the "spirit of sport" is often associated with values of fair-play, solidarity, and equality. For instance, the Olympic Charter defines the practice of sport as a human right. Access to sport is advocated "without discrimination of any kind, such as race, colour, sex, sexual orientation, language, religion, political or other opinion, national or social origin, property, birth or other status" (International Olympic Committee, 2020, Art. 6). Similar commitments are found in the FIFA Statutes or various other national sports documents.

Yet the intrinsic logic of (elite) sport and the sociocultural baggage associated with many kinds of sport are at odds with these stated values. Sport is linked to competition and performance, thus promoting a selective and exclusionary approach. Objectively fair categories, equal opportunities, and a level playing field remain a myth. As long as human beings compete against human beings, differences between top athletes of the same category in terms of body sizes, cardiac volume, financial means, or testosterone level will always exist. At the same time, a certain degree of inequality constitutes the magic of sport where an apparent "underdog" may potentially defeat an established top adversary.

Many kinds of sport also carry a history of colonialism, discrimination, and inequality. Sport such as cricket or rugby were used to promote colonialist values and attitudes. This heritage persists today, with many kinds of sport and their structures still embodying the discriminatory and colonialist tendencies of their past.

These forces lead to various forms of inequality and injustice within sport and physical activity. To understand how inequality manifests itself, an intersectional approach is necessary to recognise multiple and reinforcing strands of discrimination or favouritism. Several kinds of social stratification do not exist separately but are interwoven. Possible solutions must consider the social, political, economic, and legal environment that may contribute to discrimination and inequality.

## Sport and manifestations of (in)equality: Through the lens of gender

As made clear by the SDGs, development and greater equality will only be sustainable if everybody, regardless of sex or gender, equally benefits. But, for the moment, gender inequality remains a persistent global challenge. Female and male interactions, public infrastructure, political systems, and the labour market are deeply rooted in perceptions of binary gender roles. The global nature of gender issues also provides a useful frame to discuss examples of how inequality manifests itself in sport and physical activity. Ignoring the perspective of gender can lead to blind spots and non-consideration of crucial issues in society (Leach, 2016). A focus on gender realities does not mean concentrating on women and girls only. It involves a holistic perspective of all humans living and interacting in specific sociocultural contexts.

Thus, the following presents a selection of examples of (in)equality in sport. Even though gender is emphasised, the complexity of diversity with its multiple layers and intersectionality is brought to the fore, providing clear examples of how different aspects of diversity intersect with inequality.

### *Socio-economic barriers and physical integrity*

The socio-economic status and availability of leisure time are causally linked to sport and physical activity. When everyday survival is the order of the day, few are thinking of recreational pursuits. In terms of gender, the unequal division of labour and care responsibilities are significant barriers for many women and girls getting involved in sports programmes. Age and marital status are two additional inhibiting or enabling factors of female sports involvement. In some rather conservative, rural settings, elderly and married women exercise in the dark at night because they feel embarrassed being active and visible during the daytime.

Poverty also influences access to sports equipment and infrastructure, thus entailing safety issues. Inadequate sports facilities or defective material may cause injuries and hinder sports participation. As a result, parents who may not have access to medical care or supplies might be less willing to allow their children to participate in sport. Moreover, in some sociocultural contexts, injuries and especially scars on a female body may reduce the dowry, acting as an additional barrier to female sports participation (Meier, 2005).

### *Sport and physical activity offers*

Sport and physical activity offers must be carefully assessed and matched to the needs and sociocultural settings, traditions, and cultural values of the beneficiaries. Sport like cricket or wrestling may mainly address people from a specific ethnic background and/or social status, thus excluding others. There is still a strong focus on conventional ball games such as football, volleyball, netball, handball, and basketball, played according to defined rules on specific pitches. Due to limited infrastructure and lacking equipment in many settings, more informal sport such as fitness, dancing, or traditional games could increase the range of participation. However, many traditional or indigenous practices derive from male-dominated hunting or war scenes. Such patterns might be counterproductive by consolidating existing hierarchies and gender roles. Since movement concepts – in contrast to "classical" sport – are not as gender-stereotyped, they can be set up in a strongly inclusive manner. On the other hand, picking and consciously promoting conventional sport can also contribute to challenging sociocultural norms by increased and ongoing public visibility, e.g., of athletic women (Meier, 2005). If a public pitch in a rather traditional area is allocated, for instance, to a girls' football tournament for an entire weekend, a strong message of "normality" is delivered to the community. Risks related to such challenges and their consequences need a careful assessment and monitoring. Accompanying measures such as security guards, bus services, or fences need to be considered in certain settings to keep, e.g., female footballers safe from harm and harassment on and off the pitch. By either deliberately avoiding or safely promoting gender-stereotyped sport, all these activities require specific local knowledge, pedagogical skills, and advocacy work and must employ a "do-no-harm" approach. For example, some religions do not allow mixed-sex interaction or bodily contact in public spheres. Thus, providing equal access to sports activities may require thoughtful dialogue and compromises on issues such as physical contact, type of sport, or (gendered) team composition (Meier, 2005).

### Role models and sociocultural stereotypes

There is a historical link between sport and masculinity, and sports heroes are still often defined by traits such as bravery or muscular strength (Hargreaves, 2000). These associations contrast with stereotypical ideals of femininity. This creates an absence of – or lack of visibility for – sports role models (SRMs) for individuals, especially sportswomen, who do not meet these stereotypical conceptualisations (Vescio, Wilde and Crosswhite, 2005; Meier, 2015). Lesbian or gay, transgender or intersex athletes, for example, disturb elite-level sport, which still displays heteronormative values and norms of masculinity. Usually, such individuals are neglected as potential SRMs. And, when they do achieve role model status, it is often under the condition that they mask these so-called deviant aspects. Lacking diversity among SRMs inhibits the development of grassroots sport for the ignored groups. It reinforces notions that investments in these groups, and especially women, will not pay off. For males, on the other hand, famous SRMs, such as international footballers, help justify significant investments in infrastructure to push both grassroots and elite sport.

## Empowerment and capacity building through sport

Empowerment refers to the diverse processes for strengthening individuals, but at the same time, it focuses on organisational and decision-making processes in institutions. It should be based on a resource-oriented approach that focuses on existing capacities rather than deficits and is perceived both as a process and a result (United Nations Development Fund for Women, 2010). Strongly associated with empowerment is the process of capacity development, which encompasses the ability of people, organisations, and societies to ensure the development of capacities at the micro, meso, and macro level. At the individual, micro level, sport and physical activity serve as a medium for the promotion of individual learning and development processes, while at the meso and macro levels, actors at the local, regional, and national level are considered in terms of capacity building for equal participation and the long-term reduction of inequalities.

Despite the acknowledgement of sport as a promising catalyst, empowerment or development do not happen automatically or by coincidence. Social change rests upon pedagogical reasoning, which involves intentional teaching and transfer of skills or values from sports activities into non-sports settings (Gould and Carson, 2008). Thus, quality relationships and the influence of coaches, teachers, peers, adult leaders must be emphasised as "transmission mechanisms" (Petitpas *et al.*, 2005; Meier, 2013). More precisely, there is extensive literature indicating that sport can combat inequality by promoting intercultural life skills and dialogue.

Defined as "skills that enable individuals to succeed in the different environments in which they live" (Danish *et al.*, 2004, p. 40), life skills are an often amorphous and vague term. Life skills can include a wide range of emotional, cognitive, and social skills (Lerner *et al.*, 2005; Turnnidge, Côté and Hancock, 2014). Here, emotional skills relate to one's sense of well-being and self-worth. Cognitive skills pertain to abilities such as self-regulation and decision-making. Finally, social skills include communication skills, conflict resolution, and prosocial behaviour (Lerner *et al.*,2005 ). Overall, such skills have been shown to enhance well-being, academic performance, and job satisfaction (Zins, Weissberg and Wang, 2004; Ridder *et al.*, 2012) and, therefore, reduce many of the (individual) drivers of inequality.

Sport is seen as an ideal setting for the promotion of these skills. Positive experiences within sport can lead to improved self-esteem, and the high levels of feedback in sports settings can contribute to better self-regulation or communication abilities (Jonker, Elferink-Gemser and Visscher, 2011). To foster the development of life skills, the role of the physical education teacher or coach (i.e., a sport educator) is critical. The development of life skills must be consciously integrated into programmes, and sport educators need to create a "mastery-oriented" environment where the focus is placed on self-improvement, as opposed to competition and winning (Holt and Neely, 2011). Furthermore, sport educators need to ensure that participants reflect on how the skills developed in the sports environment can be transferred elsewhere and be given opportunities to practice those skills in different situations (Bean *et al.*, 2018).

Another line of research suggests that sport can directly influence intercultural skills and relationships, thereby working against many of the social divisions that exacerbate inequality. First and foremost, there is a rich literature concerning Allport's Contact Theory which indicates that cross-cultural contact can be beneficial (Pettigrew *et al.*, 2011). Thus, numerous sports programmes explicitly promote mixed group activities. However, contact alone is not enough to generate intercultural skills (Perry and Southwell, 2011). Sport is an inherently practical, communicative, and social activity. As such, it is considered a valuable venue for the development of intercultural skills (Puente-Maxera, Méndez-Giménez and Martínez de Ojeda, 2020). Generally, sport educators use modified sports games that are adapted to their educational context in order to generate novel experiences and promote reflection (e.g., Grimminger, 2011; Puente-Maxera *et al.*, 2020). Gieß-Stüber (2010) proposes that four mechanisms – strangeness, team challenges, belonging, and reflection – need to be integrated to foster intercultural learning. In this model, integrating strangeness refers to using new games or activities that allow for commonalities and differences to be made visible. Team tasks, meanwhile, refer to novel, collaborative challenges that enable communication and conflict management skills to be developed. Collaborative tasks and games also allow a greater sense of belonging to develop among participants. Finally, reflection permits students or athletes to connect the new games and tasks with issues and realities in their communities (Gieß-Stüber, 2010).

## Risks and challenges in empowerment through sport

Though sport holds much promise as a tool in the fight for greater equality, if programmes or educators are not careful, interventions can instead reinforce the very structures that foster inequality. The focus on individual skill-building can strengthen existing, neoliberal power structures and notions of so-called personal responsibility. By focusing so much attention on personal empowerment or capacity building, the root causes of inequality are dismissed at the expense of the individuals suffering from that inequality. As Hartmann and Kwauk (2011) argue, it is "sport's ability to resocialise and recalibrate individual youth and young people that, in turn, serves to maintain power and hierarchy, cultural hegemony, and the institutionalisation of poverty and privilege" (p. 292). In other words, sport brings a certain baggage of values and norms that often serve to reinforce current structures of power and privilege. To counteract this, sports interventions should at once question current societal structures while also giving participants the tools to succeed within society as it is currently constructed. In other words, sport educators should "provide an educational program alongside and in the sport program that actively seeks to engage participants in a mutual process of grappling with power, inequality, and identity" (Hartmann and Kwauk, 2011, p. 297). Yet, even well-intentioned and designed activities can have negative consequences. For instance, in her study, Grimminger (2011) found that an intercultural physical education initiative led to less inclusive attitudes among students.

## Building sport educator capacities

To avoid such unintended consequences, educational programmes must build the capacity of future physical education teachers and coaches to respond to these challenges. To achieve this, a crucial attitudinal shift is first required. Within education programmes, there often is a singular focus on the technical aspects of sport, and little time is spent on ethical concerns, life skills development, or social issues (Cope *et al.*, 2017). In turn, this creates an attitude whereby many sport educators believe that the "power of sport" alone is sufficient or that such developmental goals are outside of their responsibilities. To the contrary, it is our view that sport educators must be trained to seize the opportunities presented by their profession. Indeed, the popularity and inherently social nature of sport put sport educators in a unique position to attract diverse groups and combat many of the drivers of inequality. Sport educators must be given an understanding of broader societal structures, learn the skills to address relevant social issues, and be given the tools to foster intercultural, as well as personal, skill development within their sports sessions. However, research shows that many sport educators lack the competences and sport-related know-how to foster intercultural education (University of Southern Denmark, 2018; Thorjussen and Sisjord, 2020).

Referring to the already mentioned value of role models, every sport educator needs to be aware that participants constantly observe his or her behaviour. Aspects such as verbal and non-verbal language, perceptions of participants, open-mindedness, or didactical approaches are all absorbed by participants. It is crucial that sport educators "walk the talk" on values and attitudes to be credible and trustworthy. Moreover, participants will not only observe and potentially emulate their behaviour during the sports programme, but also in non-sports environments (Meier, 2013).

Even with improved sport educator training, sport managers do not always know how to integrate social components such as life skills or intercultural education into their organisational policies or programmes. Many sport management programmes focus extensively on the administrative or economic aspects of the field. They spend comparatively little time presenting how social components can be effectively integrated within organisations or programming. Changing this is key. Sport managers must create environments that facilitate empowerment and challenge inequalities. Otherwise, the contributions of the best-trained sport educators will be significantly negated.

## Future directions: Diversifying sport education

Beyond improving sport education programmes, the range of people trained in those programmes must be broadened. Currently, sport educators remain a mostly white, heterosexual, male-dominated group. For instance, research on European sports clubs shows that individuals born in a foreign country represent only four to six percent of their workforce (Steinbach and Elmose-Østerlund, 2017). Yet numerous countries, including Austria, Belgium, Germany, Sweden, and Switzerland, have more than 15% foreign-born population (Department of Economic and Social Affairs Population Division, 2019). More diversity is sorely needed to challenge inequality within sport and to enhance the personal and intercultural benefits accrued to participants. Furthermore, an understanding of diversity should take a broad view and encompass a wide range of internal and external traits, including, but not limited to, gender identity, ethnicity, religion, education, social background, and sexual orientation.

Studies suggest that diverse role models, such as sport educators, can allow individuals to observe successful people of similar backgrounds and "provide a significant key for encouraging behavioural change" (Payne *et al.*, 2003). Feeling welcomed and understood within a sports environment is an essential driver of sports participation, and the presence of individuals from similar backgrounds can support these positive feelings (Block and Gibbs, 2017). Hiring diverse, qualified individuals from different backgrounds can widen the sense of "normalcy" and generate new ideas or insights (Doherty *et al.*, 2010), hence benefiting sports organisations as well. Though we cannot provide a one-size-fits-all solution, policies and programmes need to be developed and implemented to help counteract this underrepresentation. Given the unique contexts of different countries and the myriad of factors influencing the levels of diversity in sport, it is vital to ensure that policies and programmes are evidence-based and relevant and genuinely address the national or regional issues and the needs of defined target groups. For instance, approaches such as mentoring programmes, tailored training programmes, scholarships, stipends, requirements to interview diverse candidates for open positions, or even quotas could be potential solutions. No matter the exact solution, it is past time for sport educators to reflect the increasingly diverse communities they serve.

## Conclusion

It is not sufficient to look at single aspects such as gender, ethnicity, or religion in isolation. Other factors, such as socio-economic status, sexual orientation, place of residence, or marital status must be considered holistically and in the light of how they interact with other traits. More research is necessary to disentangle the resulting complexity. Anybody, regardless of age, disability, talent, or background should have the opportunity to acquire skills or competencies through sport, including:

- Emotional skills such as self-esteem
- Social skills such as leadership, communication, or teamwork
- Cognitive skills such as concentration or decision-making
- Physical competencies such as bodily awareness and coordination

In other words, the consequences of inequality in sport lead to further inequality in benefits related to health and well-being. Moreover, the ability to build social networks and social capital as well as career pathways is limited by a lack of equal access.

The future role of education in the sport sector is crucial to overcome societal inequalities. It is not enough that curriculum designers and those responsible for the development of various educational programmes in sport acknowledge the importance of equality and diversity. It is imperative to increase the sensitivity, and skills, of sport educators regarding issues of social (in)equality, thus enabling them to challenge existing social hierarchies in educational formal and non-formal settings. Furthermore, it is of utmost importance to ensure greater diversity and, therefore, demographic representation among sport educators at all levels. Consequently, diversity must become a selection factor in all the recruitment processes of sport education programmes, and it should feed into the development of an explicit code of conducts, including monitoring and reporting mechanisms. More than anything, we need to encourage a mindset that heterogeneity and diversity, instead of being undue burdens, are an added value to society.

## References

Bean, C. *et al.* (2018) 'The implicit/explicit continuum of life skills development and transfer', *Quest*, 70(4), pp. 456–470. doi: 10.1080/00336297.2018.1451348.

Block, K. and Gibbs, L. (2017) 'Promoting social inclusion through sport for refugee-background youth in Australia: Analysing different participation models', *Social Inclusion*, 5(2), pp. 91–100. doi:10.17645/si.v5i2.903.

Conceição, P. (2019) *Human development report 2019: Beyond income, beyond averages, beyond today: Inequalities in human development in the 21st century.* New York, NY: United Nations Development Programme.

Cope, E. *et al.* (2017) 'Football, sport and the development of young people's life skills', *Sport in Society*, 20(7), pp. 789–801. doi: 10.1080/17430437.2016.1207771.

Danish, S. *et al.* (2004) 'Enhancing youth development through sport', *World Leisure Journal*, 46(3), pp. 38–49. doi: 10.1080/04419057.2004.9674365.

Department of Economic and Social Affairs Population Division (2019) *International Migrant Stock 2019.*

Doherty, A. *et al.* (2010) 'Understanding a culture of diversity through frameworks of power and change', *Sport Management Review*, 13(4), pp. 368–381. doi: 10.1016/j.smr.2010.01.006.

Gieß-Stüber (2010) 'Development of intercultural skills through sport and physical education in Europe', in Gasparini, W. and Cometti A. (eds.) *Sports policy and practice series. Sport facing the test of cultural diversity: Integration and intercultural dialogue in Europe: Analysis and practical example.* Strasbourg: Council of Europe Publ., pp. 23–30.

Gould, D. and Carson, S. (2008) 'Life skills development through sport: Current status and future directions', *International Review of Sport and Exercise Psychology*, 1(1), pp. 58–78. doi: 10.1080/17509840701834573.

Grimminger, E. (2011) 'Intercultural competence among sports and PE teachers. Theoretical foundations and empirical verification', *European Journal of Teacher Education*, 34(3), pp. 317–337. doi: 10.1080/02619768.2010.546834.

Hargreaves, J. (2000) *Heroines of sport: The politics of difference and identity/Jennifer Hargreaves.* London, New York, NY: Routledge.

Hartmann, D. and Kwauk, C. (2011) 'Sport and development: An overview, critique, and reconstruction', *Journal of Sport and Social Issues*, 35(3), pp. 284–305. doi: 10.1177/0193723511416986.

Holt, N. L. and Neely, K. C. (2011) 'Positive youth development through sport: A review', *Revista Iberoamericana De Psicología Del Ejercicio Y El Deporte*, 6(2), pp. 299–316.

International Olympic Committee (2020) *Olympic charter*. Lausanne.

Jonker, L., Elferink-Gemser, M. T. and Visscher, C. (2011) 'The role of self-regulatory skills in sport and academic performances of elite youth athletes', *Talent Development and Excellence*, 3.

Leach, M. (ed.) (2016) *Pathways to sustainability series. Gender equality and sustainable development*. Abingdon: Routledge.

Lerner, R. M. *et al.* (2005) 'Positive youth development, participation in community youth development programs, and community contributions of fifth-grade adolescents', *The Journal of Early Adolescence*, 25(1), pp. 17–71. doi: 10.1177/0272431604272461.

Meier, M. (2005) *Gender Equity, Sport and Development: Working Paper*. Biel/Bienne: Swiss Academy for Development. Available at: https://www.sportanddev.org/sites/default/files/downloads/59__gender_equity__sport_and_development.pdf (Accessed: 6 May 2021).

Meier, M. (2013) *"Sporting role models" as potential catalysts to facilitate empowerment and tackle gender issues: An empirical study in Malawi, Zambia and South Africa*. München: Universitätsbibliothek der TU München.

Meier, M. (2015) 'The value of female sporting role models', *Sport in Society*, 18(8), pp. 968–982. doi: 10.1080/17430437.2014.997581.

Payne, W. *et al.* (2003) *Sports role models and their impact on participation in physical activity: A literature review*. Ballarat.

Perry, L. B. and Southwell, L. (2011) 'Developing intercultural understanding and skills: Models and approaches', *Intercultural Education*, 22(6), pp. 453–466. doi: 10.1080/14675986.2011.644948.

Petitpas, A. J. et al (2005) 'A framework for planning youth sport programs that foster psychosocial Development', *The Sport Psychologist*, 19(1), pp. 63–80. doi: 10.1123/tsp.19.1.63.

Pettigrew, T. F. *et al.* (2011) 'Recent advances in intergroup contact theory', *International Journal of Intercultural Relations*, 35(3), pp. 271–280. doi: 10.1016/j.ijintrel.2011.03.001.

Puente-Maxera, F., Méndez-Giménez, A. and Martínez de Ojeda, D. (2020) 'Games from around the world: Promoting intercultural competence through sport education in secondary school students', *International Journal of Intercultural Relations*, 75, pp. 23–33. doi: 10.1016/j.ijintrel.2020.01.001.

Ridder, D. T. D. *et al.* (2012) 'Taking stock of self-control: A meta-analysis of how trait self-control relates to a wide range of behaviors', *Personality and Social Psychology Review: An Official Journal of the Society for Personality and Social Psychology, Inc*, 16(1), pp. 76–99. doi: 10.1177/1088868311418749.

Roberge, M.-É and van Dick, R. (2010) 'Recognising the benefits of diversity: When and how does diversity increase group performance?', *Human Resource Management Review*, 20(4), pp. 295–308. doi: 10.1016/j.hrmr.2009.09.002.

Spaaij, R., Magee, J. and Jeanes, R. (eds.) (2014) *Sport studies/Sociology. Sport and social exclusion in global society*. London: Routledge.

Steinbach, D. and Elmose-Østerlund, K. (2017) *Volunteers in sports clubs in Europe – Key demographics and characteristics*. Odense.

Thorjussen, I. M. and Sisjord, M. K. (2020) 'Inclusion and exclusion in multi-ethnic physical education: An intersectional perspective', *Curriculum Studies in Health and Physical Education*, 11(1), pp. 50–66. doi: 10.1080/25742981.2019.1648187.

Turnnidge, J., Côté, J. and Hancock, D. J. (2014) 'Positive youth development from sport to life: Explicit or implicit transfer?', *Quest*, 66(2), pp. 203–217. doi: 10.1080/00336297.2013.867275.

United Nations Development Fund for Women (2010) *Women's empowerment principles. Equality means business*. New York, NY: UNIFEM.

United Nations General Assembly (2015) *70/1. Transforming our world: The 2030 agenda for sustainable development (No. A/RES/70/1)*. New York, NY.

University of Southern Denmark (2018) *Needs analysis report – intercultural education through physical activity, coaching, and training (EDU-PACT)*. Odense.

Vescio, J., Wilde, K. and Crosswhite, J. J. (2005) *Profiling sport role models to enhance initiatives for adolescent girls in physical education and sport* (Vol. 11): Thousand Oaks, CA: Sage Publications Ltd. doi: 10.1177/1356336X05052894.

Zins, J. E., Weissberg, R. P. and Wang, M. C. (2004) *Building academic success on social and emotional learning: What does the research say? The series on social emotional learning*. New York, NY: Teachers College Press. Available at: https://ebookcentral.proquest.com/lib/gbv/detail.action?docID=4873351 (Accessed: 3 April 2021).

# Chapter 16

# Human rights in sport education

*Daniela Heerdt and William Rook*

## Introduction

Human rights are part of the DNA of modern sport – from civil rights activism by leading athletes in the 1960s, the sports boycott of apartheid South Africa, to the ongoing struggles by women athletes for equal treatment. It is increasingly recognised that there are structural issues within sport itself. The connection of sport as a business to supply chains and a vast array of stakeholders (public and private) that have the potential to lead to human rights violations is another acknowledged issue. At the same time, sport provides opportunities and may, by its very nature, be considered a vehicle for promoting human rights, for instance through its values of fair play and integrity, or development through sport.

In the past decade, the human rights discourse has infiltrated the world of sport in a way that is structured through and connected with international norms and standards. This global development arguably has two origins. First, it can be seen as reflection of a recent trend among stakeholders such as athletes, sponsors, and civil society organisations raising awareness on the importance of human rights to sport and to sports governing bodies (SGBs). Second, it is rooted in the applicability of international human rights standards to sports bodies and sporting event organisers through widespread acceptance of the United Nations (UN) Guiding Principles on Business and Human Rights (UNGPs) (Amis, 2017, pp. 138–139).

An important means of contributing to the sustainability of these developments is to integrate human rights into sport-related education at all levels so that young professionals and those interested in the world of sport can continue and consolidate this trend. The first two sections of this chapter expand on the premise that sport has a unique power to promote human rights and provide a brief overview of the development of the human rights discourse within sport. The third section presents recent examples of SGBs and other relevant stakeholders taking steps to embed human rights into their activities and reflects on how this current trend has been picked up in sport education and research. The fourth section offers several recommendations for education providers in the world of sport on how to integrate human rights into their learning experience.

DOI: 10.4324/9781003002666-21

## The unique power of sport to promote human rights

Sport and physical activity play an important role in bringing people together around common values of teamwork, excellence, respect, tolerance, and friendship. Sports bodies promote these values and help to create an environment underpinned by respect and cooperation, which strengthens the promotion of and respect for human rights.

Sport relies on a rules-based system, fair play, and the courage, cohesion, support, and goodwill of society in all its facets, including athletes, fans, workers, volunteers, and local communities, as well as governments, businesses large and small, the media, and sports bodies (Amis, 2017). The foundational principles of the world's preeminent sports bodies speak to universal humanitarian values, harmony among nations, solidarity, the preservation of human dignity, and commitment to non-discrimination. These values have much in common with international human rights principles and standards. Moreover, participation in sport and physical activity is a recognised right to which people are entitled,[1] and the Olympic Charter also sets out that the "practice of sport is a human right".[2]

In fact, many of the activities that sports bodies undertake and which happen within sport relate to human rights. Core issues like promoting safeguarding and occupational safety and health of athletes are clearly human rights issues. There are many other examples – the right to freedom from discrimination should be the basis for sport policies countering racism and homophobia; the right to equal pay for equal work is highly relevant to ongoing efforts to equalise prize money for male and female athletes; and the right to freedom from cruel, inhuman, or degrading treatment can be relevant to extreme training practices that may expose athletes to physical, emotional, or sexual abuse.[3] Furthermore, it has been recognised that sport can facilitate, enable, and, in many ways, achieve a number of other internationally recognised human rights, such as the right to education (Donnelly, 2008, pp. 386–389; United Nations General Assembly, 2014; Lemmon, 2019).[4]

Other important topics for sport, such as anti-corruption and sports integrity, are also critical to the enjoyment of human rights by participants and stakeholders. For example, corrupt practices by states and companies can undermine their duties and responsibilities to uphold human rights, with cronyism and conflicts of interest providing cover for human rights abuses to take place (Mega-Sporting Events Platform for Human Rights, 2017). This is equally true for day-to-day sport and the sporting event business. It is important therefore that efforts to fight corruption and promote integrity in sport are not siloed from a broader human rights agenda.

## The development of the sport and human rights discourse

The roots of the sport and human rights discourse run deep and have a long history of intersections with the civil rights movement, with gender discrimination, racism, athlete abuse, and exploitation in supply chains. Mega-sporting events

(MSEs) such as the Fédération Internationale de Football Association (FIFA) World Cup and the Olympic and Paralympic Games have also had human rights dimensions from the outset, and the idea of "sportswashing", improving a country's image through sport, is not a new one (Worden, 2008, 2014; Boykoff, 2019; Keys, 2019b). The labour movement and trade unions played a vital role in the development of modern sport, especially regarding the rights of athletes as workers, and in using the spotlight of MSEs to draw attention to human rights and labour rights issues, particularly in host countries of events.

It is no coincidence that there is increasing focus on sports governance and sport and human rights. In addition to the reasons outlined above, another one is that developments that started outside of sport gradually become relevant for the sports world, in particular the business and human rights movement and the discussions around human rights duties of non-state actors, which have progressed significantly in the past 20 years (Muchlinski, 2007; Deva, 2015; Bernaz, 2016; Deva and Birchall, 2020, p. Part I). While that body of work initially focused on companies as non-state actors, it is now clear that the same frameworks can apply to sports bodies as non-state actors, especially so when they are acting as economic actors. That the business and rights discourse has accelerated and developed important frameworks during a period when the connection between sport and human rights has been increasingly visible has allowed new expectations of sports bodies to be explored, and a roadmap for sport to integrate human rights to be articulated.

According to Keys, "the real watershed moment for human rights and sport mega-events" was Human Rights Watch's campaign against Beijing's bid to host the 2000 Games, which focused on the issue of discrimination in form of political repression, detention, and abuse of dissidents (Keys, 2019a, p. 116). By the time the 2000 Games were about to start, investigating human rights impacts of MSEs had become an integral part of the work of not only Human Rights Watch (HRW) but also other international human rights organisations, such as Amnesty International. Furthermore, the focus widened beyond the scope of Olympic and Paralympic Games to include other major international and regional sporting events like the FIFA World Cup (Keys, 2019a, p. 124).

In the aftermath of the London 2012 Olympic and Paralympic Games, a joint communiqué was issued on "Human Rights and the Olympic and Paralympic Games" by the governments of the United Kingdom, Russia, Korea, and Brazil.[5] After major concerns associated with the Beijing 2008 Games, London hosted the first Summer Olympics embedding sustainability from the outset and placing an emphasis on leaving a positive legacy for the city, sport in the United Kingdom, and for the wider Olympic movement. London's Organising Committee of the Olympic Games (LOCOG) also paved new ground with a Sustainable Sourcing Code that was reinforced by a grievance mechanism (London's Organising Committee of the Olympic Games [LOCOG], 2012), and the subsequent Glasgow 2014 Commonwealth Games became the first MSE to put in place a dedicated human rights policy.

The next big step was taken in June 2014, when author of the UNGPs John Ruggie and former UN High Commissioner for Human Rights Mary Robinson wrote a letter to FIFA recommending FIFA make an explicit commitment to respect human rights and establish a strategy for integrating a human rights approach based on the UNGPs. This proved to be the starting point for a multi-stakeholder effort on sport and human rights coordinated by the Institute for Human Rights and Business (IHRB),[6] and FIFA's own work on human rights, including its appointment of Ruggie to author a comprehensive set of recommendations in 2016 (Ruggie, 2016). These initiatives have since created a basis for work over the last five years to implement and operationalise human rights commitments by a number of sports bodies and event hosts, on the international as well as national level.

While these developments have focused on sports bodies, governments have also sought to align sport and human rights through several intergovernmental processes. The UN Human Rights Council (HRC) has adopted several resolutions on the issue of "Promoting human rights through sport and the Olympic ideal" in the past decade (Human Rights Council [HRC], 2016). In its Concluding Observations on the periodic reporting of Brazil under the UN Convention on the Rights of the Child in 2015, the Committee on the Rights of the Child addressed several of the potential human and children's rights risks related to the upcoming Olympic and Paralympic Games, such as police violence, sexual exploitation and abuse, forced eviction, the right to participation, and arbitrary arrests (Committee on the Rights of the Child, 2015). In July 2017, at the UN Educational, Scientific and Cultural Organization (UNESCO)'s Sixth International Conference of Ministers and Senior Officials Responsible for Physical Education and Sport, the Kazan Action Plan was adopted, which deals with sport and human rights more generally, but also explicitly mentions sporting events (UNESCO – 6th International Conference of Ministers and Senior Officials Responsible for Physical Education and Sport, 2017). The most recent development at the UN level is a report prepared by the UN High Commissioner for Human Rights and submitted pursuant to HRC resolution 40/5 on the elimination of discrimination against women and girls in sport (United Nations High Commissioner for Human Rights, 2020). Finally, in October 2020, Commonwealth member countries have unanimously adopted a statement to promote human rights in and through sport (Commonwealth Sports Ministers, 2020).

## Embedding human rights into the world of sport and sport education – Recent examples

The brief overview reveals that many of the foundations for the current sport and human rights movement were laid in 2016, with both FIFA's attention to human rights and the development of a multi-stakeholder cooperation coordinated through the Mega-Sporting Events Platform for Human Rights. Since then, several sports bodies and organising entities of MSEs have begun to embed human rights into their activities and policies. Organisations like FIFA, the International Olympic Committee (IOC), and Commonwealth Sport, in addition to other regional or national sports bodies (Deutscher Fussball-Bund, 2019), adopted human rights policies or adapted their bidding or hosting regulations to incorporate human rights provisions. Following the publication of Ruggie's recommendations to FIFA in 2016, the organisation added a commitment to human rights to its Statutes (Fédération Internationale de Football Association [FIFA], 2016, Article 3). In the years that followed, FIFA created a human rights advisory board, adopted a human rights policy, and reformed its bidding processes to include human rights standards.

More recently, since the 2018 Gold Coast Commonwealth Games, Commonwealth Sport started the process of embedding human rights into its governance structures. Human rights were made part of the strategic plan of the organisation and integrated into host city contracts for 2021 and beyond (Commonwealth Sport, 2018, p. 8). Commonwealth Sport also committed to developing a human rights strategy and implementation plan (Commonwealth Sport, 2018, p. 27). In a further major development, in late 2020 the IOC released an independent expert report that is going to inform its human rights strategy (Al Hussein and Davis, 2020).

All these changes come with explicit reference to international policy documents and instruments related to human rights, such as the International Bill of Human Rights,[7] the UNGPs, or the Organisation for Economic Co-operation and Development (OECD) Guidelines for Multinational Enterprises. Such reference is also made in the human rights provisions that the IOC added to the candidature processes and Host City Contracts for the 2024, 2026, and 2028 Olympic Games. These changes came before the IOC's decision to develop a human rights policy and amend the Olympic Charter (International Olympic Committee, 2020).

Another area where the link to human rights is already present is the sport for development and peace (SDP) agenda. Existing research in the field ranges from straightforward philanthropic supports for charitable activities to programmes claiming more concrete outcomes in terms of either developmental impact or good governance (Giulianotti, 2004, p. 355). However, work clearly needs to be done to align the SDP agenda with the sport and human rights movement – in particular to ensure that SDP initiatives consider their human rights impacts and embed safeguarding, accountability, and remedy in SDP programmes (Institute for Human Rights and Business, 2018).

The various agendas and processes outlined above gave momentum to the growing movement, resulting in a wave of new frameworks and policies, and concrete examples of sport promoting human rights. Perhaps the most high profile case has been the progress on labour rights seen in Qatar as a result of concerted advocacy and campaigning for the rights of migrant workers (HRW, 2020). The Supreme Committee (SC), responsible for developing the stadia and infrastructure for the 2022 FIFA World Cup, became the first MSE organising entity to publicly accept its responsibilities in line with the UNGPs. By adopting Worker's

Welfare Standards and independent performance checks against these standards, and by instigating joint health and safety inspections with Building and Woodworkers International, the global trade union of construction workers, the SC triggered several groundbreaking developments for the region. In fact, the focus on the World Cup in Qatar has led to substantive reforms of the country's labour laws, which effectively dismantled the "kafala" system and provide more protection to migrant workers (International Labour Organisation [ILO], 2020).

The timing of this concerted focus over the past five years in some ways comes as a reaction to increasing awareness of cases of corruption, poor governance, and human rights abuses connected to sport (Ruiz, Apuzzo and Borden, 2015). A number of other forces have also played a role in stimulating this action: sponsors and investors have become increasingly sensitive to the risks associated with MSEs, and local communities in many locations are more and more hostile to the prospect of hosting MSEs (Ramaswamy, 2015; Boykoff, 2020).

Slowly, human rights developments in sport at international, national and sports body levels have also started to find their way into education. For example, the "Teaching Business and Human Rights Handbook" includes a teaching note on MSEs and human rights.[8] For a couple of years now, the FIFA Master, run by the International Centre for Sports Studies, includes a session on human rights. In addition, case studies on MSEs have been integrated in business and human rights programmes, and so have guest lectures on sport and human rights more generally. Specific cases of adverse human rights impacts caused by MSEs can increasingly be found as part of human rights courses.

At the same time, there is a growing body of research and literature on human rights and sport (Caudwell and McGee, 2018, p. 2). The number of books looking into this connection more generally, or into specific dimensions of it, is growing (see for instance David, 2005; Heerdt, 2019; Keys, 2019b). The same can be said about academic journals from the various disciplines that sport relates to, be it sociology, history, health studies, or law. Not only single articles but even entire issues are dedicated to sport and human rights-related topics (Duval and Heerdt, 2020; Centre for Sports and Human Rights, 2020). Several studies were and are being conducted, some with a focus on a specific group of affected people such as children in sport (Dowse, Powell and Weed, 2015; Petry and Müller Schoell, 2015, 2018). Finally, there is also a rise in research consortia and networks that explicitly address a human rights dimension of sport (See "Olympic Compliance Task Force Project" or "EventRights" project).[9]

## Responsibility of education providers in the world of sport

To consolidate the current sport and human rights movement and ensure that recent developments in sport and human rights are sustainable, there is a need to embed this trend more strongly into sport education. Thereby, future professionals in the field of sport will have a better understanding of the human rights risks related to sport and sporting events from the outset. It is important that this endeavour is integrated at all levels where sport education is taking place, from university programmes to traineeships at sports organisations, trainer education, or referee training.

University programmes related to sport offer numerous opportunities for integrating human rights into the curriculum. This could for instance mean that study programmes on sociology and sport include topics like discrimination, equality, and inclusion from a human rights perspective, or that study programmes on physical education teach students about the human right to mental and physical health and bodily integrity and the related risks. With respect to sport studies on management or economics, a lot can be learned from existing business and human rights education, for which a significant number of materials and teaching guides have been developed.[10] Where the planning of an MSE is included as exercise or case study in sports business schools, the development of a human rights strategy for these events should be part of it, in line with the updated requirements of SGBs like FIFA or the IOC.

Specifically, regarding university education, it is not only sports programmes that should integrate human rights, but the argument also applies vice versa. Human rights studies should integrate sport in their curricula, be it as module in a human rights course on current issues, as research seminar, or as part of a business and human rights track. A concrete idea is for human rights law clinics, of which there are many, to include cases that deal with sport-related human rights abuses linked to MSEs or day-to-day sport.

Furthermore, programmes for educating trainers and coaches offer room to build capacity on human and children's rights. Relevant studies on coach and trainer education and certification are being conducted, but it is unknown to what extent human rights issues related to sport are part of these programmes or studies. Especially children's rights risks should be integrated to foster prevention of child abuse in the context of sport and strengthen safeguarding. At the same time, this can help to spread awareness on sport-related human and children's rights issues and thereby increase chances for cases of abuse being identified and reported. A similar argument can be made for referee trainings. Here, for instance, a proper education on the right to non-discrimination can help to address racist behaviour or unequal treatment among athletes.

Finally, by integrating human rights into sport education, the world of sport also helps to achieve Sustainable Development Goal number four on inclusive and equitable quality education and lifelong learning opportunities. This is as relevant in relation to physical education and ensuring a holistic education as it is when it comes to using sport as means to educate participants, including athletes and fans, about human rights and sustainable development. The Youth Olympic Games have for instance been used by children's rights organisations to raise awareness. MSEs more broadly could and should be used to raise awareness and educate on human rights issues present in the hosting countries. This could be organised with local universities and schools, through project weeks or guest lectures, coupled with extracurricular events and activities on sport and human rights more generally.

## Conclusion

To ensure that sport's unique power to promote human rights is harnessed and used in the right way, human rights and a human rights-based approach should be integrated into sport education programmes across the board. Human rights are universal, which primarily means that they are the same everywhere and for everyone and in the present context means that they play a role for any education programme related to sport, be it sport management, sports law, sport sociology, or physical education. Furthermore, this equally applies to all parts of the globe, and a few relevant initiatives already exist which can be built upon. To foster and advance these initiatives and ensure that lessons learned in certain parts of the world in the context of sport and human rights are shared globally, connections should be made between the different programmes and the establishment of a global network of sport and human rights education programmes would be a desired approach.

However, the true value of sport's potential in human rights can only be realised if those actors within the sports ecosystem who bear obligations and responsibilities uphold and fulfil their duties. Indeed, many of the harmful human rights violations and impacts seen in recent years have taken place within elite sport and within the context of MSEs. These are extremely well-resourced sectors, with highly competitive processes to bid for and host major events. It is therefore reasonable to expect high profile sports organisations and events to uphold exemplary standards in their governance, in their delivery, and in their operations. This means sport taking a leading role, setting standards, and providing best practice examples. Concretely required actions include preventing and mitigating harm, de-risking operations, and maintaining trust in sport and, through that, assuring its future. A growing integration of human rights into sport education will lead to a generation of professionals within sports governance which is sufficiently qualified to ensure a world of sport that respects and promotes human rights.

## Notes

1. See for example Article 1 of the Revised International Charter of Physical Education, Physical Activity and Sport adopted by UNESCO's General Assembly (2015), which states that: "The practice of physical education, physical activity and sport is a fundamental right for all"; Article 30 of the UN Convention on the Rights of Persons with Disabilities, which affirms the right of persons with disabilities to: "Participation in cultural life, recreation, leisure and sport"; Article 31 of the UN Convention on the Rights of the Child, which states that: "Children have the right to relax and to join in a wide range of cultural, artistic and other recreational activities"; Article 10 of the UN Convention on the Elimination of All Forms of Discrimination against Women (CEDAW), which provides for men and women having "the same Opportunities to participate actively in sports and physical education"; and Article 13 which states that women have the "right to participate in recreational activities, sports and all aspects of cultural life". Available at https://en.unesco.org/themes/sport-and-anti-doping/sport-charter

# Human rights in sport education 203

2. International Olympic Committee (2020), Olympic Charter, Principle 4, available at https://stillmedab.olympic.org/media/Document%20Library/OlympicOrg/General/EN-Olympic-Charter.pdf#_ga=2.40626978.1643278620.1610056030-1090094817.1587547475.
3. The right to freedom from discrimination is guaranteed by Article 7 of the Universal Declaration of Human Rights, the right to equal pay for equal work is covered by Article 7 of the International Covenant on Economic Social and Cultural Rights, and the right to freedom from cruel, inhuman, or degrading treatment is stated in Article 5 of the Universal Declaration of Human Rights.
4. The right to participate in cultural life, enshrined in Article 27 of the Universal Declaration of Human Rights and Article 15 of the International Covenant on Economic, Social and Cultural Rights (ICESCR). The right to health, enshrined in Article 25 of the UDHR, Article 12 of the ICESCR, Article 5 of the Convention on the Elimination of All Forms of Racial Discrimination, and Articles 11 and 12 of CEDAW. The right to rest and leisure, included in Article 24 of the UDHR and Article 7 of the ICESCR.
5. The communiqué on "Human Rights and the Olympic and Paralympic Games" between the United Kingdom, The Russian Federation (host of the Sochi 2014), Brazil (host of Rio 2016), and South Korea (host of PyeongChang 2018) was launched on August 29, 2012 at the UK Foreign & Commonwealth Office, available at: https://www.rusemb.org.uk/press/843.
6. This eventually resulted in the Mega-Sporting Events Platform for Human Rights. The starting point was a joint statement on the occasion of the Wilton Park Meeting on Human Rights and Mega-Sporting Events on November 17, 2015, by the International Labour Office, the International Organization of Employers, the International Trade Union Confederation, and OHCHR, available at https://www.ihrb.org/focus-areas/mega-sporting-events/ilo-ituc-ioe-ohchr-joint-statement-mse-human-rights.
7. The International Bill of Human Rights consists of the UDHR, the International Covenant on Economic, Social and Cultural Rights, the International Covenant on Civil and Political Rights, and its two Optional Protocols.
8. See https://teachbhr.org/resources/teaching-bhr-handbook/teaching-notes/mega-sporting-events-and-human-rights-2/.
9. See https://blog.richmond.edu/olympicscompliance/ & http://eventrights.net/.
10. See for instance https://teachbhr.org/resources/teaching-bhr-handbook/.

## References

Al Hussein, Z. R. and Davis, R. (2020) *Recommendations for an IOC Human Rights Strategy Independent Expert Report by Prince Zeid Ra'ad.*

Amis, L. (2017) 'Mega-sporting events and human rights – A time for more teamwork?', *Business and Human Rights Journal*, 2(01), pp. 135–141. doi: 10.1017/bhj.2016.29.

Bernaz, N. (2016) *Business and human rights: History, law and policy – Bridging the accountability gap.* 1st edn. Abingdon: Routledge. doi: 10.4324/9781315626055.

Boykoff, J. (2019) 'Hosting the Olympic games in developed countries – Debating the human rights ideals of sport', in Keys, B. (ed.) *The ideals of global sport – From peace to human rights 2.* Philadelphia, PA: University of Pennsylvania Press.

Boykoff, J. (2020) *NOlympians –Inside the fight against capitalist mega-sports in Los Angeles, Tokyo and beyond.* Halifax: Fernwood Publishing.

Caudwell, J. and McGee, D. (2018) 'From promotion to protection: Human rights and events, leisure and sport', *Leisure Studies*, 37(1), pp. 1–10. doi: 10.1080/02614367.2017.1420814.

Centre for Sports and Human Rights (2020) *Call for Papers: Special Issue*. Available at: https://www.sporthumanrights.org/en/news-events/call-for-papers-special-issue (Accessed: 24 September 2020).

Committee on the Rights of the Child (2015) *CRC/C/BRA/CO/2-4 – Concluding Observations on the Combined Second to Fourth Periodic Reports of Brazil*.

Commonwealth Sport (2018) *Transformation 2022 Refresh – Strategic Plan 2019–2022*. Available at: https://thecgf.com/sites/default/files/2019-10/CGF_TRANSFORMATION22_BROCHURE_FINAL_16-08-19_LOWRES.pdf (Accessed: 2 December 2020).

Commonwealth Sports Ministers (2020) *The Commonwealth Consensus Statement on Promoting Human Rights in and through Sport*. Available at: https://thecommonwealth.org/sites/default/files/inline/CWConsensusStatement-ADOPTEDv2.pdf (Accessed: 2 December 2020).

David, P. (2005) *Human rights in youth sport*. 1st edn. London: Routledge (Ethics and sport).

Deutscher Fussball-Bund (2019) *Bekenntnis zu Menschenrechten in Satzung*. Available at: https://www.dfb.de/news/detail/bekenntnis-zu-menschenrechten-in-satzung-208027/ (Accessed: 2 December 2020).

Deva, S. (2015) 'Multinationals, human rights and international law: Time to move beyond the "state-centric" conception', in Van Ho, T. and Letnar Cernic, J. (eds) *Human rights and business: Direct corporate accountability for human rights*. Chicago, IL: Wolf Legal Publishers.

Deva, S. and Birchall, D. (2020) *Research Handbook on Human Rights and Business*. Available at: https://www.e-elgar.com/shop/gbp/research-handbook-on-human-rights-and-business-9781786436399.html (Accessed: 7 January 2021).

Donnelly, P. (2008) 'Sport and human rights', *Sport in Society*, 11(4), pp. 381–394. doi: 10.1080/17430430802019326.

Dowse, S., Powell, S. and Weed, M. (2015) *Children's Rights and Mega Sporting Events: An Evidence-based Review of the Intersections in Relation to the Following Themes*. Available at: https://www.academia.edu/24736907/CHILDRENS_RIGHTS_AND_MEGA_SPORTING_EVENTS_AN_EVIDENCE_BASED_REVIEW_OF_SELECTED_INTERSECTING_THEMES_FINAL_REPORT (Accessed: 15 January 2021).

Dowse, S., Powell, S. and Weed, M. (2018) 'Mega-sporting events and children's rights and interests – Towards a better future', *Leisure Studies*, 37(1), pp. 97–108. doi: 10.1080/02614367.2017.1347698.

Duval, A. and Heerdt, D. (2020) 'FIFA and human rights – A research agenda', *Tilburg Law Review*, 25(1). doi: 10.5334/TILR.189.

Fédération Internationale de Football Association (FIFA) (2016) *FIFA Statutes. FIFA Congress*. Available at: https://resources.fifa.com/mm/document/affederation/generic/02/78/29/07/fifastatutsweben_neutral.pdf (Accessed: 13 March 2017).

Giulianotti, R. (2004) 'Human rights, globalization and sentimental education: The case of sport', *Sport in Society*, 7(3), pp. 355–369. doi: 10.1080/1743043042000291686.

Heerdt, D. (2019) 'The human rights impacts of Olympic games', in Krieger, J. and Wassong, S. (eds.) *Dark sides of sport*. Champaign, IL: Common Ground Research Networks.

Human Rights Council (HRC) (2016) *A/HRC/RES/31/23 - Resolution Adopted by the Human Rights Council on 24 March 2016 31/23. Promoting Human Rights through Sport and the Olympic Ideal*. Available at: https://undocs.org/A/HRC/RES/31/23 (Accessed: 13 January 2020).

Human Rights Watch (HRW) (2020) *'How Can We Work Without Wages?'* Available at: https://www.hrw.org/sites/default/files/media_2020/08/qatar082

0_web_3.pdf (Accessed: 16 September 2020).

Institute for Human Rights and Business (2018) *Rights Through Sport – Mapping 'Sport for Development and Peace'*. Available at: https://www.ihrb.org/uploads/reports/Rights_Through_Sport_-_Mapping_SDP%2C_IHRB_2018.pdf (Accessed: 7 January 2021).

International Labour Organisation (ILO) (2020) *Dismantling the Kafala System and Introducing a Minimum Wage Mark New Era for Qatar Labour Market, Press release*. Available at: http://www.ilo.org/beirut/projects/qatar-office/WCMS_754391/lang–en/index.htm (Accessed: 16 September 2020).

International Olympic Committee (2020) *IOC Moves Forward with Its Huma Rights Approach, Olympic News*. Available at: https://www.olympic.org/news/ioc-moves-forward-with-its-human-rights-approach (Accessed: 2 December 2020).

Keys, B. (2019a) 'Reframing human rights', in Keys, B. (ed.) *The ideals of global sport – From peace to human rights*. Philadelphia, PA: University of Pennsylvania Press, pp. 109–135.

Keys, B. (2019b) *The ideals of global sport – From peace to human rights*. Philadelphia, PA: University of Pennsylvania Press.

Lemmon, M. (2019) 'Evening the playing field: women's sport as a vehicle for human rights', *International Sports Law Journal*, 19(3–4), pp. 238–257. doi: 10.1007/s40318-019-00148-5.

London's Organising Committee of the Olympic Games (LOCOG) (2012) *LOCOG Sustainable Sourcing Code*. Available at: https://library.olympic.org/Default/doc/SYRACUSE/47420/locog-sustainable-sourcing-code-london-organizing-committee-for-the-olympic-and-paralympic-games?_lg=en-GB (Accessed: 15 January 2021).

Mega-Sporting Events Platform for Human Rights (2017) *Corruption and Human Rights in the Sports Context*. Available at: www.megasportingevents.org (Accessed: 12 June 2020).

Muchlinski, P. (2007) *Multinational enterprises & the law*. Oxford: Oxford University Press. doi: 10.1093/law:iic/9780199227969.book.1.

Petry, K. and Müller Schoell, T. (2015) *Children Rights and Mega Sporting Events in 2014*. Available at: http://www.childrenwin.org/wp-content/uploads/2015/08/ITDH_report_final.pdf (Accessed: 16 October 2017).

Ramaswamy, C. (2015) 'Hosting the Olympics: the competition no one wants to win', *The Guardian*. Available at: https://www.theguardian.com/sport/shortcuts/2015/nov/30/hosting-olympics-hamburg-drop-out-2024-games (Accessed: 14 January 2021).

Ruggie, J. G. (2016) *'For the Game. For the World.' – FIFA and Human Rights, Harvard University*. Available at: https://www.hks.harvard.edu/sites/default/files/centers/mrcbg/programs/cri/files/Ruggie_humanrightsFIFA_reportApril2016.pdf (Accessed: 15 January 2021).

Ruiz, R., Apuzzo, M. and Borden, S. (2015) 'FIFA Corruption: Top Officials Arrested in Pre-Dawn Raid at Zurich Hotel', *The New York Times*. Available at: https://www.nytimes.com/2015/12/03/sports/fifa-scandal-arrests-in-switzerland.html (Accessed: 7 January 2021).

UNESCO – 6th International Conference of Ministers and Senior Officials Responsible for Physical Education and Sport (2017) *Kazan Action Plan*. Available at: https://unesdoc.unesco.org/ark:/48223/pf0000252725 (Accessed: 5 June 2020).

United Nations General Assembly (2014) *UN Doc A/69/L.5Sport as a Means to Promote Education, Health, Development and Peace*.

United Nations High Commissioner for Human Rights (2020) *A/HRC/44/26 – Intersection of Race and Gender Discrimination in Sport*.

Worden, M. (2008) *China's great leap: The Beijing games and Olympian human rights challenges*. New York, NY: Seven Stories Press.

Worden, M. (2014) *Raising the Bar – Mega-Sporting Events and Human Rights*.

Chapter 17

# Developing intercultural sport educators in Europe

## Opportunities, challenges, and future directions

*Louis Moustakas, Eleftheria Papageorgiou, and Karen Petry*

## Introduction

The demographic composition of Europe has shifted dramatically over the last 20 years: European populations have become older and migration within and from outside the European Union has also significantly risen. This increase in migration and cultural diversity presents both challenges and opportunities. To maximise the opportunities, the successful, positive social integration of these new groups is paramount. Yet integration is not always understood in positive terms and does not happen automatically. It can take multiple forms, from assimilation to segregation or marginalisation. In particular, while the process of assimilation requires the "other" to adapt to the majority's own culture, integration maintains and values the cultural individuality of majority and minority groups (Berry, 1997). Thus, moving forward, we use the term integration to refer to this latter understanding of the term.

Sport has become increasingly recognised as a valuable tool to promote this latter, positive form of social integration. Sport is positioned as a shared cultural manifestation and as an inherently social, interactive activity that can provide opportunities to foster tolerance and intercultural skills (Cardenas, 2013; Puente-Maxera, Méndez-Giménez and Martínez de Ojeda, 2020). At the European level, the potential of sport to contribute to social integration is acknowledged in numerous policy documents. For instance, the European Commission has noted that sport can contribute to "inclusive growth" and that "it contributes to social cohesion by breaking down social barriers" (European Commission, 2011). Yet, there are limited training or education opportunities to support sport educators towards achieving these lofty societal goals. Instead, sport is often positioned as inherently good that confers automatic benefits. As a result, sport educators are increasingly tasked with supporting social cohesion and intercultural education without necessarily possessing the skills or tools to do so successfully. Overall cultural understanding, implementing appropriate learning activities, and fostering reflection are especially prominent challenges for sport educators (Forde *et al.*, 2015). More generally, there is a limited picture of the opportunities or challenges

DOI: 10.4324/9781003002666-22

faced in intercultural sport education, and few curricula have been developed to support current or future sport educators.

It is against this background that the European project "Intercultural Education through Physical Activity, Coaching and Training" (EDU:PACT) was launched with financial support from Erasmus+ and the European Commission. The EDU:PACT project explored the realities, opportunities, and challenges for sport-related intercultural education across Austria, Denmark, Germany, Greece, and Italy. Based on these findings, the consortium of universities from these countries developed and realised a module to train physical education teachers and sport coaches on how to implement intercultural education within their sports sessions. In short, EDU:PACT aimed to prepare physical education teachers and sport coaches for inclusive intercultural education in and through sport by improving the quality of their pre-service and in-service education. From 2018 to 2021, the consortium worked to understand sport educators' needs and develop an appropriate educational approach. Thus, in the following, we will map out the challenges and opportunities inherent to intercultural sport education and present the EDU:PACT Module as a potential approach to help address these challenges and capitalise on existing opportunities. Finally, we will combine the various findings and outcomes to propose future avenues for the development of intercultural sport education.

## The opportunities and challenges of sport and intercultural education

Before moving forward, it is important to precisely define the term "intercultural education". To some, intercultural education promotes a relatively narrow set of socio-technical skills that allow individuals to deal with specific social groups. In turn, this leads to an overemphasis on cultural traits, whereby individual characteristics are reduced to a mere by-product of cultural membership and the risk of stereotyping increases (Abdallah-Pretceille, 2006; Grimminger, 2011). We do not share this view of intercultural education and instead follow the definition put forward by Bennett (2009), who states that intercultural education is about "acquiring increased awareness of subjective cultural context (world view), including one's own, and developing greater ability to interact sensitively and competently across cultural contexts as both an immediate and long-term effect of exchange" (p. 2). Essential in this is both the understanding of one's unique sociocultural context and the associated biases that may bring, as well as the ability to act and interact in intercultural settings. In short, intercultural education fosters a multidimensional skill set that can be promoted by culturally responsive pedagogy (Ladson-Billings, 1995).

To achieve this holistic, inclusive view of intercultural education, three common pedagogical characteristics were identified by educators and experts: mixed-group, cooperative activities; discussion and reflection; and educator-participant relationships. Indeed, these characteristics largely echo the basic principles of methodologies and approaches developed elsewhere in the sports context (e.g. Gieß-Stüber, 2010; Grimminger, 2011; Puente-Maxera *et al.*, 2020; Smith *et al.*, 2020). Yet, though there was general agreement on these characteristics, a number of perceived external barriers, a lack of intercultural sensitivity, and individual biases limited sport educators' ability to successfully deliver intercultural education through sport (cf. Gasparini and Cometti, 2010; Block and Gibbs, 2017).

First and foremost, there was a recognition that sport is a practical, social, and interactive activity that is a potentially valuable venue for exchange and intercultural education. For many educators, sport provides an opportunity to transcend the barriers or closed-off nature of their societies. For instance, Danish participants noted that Danes are reticent to talk with strangers. Rather, it is more common for Danes to meet new people through formalised social settings such as events or sports clubs. Therefore, sports activities were seen as a crucial way to bridge the gap between Danes and other ethnic groups. Despite this widespread acknowledgement, there were numerous questions regarding how to bring groups together successfully. In particular, there was a sense that the cultural background of immigrants poses a significant challenge. In line with previous research (Norman *et al.*, 2014), participants of our study referred to the challenges posed by racial and gender stereotypes, both among educators and between students. These stereotypes often lead to discriminatory behaviours and translate to an inability to manage diverse groups. For instance, many sport educators believed that individuals' religious background prevented them from participating in sport or that they did not value participation in a sports club to the same extent as the "local" populations. And, though mixing groups was seen as beneficial, for some, there was a notion that too many immigrants may pose a problem: "having an ethnically mixed context helps and it is very important since groups with a dominant ethnicity can be an obstacle. This fact must be considered negative also with groups with a majority of non-Italians" (Quote from an Expert, Italy).

Beyond merely mixing groups, many of the educators we interviewed also felt that sport alone is not sufficient to achieve intercultural education goals. Though sport can sometimes provide the impetus to bring groups together, sports sessions must be intentionally designed and implemented with intercultural education goals in mind. At the most basic level, there was a recognition that "team sport" or "cooperative activities" could be promising avenues to break down cultural barriers and facilitate exchange. Going more deeply, many respondents acknowledged the need to give equal status and shared goals to the participants: "games and activities that include specific roles for children can promote teamwork in the direction of a common goal" (Quote from an Expert, Greece). These notions of equal status and shared goals are essential preconditions within Allport's famous Contact Theory (Allport, 1954) and are prevalent in many of the aforementioned sport-pedagogical approaches. Consistently working towards clear, shared goals was seen as a mean to foster not only intercultural education but also promote a greater sense of identity: "because something was expected from them, the boys felt like they were a part of the club and community" (Quote from an Expert, Denmark).

However, even when groups are mixed in this positive and collaborative way, this contact alone is not necessarily enough to generate sustainable intercultural education (Perry and Southwell, 2011). This kind of contact must also seek to gradually change the mentality and foster self-analysis to shape attitudes and behaviour positively. Transformation learning theory describes this process as "metacognitive reasoning" (Mezirow, 2003, p. 61) and often takes the form of a targeted reflection and discussion sessions. As numerous educators recognised, there is an accompanying need to foster discussion and reflection in the sports context. This reflection allows students or athletes to connect the new experiences with issues and realities in their communities and consider how to use acquired skills outside of the sports setting. German sport educators noted that, following each session, it is necessary to implement a reflection phase that embeds the relationship between the experiences in the context of the game and the participants' own experiences. Indeed, without reflection, even well-designed and well-delivered activities are "just sport". The management of the reflection process is the part where the "intercultural ethos" (Tarozzi, 2014) and the "art of teaching" (Quennerstedt, 2019) of sport educators are most highlighted and can have the largest impact on the athletes or students. Conversely, this means that the reflection process must be adequately planned and appropriately delivered to achieve the desired impact.

Finally, underpinning the above characteristics, positive relationships between educators and participants were viewed as an overarching requirement. The need to both understand the perspectives and lived realities of diverse students, as well as build positive, trusting relationships, are paramount (e.g. Van der Veken *et al.*, 2021). Yet, arguably, this is where sport educators struggle the most. As such, this limits their ability to implement the pedagogical features described above. Classic sport education programmes, clubs, and schools do not focus on these intercultural, relational elements. As a result, sport educators may feel unsure and unprepared to tackle issues arising from sociocultural differences. Many educators reported uncertainties about dealing with religious issues, linguistic barriers, and mixed-gender activities. Though often these concerns are born from a lack of information or intercultural sensitivity, others have more negative, in-built biases that limit the development of relationships: "Quite often, even teachers or coaches are suspicious of children from various cultural backgrounds. Thus, their attitudes influence both their teaching style and their pupils' attitudes" (Quote from an Expert, Greece). Either way, sport educators have a nascent sense of the intercultural education opportunities present in sport but often feel uncertain about mixing groups, integrating reflections, or dealing with cultural differences.

## The EDU:PACT Module

The above understanding of both opportunities and challenges ultimately significantly influenced the final EDU:PACT Module's conception (for the full Module, see Reynard, Moustakas and Petry, 2020). This Module, which is meant to be used by individuals training current and future sport educators, is divided into four distinct units:

- Understanding Yourself
- Understanding Others
- Planning and Delivering Intercultural Education Sessions
- Monitoring and Evaluation

Each unit includes a guided learning section through which the reader gains access to theoretical information and knowledge meant to support that particular unit. Additionally, each unit incorporates a practical section where the reader is presented with related activities that can be facilitated with other physical education teachers or coaches, or with students and athletes. These activities reinforce each unit's core learning while also providing concrete examples of how to integrate new experiences, shared goals, and reflection into sports sessions (Figure 17.1).

Overall, these units are meant to build on each other and form a coherent whole to foster intercultural sport education. The four units combine to provide sport educators with the understanding, awareness, pedagogical tools, and competences to design, deliver, and evaluate intercultural sport education sessions. The first unit focuses on self-understanding. The Module begins from the starting point that self-understanding is a prerequisite for greater intercultural competence. Though intercultural education is often framed as an issue of understanding the foreign "other" (Abdallah-Pretceille, 2006; Grimminger, 2011), intercultural education must begin with a fundamental understanding of one's personal and social background (Bennett, 2009). Once sport educators comprehend how that background influences their actions and attitudes, they can then more effectively develop open, positive, trusting relationships with their participants. This unit presents critical concepts related to self-identity, illustrates how

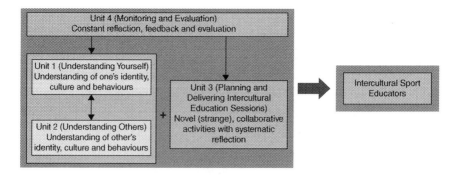

*Figure 17.1* Overview of the EDU:PACT Module.

that identity shapes behaviour, and how to challenge or change those behaviours when needed.

Once sport educators have acquired a greater appreciation of their identity and how that identity influences their perspectives and behaviours, they can then begin the work of understanding others and building positive relationships. In the second unit, the focus is not on reducing others to their cultural membership or perceived cultural traits, but rather to develop core communication and leadership skills that allow for consistent, continuous understanding to develop. Moving forward, it is also important for us to clarify what we mean when using words such as "communication" or "leadership", both of which may have very top-down connotations. First, in terms of communication, we focus explicitly on all elements associated with the word, most especially on active listening and effective discussions. Second, leadership here does not refer to neoliberal managerial notions of visionary leadership, but rather to the inherent leadership role sport educators play in building and maintaining relationships within a group. Numerous interviewees recognised this as well, noting that "leadership can function as a role model and therefore facilitate intercultural learning", but that bottom-up approaches that include participants in decision-making must also be integrated (Quote from an Expert, Germany).

After exploring notions of self and mutual understanding, the third unit aims to prepare coaches and physical education teachers to plan effective activities designed to contribute to intercultural education. Though numerous sample activities are proposed, the goal here is to give sport educators the tools to create or adjust their own activities. Providing the most suitable design for a well-organised programme and including the most appropriate activities is not a robotic process but requires specific knowledge and skills. This includes establishing clear goals, the awareness of groups and sub-groups, understanding the relations between them, and combining this knowledge to design and implement culturally appropriate activities (Kreuter *et al.*, 2003). To foster these skills, the Module proposes two didactical-pedagogical concepts: the experiential learning model (Kolb, 1984) and the intercultural education model from Gieß-Stüber (2010). These two models combine to guide educators in designing an interculturally appropriate session while also unifying the necessary experiences and reflections needed for successful experiential learning.

Finally, the Module concludes with a unit dedicated to monitoring, evaluation, and reflection. Integrating continuous feedback, evaluation, and reflection are essential components of delivering intercultural education programmes. The EDU:PACT Module aims to develop the intercultural management of sport educators and to build behavioural and emotional competences to foster intercultural integration. For sustainability, reflection should become a routine in all sports sessions, and the sport educators must find a good balance between play and reflection. Likewise, sport educators should integrate feedback, self-reflection, and evaluation throughout. This allows their sessions to improve continuously while also engaging participants and building relationships. To do so, this unit proposes interactive evaluation activities and numerous conceptual tools such as problem trees, Theory of Change models, and other evaluation tools.

## The future of intercultural sport education

Obviously, many opportunities and challenges were shared across Europe. Sport educators understand that the social and interactive nature of sport confers it with significant potential in the context of intercultural education. Yet, dealing with mixed groups, facilitating reflections, or engaging with stereotypes remain significant barriers to the delivery of intercultural sport education. These barriers primarily emerge from the current gap in educational programmes that train sport educators for intercultural education. Though policy and politics often position sport as a tool for social cohesion and intercultural dialogue, the expectation largely remains that this will occur more or less automatically. There is not always a strong perceived need for additional development or training, as sport is viewed as conveying inherently positive social values already.

Many are convinced that sports activities or sports practice are subject to a canon of ideal values, which, among other things, practise and implement normative behaviour based on respect, fairness, cooperation, compliance with rules, and incorruptibility (e.g. Hartmann and Kwauk, 2011). For this reason, sport and exercise are seen as particularly suitable as instruments or tools for addressing and acquiring socially desirable behaviour patterns among children and young people in all countries of the world. Sports activities are believed to offer an ideal learning field for a fair and respectful social interaction characterised by a sense of community, teamwork, and empathy. Here, sport, play, and exercise can contribute to personality development and a more stable self-concept, strengthen self-confidence and resilience, and encourage responsibility.

This discourse serves the function of pushing discussions about the role of sport and physical education in intercultural learning to the background. With the EDU:PACT project, it was aimed to address this misconception and provide a targeted, deliberate intercultural education approach. Sport is not integrative, social, or fair per se – on the contrary: sport often manifests existing inequalities in our societies (Coakley, 2011). To tap into the social and interactive potential of sport, culturally aware, intentional pedagogical approaches must be designed and disseminated. As a result from the EDU:PACT project, the Module was systematically integrated into the curricula of many of the partner organisations. Despite this, there remain significant challenges in Europe and beyond integrating such content into formal physical education or coaching curricula. Not all universities or training providers are equally receptive to incorporating such socially oriented content in sport or physical education programmes.

Part of this is because of the overarching assumption that sport is an inherently positive force and does not necessarily require new or modified approaches. In addition, within sport education programmes, there often is a singular focus on the technical aspects of sport, but little time focus on social or cultural issues

(Cope *et al.*, 2017). The promotion of physical activity and the improvement of motor skills often subordinate intercultural education activities to a lower position. Accordingly, this fosters an attitude where many programmes or sport educators believe that addressing these issues is outside their purview. Therefore, future work should not only focus on pedagogy but also advocacy. It is imperative not only to outline *how* intercultural education can be fostered in sport but also *why* sport educators should take on that role.

Viewing the development of sport-specific behaviours and competences as separate from the goals of intercultural education is, in our view, a mistake. A positive, inclusive intercultural pedagogical climate should be understood as a prerequisite for successful sports participation and skill development. Studies regularly show that fostering a positive, inclusive intercultural climate encourages sports participation and improves enjoyment (e.g. Kamphuis *et al.*, 2008). In other words, even if one views sports participation and skill development as the core goals of sport education, intercultural competences are a key tool to ensure all participants achieve those goals.

For those who specifically aim to foster intercultural education through sport, significant gaps also persist. Important questions remain of whether sport and physical education are truly suitable to contribute to intercultural learning. The general question of whether and under what conditions sport and physical education can contribute to intercultural learning is currently the subject of extensive research and debate. In particular, how intercultural competences learned in and through sport can be adopted in everyday activities is seldom or not at all addressed. Furthermore, there is a need to develop and tailor intercultural education approaches to specific regional and country contexts. At present, much of the work – including EDU:PACT – has emerged from Europe or elsewhere in the Global North.

## Conclusion

In this chapter, we have shown how sport is increasingly positioned as a tool to foster intercultural skills and that sport educators are often delegated the responsibility to support these goals. However, though sport educators understand that sport's social, goal-oriented nature may provide intercultural education opportunities, many face difficulties mastering the (self-)reflective and relational skills required for successful intercultural sport education. To help address these gaps, we have presented the EDU:PACT Module as one potential solution for pre-service and in-service sport educators. This Module, however, is but a first step. There is certainly room for more rigorous and contextually adapted educational tools. Similarly, there remains much work to properly understand the role of sport in fostering intercultural competences, both on and off the pitch. Despite these gaps, one thing is clear: unless sport educators are given the tools and skills to deliver intercultural sport education, sport's power to "break down barriers" will be greatly limited.

## References

Abdallah-Pretceille, M. (2006) 'Interculturalism as a paradigm for thinking about diversity', *Intercultural Education*, 17(5), pp. 475–483. doi: 10.1080/14675980601065764.

Allport, G. W. (1954) *The nature of prejudice*. Boston, MA: Addison-Wesley.

Bennett, M. J. (2009) 'Defining, measuring, and facilitating intercultural learning: A defining, measuring, and facilitating intercultural learning: A conceptual introduction to the intercultural education double supplement', *Intercultural Education*, 20(S1–2).

Berry, J. W. (1997) 'Immigration, acculturation, and adaptation', *Applied Psychology*, 46(1), pp. 5–34. doi: 10.1111/j.1464-0597.1997.tb01087.x.

Block, K. and Gibbs, L. (2017) 'Promoting social inclusion through sport for refugee-background youth in Australia: Analysing different participation models', *Social Inclusion*, 5(2), pp. 91–100. doi: 10.17645/si.v5i2.903.

Cardenas, A. (2013) 'Peace building through sport? An introduction to sport for development and peace', *Journal of Conflictology*, 4(1). doi: 10.7238/joc.v4i1.1493.

Coakley, J. (2011) 'Ideology doesn't just happen: Sports and neoliberalism', *The Journal of Latin American Socio-Cultural Studies of Sport*, 1(1), pp. 67–84.

Cope, E. *et al.* (2017) 'Football, sport and the development of young people's life skills', *Sport in Society*, 20(7), pp. 789–801. doi: 10.1080/17430437.2016.1207771.

European Commission (2011) *Developing the European dimension in sport*. Brussels.

Forde, S. D. *et al.* (2015) 'Moving towards social inclusion: Manager and staff perspectives on an award winning community sport and recreation program for immigrants', *Sport Management Review*, 18(1), pp. 126–138. doi: 10.1016/j.smr.2014.02.002.

Gasparini, W. and Cometti, A. (eds.) (2010) *Sports policy and practice series. Sport facing the test of cultural diversity: Integration and intercultural dialogue in Europe: Analysis and practical examples*. Strasbourg: Council of Europe Publ.

Gieß-Stüber (2010) 'Development of intercultural skills through sport and physical education in Europe', in Gasparini, W. and Cometti, A. (eds.) *Sports policy and practice series. Sport facing the test of cultural diversity: Integration and intercultural dialogue in Europe: Analysis and practical examples*. Strasbourg: Council of Europe Publ, pp. 23–30.

Grimminger, E. (2011) 'Intercultural competence among sports and PE teachers. Theoretical foundations and empirical verification', *European Journal of Teacher Education*, 34(3), pp. 317–337. doi: 10.1080/02619768.2010.546834.

Hartmann, D. and Kwauk, C. (2011) 'Sport and development: An overview, critique, and reconstruction', *Journal of Sport and Social Issues*, 35(3), pp. 284–305. doi: 10.1177/0193723511416986.

Kamphuis, C. B. M. (2008) 'Socioeconomic status, environmental and individual factors, and sports participation', *Medicine and Science in Sports and Exercise*, 40(1), pp. 71–81. doi: 10.1249/mss.0b013e318158e467.

Kolb, D. A. (1984) *Experiential learning: Experience as the source of learning and development*. Englewood Cliffs, NJ: Prentice-Hall.

Kreuter, M. W. *et al.* (2003) 'Achieving cultural appropriateness in health promotion programs: Targeted and tailored approaches', *Health Education & Behavior: The Official Publication of the Society for Public Health Education*, 30(2), pp. 133–146. doi: 10.1177/1090198102251021.

Ladson-Billings, G. (1995) 'Toward a theory of culturally relevant pedagogy', *American Educational Research Journal*, 32(3), p. 465. doi: 10.2307/1163320.

Mezirow, J. (2003) 'Transformative learning as discourse', *Journal of Transformative Education*, 1(1), pp. 58–63. doi: 10.1177/1541344603252172.

Norman, L. *et al.* (2014) *Sporting experiences and coaching aspirations among black and minority ethnic (BME) groups: A report for sports coach UK*. Leeds.

Perry, L. B. and Southwell, L. (2011) 'Developing intercultural understanding and skills: Models and approaches', *Intercultural Education*, 22(6), pp. 453–466. doi: 10.1080/14675986.2011.644948.

Puente-Maxera, F., Méndez-Giménez, A. and Martínez de Ojeda, D. (2020) 'Games from around the world: Promoting intercultural competence through sport education in secondary school students', *International Journal of Intercultural Relations*, 75, pp. 23–33. doi: 10.1016/j.ijintrel.2020.01.001.

Quennerstedt, M. (2019) 'Physical education and the art of teaching: Transformative learning and teaching in physical education and sports pedagogy', *Sport, Education and Society*, 24(6), pp. 611–623. doi: 10.1080/13573322.2019.1574731.

Reynard, S., Moustakas, L. and Petry, K. (eds.) (2020) *EDU:PACT module handbook: Teaching and learning guidelines on intercultural education through physical activity, coaching and training*. Vienna.

Smith, W. *et al.* (2020) 'School HPE: Its mandate, responsibility and role in educating for social cohesion', *Sport, Education and Society*, 33(2), pp. 1–14. doi: 10.1080/13573322.2020.1742103.

Tarozzi, M. (2014) 'Building an 'intercultural ethos' in teacher education', *Intercultural Education*, 25(2), pp. 128–142. doi: 10.1080/14675986.2014.888804.

Van der Veken, K. *et al.* (2021) 'Looking for boundary spanners: An exploratory study of critical experiences of coaches in sport-for-development programmes', *Sport, Education and Society*, pp. 1–14. doi: 10.1080/13573322.2021.1871726.

Chapter 18

# Careers of European athletes

## Who is ultimately responsible?

*Stefan Walzel, Niklas A. Rotering,
and Ruth Crabtree*

## Introduction

Research suggests that the practice of high-performance sport requires the investment of substantial personal resources (Conzelmann, Gabler and Nagel, 2001). Due to the time-consuming character of a high-performance sports career and the necessity to be geographically flexible, high-performance athletes (HPA) in many sports disciplines face more difficulties in receiving formal education that enables them to develop a professional or academic career compared to their non-athlete peers of the same age (Aquilina and Henry, 2010). Since the achievable income from sport alone is often insufficient to provide an adequate standard of living during and especially after the sports career, dual career planning – i.e., the parallel pursuit of sports and professional careers – is crucial for most HPAs.

As numerous studies (Wylleman, Alfermann and Lavallee, 2004; Aquilina and Henry, 2010; Henriksen *et al.*, 2020; Morris *et al.*, 2020) have shown, this double burden challenges HPAs enormously and rarely do they succeed in optimally combining a sports career with professional development, resulting often in resignation and the end of a top sports career. Junior HPAs frequently decide against a sports career (aligned with dropout) after school due to the lack of compatibility with professional goals. Uncertain prospects for a high-performance sports career and associated risks like injuries contribute to their decision (Aquilina and Henry, 2010; Bendrich, 2015). According to the EU Guidelines on the Dual Careers of Athletes, "one-third of all participants between the ages of 10 and 17 withdraw from sport each year as they consider that sport takes up too much of their time and prevents them from pursuing other things in life (e.g., study)" (European Commission, 2012, p. 5).

A recent study suggests a positive trend regarding the satisfaction of German HPAs with their vocational and professional career since 2009, but satisfaction significantly decreases as the competitive level of the HPAs increases (Breuer *et al.*, 2018), hence, HPAs are increasingly faced with the dilemma of having to choose between a career in sport or a professional career (Nagel and Conzelmann, 2006; Aquilina, 2013).

DOI: 10.4324/9781003002666-23

HPAs face difficult challenges when they attempt to pursue a dual career (Wylleman *et al.*, 2004). Research in this field has its origins in the 1970s and can essentially be reduced to two research streams. Firstly, the focus was on the conditions for the compatibility of a sports career with a professional career. In transition research (e.g., Wylleman *et al.*, 2004; Wylleman and Lavallee, 2004; Alfermann, 2006; Wylleman and Reints, 2010), a distinction is made between different phases of a dual career (e.g., secondary school education, higher education, vocation) in which HPAs require suitable support and services to continue their sports career and to reach the next stage of professional development (Wylleman, Reints and De Knop, 2013). The transition from school to vocational training or university studies as well as the transition to the labour market at the end of their sports career were identified as particularly critical phases. Especially the late entry into a profession, which is referred to as "occupational delay" (Naul, 1994), is often associated with professional disadvantages (Wylleman and Reints, 2010).

The second research stream is dedicated to the biographical analysis of HPAs, with older studies (e.g., Conzelmann *et al.*, 2001) suggesting that high-performance sport tends to positively influence professional careers, although participating in top-level sport often leads to longer school training periods and, in some cases, even to poorer school and training performance. Institutional support measures and structures (especially in the school sector) mean that the high requirements of top-level sport do not normally have a negative impact on the quality of educational qualifications. Since high-performance sports involvement can be conducive to a professional career due to specific soft skills (e.g., high resilience, working in teams), experience, and factors such as athlete's recognition and popularity, it can compensate for delayed career entry, especially if the athletes find professional employment in the high-performance sport system (Conzelmann *et al.*, 2001). However, the increasing temporal demands in high-performance sport may lead to greater doubts as to whether these findings are still valid today. For example, Borggrefe (2013) concludes that the compatibility of sport and professional careers has significantly deteriorated in recent years.

Comparatively few studies engage with investigating dual careers of HPAs from the perspective of universities. As the following elaborations will show, especially universities with sport science degree programmes offer great opportunities for HPAs, whilst acknowledging at the same time that several challenges are associated with university careers which cannot be solved by the universities alone, but require contributions from both politics and sport federations.

The following section will outline the political framework conditions in Europe along with the associated challenges faced by universities. Also, the impact regarding managerial implications will be presented.

## Dual career and European policies

Politicians at both the national and the European level have recognised the increasing sports performance requirements for HPAs and acknowledged that a dual career under these circumstances is becoming progressively more difficult to master for HPAs. The European Commission (2016) stresses that "the employability of an athlete beyond their sports career should be a joint responsibility" (p. 10) between the athlete and further stakeholders, such as policy makers, sport federations, sports clubs, and education providers. Politicians, sports organisations, companies, and universities must face up to this shared responsibility, and each actor should contribute to solving the problem within their own area of expertise and available means.

The conditions for and stages of HPAs' dual career development differ, in some cases dramatically, within Europe (European Commission, 2016). Due to the increasing mobility of students, and particularly HPAs, the European Commission in 2016 called for a generic European solution with individual adaptability instead of pursuing country-specific individual solutions. The development and application of flexibility regarding time and location of study, supported through independent learning forms and methods (e.g., e-learning, blended learning), were recognised as an important starting point, especially for programmes offered by universities, to enable HPAs to successfully complete their studies alongside their sports careers. According to the Dual Career Quality Framework of the European Commission (2016), the athlete is at the centre of considerations. Hence, based on the HPAs' needs and conditions, the European Commission as well as European and national sport federations called on universities to create the matching conditions and opportunities enabling a dual career for HPAs (European Commission, 2016), for example by providing specific e-learning programmes for HPAs.

The document "White Paper on Sport" highlights the specific relevance of and connection between sport and education (European Commission, 2007), and this was reinforced in the recent paper (EU Work Plan for Sport 2017–2020) to which the subject of dual careers got added (Council of European Union, 2017), emphasising that "in particular those coming from third countries to train and compete in Europe, face multiple risks linked to their vulnerability" (European Commission, 2011, p. 5).

The idea of improving dual career opportunities for HPAs is supported by researchers who suggest that many commercialisation problems in sport (e.g., doping, match fixing, corruption in sport) can in part be attributed to a lack of alternative career paths once the HPA has decided to focus on their sports career. In a study, 58% of German HPAs stated that, in addition to the pressure to succeed (89%) and pressure from the environment (80%), existential anxiety is a major reason for misconduct such as doping (Breuer and Hallmann, 2013). Due to a lack of career prospects and/or low-income prospects, HPAs may have a keen interest in prolonging their sports career, and taking performance-enhancing drugs is one option. By improving the dual career opportunities for HPAs, their existential anxiety can be reduced including its side effects (e.g., doping incidents), and a contribution can be made to improving the integrity of sport.

## Challenges for universities providing dual career opportunities for HPAs in sport science

It is not only the HPAs who face some challenges in managing their dual career. Universities also experience several problems and challenges that make it difficult to improve HPAs' study conditions. The services and support offered to HPAs differ enormously between European countries and individual universities. According to Aquilina and Henry (2010), the level of support provided for HPAs by universities very much depends on the decision makers within higher education and their attitude to sport and athlete support.

Research has shown that HPAs face numerous challenges when studying at a university, including the following:

- Due to structural reforms at many universities and the introduction of Bachelor's and Master's degree programmes, a decreasing flexibility and therefore compatibility of studies and high-performance sport was observed (Bendrich, 2015; Brustio et al., 2020).
- HPA students are still dependent on the goodwill of individual professors and lecturers because specific policies and guidelines for promoting HPA students are missing or not binding (Bette, 1984; Borggrefe, Cachay and Riedl, 2009).
- Various studies have shown that the individual support programmes for a dual career of HPAs offered by different institutions (sports club, sports association, university) are not harmonised with each other and this even causes conflicts (e.g., Bendrich, 2015).
- Better conditions regarding the compatibility of studying and high-performance sport lead to a migration of HPAs to the USA. Even if the athletes usually return to their home country after their studies, this may harm the high-performance sport system in the respective European country because the sports talents are abroad for several years (Bendrich, 2015; Hottenrott and Braumann, 2015; Ridpath, Rudd and Stokowski, 2019).
- The location dependency of HPAs' training sessions and competitions (e.g., alpine winter sport in the mountains) limits their opportunities and makes studying at a university more difficult (Flatau and Emrich, 2013).
- HPAs from particularly training-intensive sport as well as seasonal winter or summer sport face bigger problems to successfully complete their studies in traditional university programmes requiring physical attendance (Borggrefe, 2013).
- Depending on the athletes' life phase, a third burden is added to the double career pursuit when they start a family, which is especially relevant for female athletes (Conzelmann et al., 2001).

Condello *et al.* (2019) suggest building up networks between universities and associated stakeholders involved with HPAs, allowing them to work together on overcoming these barriers by providing suitable support mechanisms regarding dual careers.

### Focus on sport science

Borggrefe's (2013) study on HPAs' careers shows that many of them face issues that their non-athlete peers do not, such as a lack of qualified vocational training or study degree as well as working experience, insufficient financial security, and physical restrictions due to injuries and/or extreme physical strain. Such findings seem to be at odds with the fact that HPAs have a few advantageous skills and experiences that are especially functional for jobs in sport or related to sport. The pertinent experience athletes have in the field can be highly advantageous for such jobs. Acquiring the same depth of experience exclusively through education or training programmes is only achievable with great difficulty. Some advantages athletes have include an extraordinarily high level of expertise in sport, international experience through competitions and championships, a high degree of familiarity with the professional athletes, and an established network in sport in general.

In addition, HPAs are often attributed with having soft skills, such as high resilience, a strong ability to work in a team, ambition, and determination (Borggrefe, 2013), which are highly required for a number of jobs in sport. Therefore, sports organisations should have a strong interest in taking advantages of these soft skills. In combination with developing improved dual career options for HPAs in the field of (high-performance) sport, sports organisations could tremendously benefit from HPAs in the future. Jobs in sport, such as coaching positions, sport managers, or officials are particularly interesting as they are often in line with the athletes' interests, and they can benefit from their respective experience.

Their high affinity to sport as well as their own experiences and competences in high-performance sport predestine HPAs for studying sport science. The athletes' social environment can be extremely conducive to their study pursuit. Vice versa, the knowledge and competences gained from the studies might positively affect the HPAs' sports performance and overall career in sport. Despite such seemingly favourable preconditions, only a relatively low number of HPAs decide to study sport science (e.g., 19% of the German athletes of the Olympic team in Rio de Janeiro 2016 [Schneider and Fischer, 2019]).

According to Latinjak (2018) and Mateu *et al.* (2020), the causes associated with the unexpectedly low uptake of sports studies by HPAs could be the following:

- The risk of injury increases due to the plenitude of practical sports courses included in the programmes. The additional physical activities often result in atypical strains, movement sequences, and techniques which are counterproductive for the sport performed competitively.

- A degree in sport science typically involves practical and theoretical activities in various sport, which usually requires attendance on site. However, this is not compatible with HPAs' training and competition schedule.
- HPAs' unique physical characteristics (e.g., height, weight, length of their limbs) are often decisive for their sporting success but can be extremely dysfunctional for passing the required sports aptitude tests and practical exams, which involve the performance of different sport. Thus, they may have a negative impact on both the admission and successful completion of sport science programmes.

Therefore, sport science programmes should remove admission barriers for HPAs and facilitate study conditions which can be brought in line with being an HPA.

Furthermore, sport science programmes designed for HPAs would be an important contribution to the sustainable development of sports organisations, specifically in high-performance sport. In many countries, there is a lack of highly qualified and experienced coaches, officials, managers, and journalists with sport-specific expertise in high-performance sport (Wicker, Orlowski and Breuer, 2018). Subsequently, better-educated athletes are more mature, confident, and responsible in dealing with threats to the integrity of sport and thus contribute to ensuring the uprightness of sport. For voluntary positions in national and international sports organisations and federations, well-educated athletes (and potentially later officials) with a solid knowledge foundation in sport science bring added value.

### Network approach and online learning

Previous programmes and measures promoting the dual career of HPAs have primarily aimed to create appropriate conditions for them to successfully participate in and complete existing university study programmes. Considering the small number of HPA students in the study programmes, the additional costs for providing individual services to them and offering extra support are extremely high and difficult to justify in relation to limited resources within universities.

Therefore, instead of customising existing programmes to meet the specific needs of HPAs, it would be useful to think about developing a tailor-made study programme in sport science based on the needs of HPAs. Taking into account the resource argument and the e-learning opportunities, it would be advisable for universities to form a network and work together with sport federations and sport policy to develop a study programme of sport science tailored to athletes' needs.

Developing technical possibilities turn e-learning or blended learning into a good and meaningful approach to support the HPA in their study progress and thus a dual career. However, the preparation of e-learning or blended learning modules and subsequent supervision are as well very resource-intensive; therefore, many universities refrain from implementing specific e-learning/blended learning opportunities for HPAs (Jahn, 2019).

Regarding the great diversity of study programmes and the comparatively small number of HPA students, economically it is not very conducive to offer support services throughout all study programmes to reconcile studying and a competitive sports career. In a first step, the focus on sport science study programmes seems promising, as many HPAs do pursue a professional career in sport after finishing their active sports career. This observation supports the previous statements on the athletes' interest, experience, and special expertise in the field of (high-performance) sport. Adapting sports study programmes would not only improve the dual career opportunities for HPAs, but at the same time it might also contribute to the sustainable development of sport, since well-trained coaches, managers, sports journalists, physiotherapists, and so on are needed in leisure sport as well as in competitive sport for their future development.

In view of the problems and challenges related to the dual careers of HPAs, the following considerations should be made to help overcome the issues raised:

- Resources and solutions should be developed in partnership with key stakeholders, resulting in potentially significant positive outcomes for HPAs.
- Good career prospects in sport following a career as an athlete justify the focus on sport science.
- However, sport science programmes will only be compatible with HPAs sports career if a large proportion of modules are offered in the form of e-learning or blended learning.

The importance of e-learning as a starting point for flexible study options has already been emphasised in the EU Guidelines on Dual Careers of Athletes. In general, all forms of teaching and learning supported by electronic or digital media can be subsumed in the term e-learning (Reinmann, Lames and Kamper, 2010). E-learning tools range from online learning scenarios, the processing of linear or branched multimedia learning offers, to constructivist forms of learning using Web 2.0 technologies (Schulz-Zander and Tulodziecki, 2011) and complex virtual learning environments (Dillenbourg, Schneider and Synteta, 2002). Due to the many opportunities and applications, e-learning has great potential to be used in diverse contexts and areas. A distinction can be made between:

- Traditional educational programmes that are enriched by e-learning
- Hybrid programmes, in which e-learning plays an equally important role as traditional teaching methods
- Pure e-learning scenarios (de Witt, 2005)

The latter completely comprises of virtual learning offers without physical presence and allow knowledge transfer, communication, and interaction online (Jahn, 2019). Thus, new information and communication technologies can be used

# Careers of European athletes    223

*Table 18.1* Advantages and Opportunities Versus Disadvantages and Risks Related to Online Learning

| Advantages and opportunities | Disadvantages and risks |
| --- | --- |
| • Learning independent of time and place<br>• Flexible and individual design of the study programme with regard to pace, scope and personal living conditions<br>• Adaptability of learning content to the prerequisites and needs of the students; the associated proactive examination of the learning material additionally promotes learning<br>• Students are at the centre of learning and studying<br>• Students acquire comprehensive e-skills on the side (Jahn, 2019)<br>• Teachers/lecturers can respond to students' needs on a very short notice (Köhler *et al.*, 2019)<br>• Inclusion problems of HPA students in the social fabric of the university are substantially reduced | • High degree of self-discipline and self-learning competence demanded from HPAs<br>• Increased organisational and supervision-related efforts by teachers/lecturers<br>• Challenge for teachers/lecturers to include HPAs in the interactive learning process<br>• Opportunities for exchange with fellow students and teachers/lecturers is fully based on virtual platforms and, hence, might be challenging<br>• Not being able to provide sufficient infrastructural conditions and resources in financial, personnel and temporal respects for online learning programmes<br>• Lack of knowledge and competence in the didactic and methodical implementation of high-quality e-learning offerings by the teachers/lecturers (Jahn, 2019)<br>• Legal challenges when it comes to grading examinations via electronic platforms (Ibabe and Jauregizar, 2009) |

for quality assurance and development in sport, movement sciences, sport education and training, and in sports organisations (Igel and Daugs, 2003; Eickhoff, 2008; Reinmann *et al.*, 2010; Hebbel-Seeger, Kretschmann and Vohle, 2013).

The advantages and opportunities of using electronic forms and methods of learning are accompanied by several disadvantages and risks, which must not be ignored and underestimated. These are summarised in Table 18.1.

A particularly promising approach to improve the compatibility of study and high-performance sport is blended learning, which has been established in recent years as an effective teaching and learning method. The basic idea of blended learning is to combine presence (offline) and virtual events (online) in such a way that the educational advantages of both respective formats are used for an optimal learning process and the social aspects of joint learning are combined with the effectiveness and flexibility of electronic forms of learning (Koop and Mandl, 2011; Kallischnigg, 2012; Jahn, 2019). Hybrid learning scenarios, such as flipped classroom, are therefore very suitable for HPA students and their dual career (Jahn, 2019). In a pilot project in sport-oriented schools of adolescent HPAs, it was shown that e-learning formats are very suitable for students who do not take part in regular classes due to competitions or training camps and were rated extremely positively by both teachers and students. The cost-benefit ratio and the development of self-learning competence in adolescent HPAs were identified as critical success factors (Köhler, Börner and Drummer, 2019).

In summary, in reaction to the increasing internationalisation of sport, for example through competitions and training camps abroad or the formation of international cadres (especially in team sport), e-learning is an appropriate approach to individualising learning for HPAs. They can that way not only study adapted to their individual sports schedule, but they can also determine the progress of their study depending on their individual situation. Retrieving content digitally, participating in online lectures and exercises and communicating actively with fellow students and lecturers, even during intensive training and competition periods at home and abroad, allows HPAs to follow their studies continuously and thus complete their studies more quickly. E-learning makes it possible to create important foundations for the compatibility of high-performance sport and athletes' professional future. A study programme that consists of (predominantly) e-learning/blended learning units thus represents a valuable element for a better compatibility of high-performance sport and university studies.

## Conclusion

The issues concerning HPAs, dual careers, and educational accomplishment continue to be prevalent for many athletes across Europe. The evidence suggests that many of the challenges faced can be overcome if a systematic and joined-up approach is taken by the key stakeholders. Such stakeholders include not only the HPAs themselves, but also universities, coaches, sport federations, and sports governing bodies. Working in partnership and understanding the concerns of all invested parties are essential to developing flexible solutions that ultimately help to achieve the associated goals. As many countries within Europe focus on achieving sporting success, the number of HPAs will increase further. It involves everyone's responsibility that resources are not only concentrated on their sports career but also on their education, ensuring that the athletes' career aspirations are not compromised long term.

## References

Alfermann, D. (2006) 'Karriereübergänge', in Tietjens, M. and Strauß, B. (eds.) *Handbuch Sportpsychologie*. Schorndorf: Hofmann, pp. 118–125.
Aquilina, D. (2013) 'A study of the relationship between elite athletes' educational development and sporting performance', *The International Journal of the History of Sport*, 30(4), pp. 374–392.
Aquilina, D. and Henry, I. (2010) 'Elite athletes and university education in Europe: A review of policy and practice in higher education in the European Union member states', *International Journal of Sport Policy*, 2(1), pp. 25–47.
Bendrich, B. (2015) *Studentische Spitzensport zwischen Resignation, Mythos und Aufbruch. Eine Studie zu dualen Kariere in Deutschland und den USA*. Göttingen: Optimus.
Bette, K. H. (1984) *Strukturelle Aspekte des Hochleistungssports in der Bundesrepublik*. Sankt Augustin: Richarz.

Careers of European athletes 225

Borggrefe, C. (2013) *Spitzensport und Beruf. Eine qualitative Studie zur dualen Karriere in funktional differenzierter Gesellschaft*. Schorndorf: Hofmann.

Borggrefe, C., Cachay, K. and Riedl, L. (2009) *Spitzensport und Studium. Eine organisationssoziologische Studie zum Problem Dualer Karrieren*. Schorndorf: Hofmann.

Breuer, C. and Hallmann, K. (2013) *Dysfunktionen des Spitzensports: Doping, Match-Fixing und Gesundheitsgefährdungen aus Sicht von Bevölkerung und Athleten*. Bonn: Bundesinstitut für Sportwissenschaft.

Breuer, C. et al. (2018) *Die Lebenssituation von Spitzensportlern und -sportlerinnen in Deutschland*. Bonn: Bundesinstitut für Sportwissenschaft.

Brustio, P. R. et al. (2020) 'Italian student – Athletes only need a more effective daily schedule to support their dual career', *Sport Sciences for Health*, 16, pp. 177–182.

Condello, G. et al. (2019) 'Dual-career through the elite university student-athletes' lenses: The international FISU-EAS survey', *PLoS ONE*, 14(10). doi: 10.1371/journal. pone.0223278.

Conzelmann, A., Gabler, H. and Nagel, S. (2001) *Hochleistungssport – persönlicher Gewinn oder Verlust?* Tübingen: Attempto Verlag.

Council of the European Union (2017) *European work plan for Sport 2017–2020*. Available at: http://data.consilium.europa.eu/doc/document/ST-9639-2017-INIT/en/pdf (Accessed: 07 Sep 2020).

Dillenbourg, P., Schneider, D. and Synteta, P. (2002) 'Virtual learning environments', in Dimitracopou, I. (ed.) *3rd Hellenic conference 'Information & communication technologies in education'*. Rhodos, pp. 3–18.

Eickhoff, L. A. (2008) *eLearning in der Sportausbildung und -weiterbildung, Probleme, Perspektiven und Tendenzen*. Dissertationsschrift, Köln.

European Commission (2007) *White Paper on Sport*. Available at: https://eur-lex.europa. eu/legal-content/EN/TXT/PDF/?uri=CELEX:52007DC0391&from=EN (Accessed: 07 Sep 2020).

European Commission (2011) *Developing the European Dimension in Sport*. Available at: https:// eur-lex.europa.eu/legal-content/EN/TXT/PDF/?uri=CELEX:52011DC0012&from=EN (Accessed: 24 Nov 2020).

European Commission (2012) *EU Guidelines on Dual Careers of Athletes*. Available at: https://op.europa.eu/en/publication-detail/-/publication/3648359d-61c4-4132-b247-3438ee828450 (Accessed: 02 Dec 2020).

European Commission (2016) *Study on the Minimum Quality Requirements for Dual Career Services*. Luxembourg: Publications Office of the European Union. Available at: https:// publications.europa.eu/en/publication-detail/-/publication/e06e5845-0527-11e6-b713-01aa75ed71a1 (Accessed: 24 Nov 2020).

Flatau, J. and Emrich, E. (2013) 'Asset specificity in the promotion of elite sports: Efficient Institutions of governance for the 'Production' of long-term future sporting success', *International Journal of Sport Finance*, 8(4), pp. 327–340.

Hebbel-Seeger, A., Kretschmann, R. and Vohle, F. (2013) 'Bildungstechnologien im Sport. Forschungsstand, Einsatzgebiete und Praxisbeispiele', in Ebner, M. and Schön, S. (eds.) *L3T. Lehrbuch für Lernen und Lehren mit Technologien*. Berlin u.a: Epubli, pp. 557–568.

Henriksen, K. et al. (2020, in print) 'A holistic ecological approach to sport and study: The case of an athlete friendly university in Denmark', *Psychology of Sport & Exercise*. doi: 10.1016/j.psychsport.2019.101637.

Hottenrott, K. and Braumann, K. M. (2015) 'Aktuelle situation im deutschen Spitzensport. Current situation in German elite sport', *Sportwissenschaft*, 45(3), pp. 111–115.

Ibabe, I., & Jauregizar, J. (2008). Formative Online Assessment in E-Learning. In F. García-Peñalvo (Ed.), *Advances in E-Learning: Experiences and Methodologies* (pp. 279-300). IGI Global. http://doi:10.4018/978-1-59904-756-0.ch016

Igel, C. and Daugs, R. (2003) 'eLearning in der Bewegungs- und Trainingswissenschaft: Das Engineering des BMBF-Projektes "eBuT"', *dvs-Informationen*, 18(3), pp. 5–8.

Jahn, V. (2019) 'Back flip meets flipped classroom – Die Ermöglichung von dualen Karrieren für studierende Spitzensportlerinnen und Spitzensportler durch innovative E-learning-Ansätze', in Schneider, A. and Wendeborn, T. (eds.) *Spitzensport und Studium. Herausforderungen und Lösungsansätze zur Ermöglichung dualer Karriere.* Wiesbaden: Springer, pp. 77–95.

Kallischnigg, M. (2012) 'Perspektiven der Vereinbarkeit von Spitzensport und beruflicher Karriereplanung dank Blended-Learning-Arrangement in der akademischen Ausbildung für Spitzensportler/-innen (Praxisreport)', in Csanyi, G., Reichl, F. and Steiner, A. (eds.) *Digitale Medien – Werkzeuge für exzellente Forschung und Lehre, Medien in der Wissenschaft.* Münster: Waxmann, pp. 263–265.

Köhler, T., Börner, C. and Drummer, J. (2019) 'E-learning an Sportgymnasien – Ergebnisse eines Schulversuchs an den Sportgymnasien im Freistaat Sachsen', in Schneider, A. and Wendeborn, T. (eds.) *Spitzensport und Studium. Herausforderungen und Lösungsansätze zur Ermöglichung dualer Karriere.* Wiesbaden: Springer, pp. 131–151.

Koop, B. and Mandl, H. (2011) 'Blended learning: Forschungsfragen und Perspektiven', in Klimsa, P. and Issing, L. J. (eds.) *Online-Lernen, Handbuch für Wissenschaft und Praxis.* Munich: Oldenbourg, pp. 139–150.

Latinjak, A. T. (2018) *La Carrera Dual en la Formacio de Futurs Professoals de L'Esport.*

Mateu, P. *et al.* (2020) 'Living life through sport: The transition of elite Spanish student-athletes to a university degree in physical activity and sports sciences', *Frontiers in Psychology*, 11, 1367.

Morris, R. *et al.* (2020, in print) 'A taxonomy of dual career development environments in European countries', *European Sports Management Quarterly*.

Nagel, S. and Conzelmann, A. (2006) 'Zum Einfluss der Hochleistungssport-Karriere auf die Berufskarriere–Chancen und Risiken', *Sport und Gesellschaft*, 3(3), pp. 237–261.

Naul, R. (1994) 'The elite athlete career: Sport pedagogy must counsel social and professional problems in life development', in Hackfort, D. (ed.) *Psycho-social issues and interventions in elite sport.* Frankfurt: Lang, pp. 237–258.

Reinmann, G., Lames, M. and Kamper, M. (2010) *E-Learning für die Qualifizierung im organisierten Sport.* Frankfurt: DOSB.

Ridpath, B. D., Rudd, A. and Stokowski, S. (2019) 'Perceptions of European athletes that attend American colleges and universities for elite athletic development and higher education access', *Journal for Global Sport Management*, 5(1), pp. 34–61.

Schneider, A. and Fischer, C. (2019) 'Studierende Spitzensportlerinnen und Spitzensportler bei den Olympischen Spielen in Rio – Analyse zur Struktur und Erfolg der deutschen Olympiamannschaft 2016', in Schneider, A. and Wendeborn, T. (eds.) *Spitzensport und Studium. Herausforderungen und Lösungsansätze zur Ermöglichung dualer Karriere.* Wiesbaden: Springer, pp. 19–52.

Schulz-Zander, R. and Tulodziecki, G. (2011) 'Pädagogische Grundlagen für das Online-Lernen', in Klimsa, P. and Issing, L. J. (eds.) *Online-Lernen – Handbuch für Wissenschaft und Praxis.* Munich: Oldenbourg, pp. 35–45.

Wicker, P., Orlowski, J. and Breuer, C. (2018) 'Coach migration in German high performance sport', *European Sport Management Quarterly*, 18(1), pp. 93–111.

de Witt, C. (2005) 'Integration von e-learning in die Bildung', in Kleber, H. (ed.) *Perspektiven der Medienpädagogik in Wissenschaft und Bildungspraxis*. Munich: kopaed, pp. 204–217.

Wylleman, P. and Lavallee, D. (2004) 'A development perspective on transitions faced by athletes', in Weiss, M. (ed.) *Developmental sport and exercise psychology. A lifespan perspective*. Morgantown: FIT, pp. 507–527.

Wylleman, P. and Reints, A. (2010) 'A lifespan perspective on the career of talente dand elite athletes: Perspectives on high-intensity sports', *Scandinavian Journal of Medicine and Science in Sport*, 20(S2), pp. 88–94.

Wylleman, P., Alfermann, D. and Lavallee, D. (2004) 'Career transitions in sport', *Psychology of Sport and Exercise*, 5, pp. 7–20.

Wylleman, P., Reints, A. and De Knop, P. (2013) 'A developmental and holistic perspective on athletic career development', in Sotiriadou, P. and De Bosscher, V. (eds.) *Managing high performance sport*. London: Routledge, pp. 159–182.

Chapter 19

# Transforming coach education for the 21st century

*Christian Thue Bjørndal, Tynke Toering, and Siv Gjesdal*

## Introduction

Participation in sport can impact lives in profound ways by promoting physical and mental health and well-being, and aiding psychosocial development (Eime *et al.*, 2013). However, participation in itself does not guarantee these outcomes, and young athletes who partake in organised sport often face multiple pressures, including competing time demands with other youth activities (Bakken, 2019), high dropout rates (Bakken, 2018), and health risks associated with overuse injuries and burnout (DiFiori *et al.*, 2014). The abuse of power in elite and grassroots level sport has also become a growing concern (Johnson *et al.*, 2020). Misconceptions about best practice in organised sport continue to be presented as evidence-based knowledge (Collins and Bailey, 2013), and the ability to predict future successes remains elusive (Johnston *et al.*, 2018).

One way to address current challenges in sport is to examine the ways in which coach expertise can be improved through coach education. Coaches are essential stakeholders in athlete development processes but coach education itself needs to be reformed. Current coach education programmes are structured in ways that often reflect and, to some extent, maintain the separateness and uniqueness of scientific disciplines. Similarly, coach education programmes often focus on ways to measure and track performance rather than giving attention to how coach behaviours and routines are shaped and developed (Denison, Jones and Mills, 2019). Typically, coaching behaviours are informed by separate, compartmentalised modules of knowledge that focus on the individual elements of coaching. This has led to a preoccupation with scientific disciplines, such as sport and exercise physiology and psychology, that are underpinned by strongly reductionist philosophies (Pol *et al.*, 2020). Typically, coach education content is normative, decontextualised, and centred on knowledge about coaching rather than of coaching practice and performance (Vaughan *et al.*, 2021).

Coaches have their own implicit orientations and ways of thinking about athlete performance and are heavily influenced by distinct sport coaching cultures (Zehntner and McMahon, 2015). Approaches to coach learning and development reflect the particular paradigms in which coaches are socialised. These mirror,

DOI: 10.4324/9781003002666-24

for instance, their values, their beliefs, and their dispositions towards the social world (Mallett and Tinning, 2014). How coaches understand their own professional identity and their approaches to athlete development will impact on how they coach, whether they are able to advance in their coaching careers, and which values they will prioritise. To enable sport coaches to challenge current knowledge and praxis, coach education needs to focus not only on how knowledge is reproduced but also on the critical ways in which meaning is sought. Coaches also need to better understand the contexts in which their coaching is located (Cushion, Armour and Jones, 2006) and how these contexts shape their own preferred practices through particular relations of power (Denison *et al.*, 2019).

The present chapter is an attempt to critically discuss the scientific and cultural premises on which current coach education in sport is based and to offer reflections on how this education can be developed and improved. In the first section, we look at coach education programmes and explore how current reductionist sport science models may limit holistic approaches to sport coaching. In the second section, we explore how systems of knowledge produce ideas about sport coaching and athlete development and how new knowledge can develop through probing the power dynamics that are explicitly and implicitly valued in coach education. We examine how these permeate current sociocultural contexts and have hindered more effective, ethical, and athlete-centred approaches to coaching. Finally, we conclude by sharing some ideas that we believe can contribute to transforming coach education through the design of more transdisciplinary approaches in coaching courses.

## The need for transdisciplinary perspectives

Coach education needs to become more relevant to the people, contexts, and cultures in which it is located. To achieve this goal, a common understanding is needed of how science and praxis enable and limit the knowledge and work of coaches. Modern coach education attempts to base itself on sport science evidence, and this web of available knowledge offers important opportunities for understanding athlete development and performance. However, such knowledge is shaped by the paradigmatic approaches used within particular disciplines. Most positivist approaches, for example, are rooted in experimental control, and coach education that relies too heavily on such traditions can be problematic if the learning effects of context, emotion, and the world beyond coaching routines are dismissed or ignored (Denison *et al.*, 2019). The behavioural and learning effects observed in controlled settings may well be different from those observed in real-world competitive settings (Headrick *et al.*, 2015), as shown in recent studies of perception and action in sport (Aksum *et al.*, 2020). Many of the approaches that inform coach education have tended to focus on distinct aspects of particular phenomena (Mills, Denison and Gearity, 2020). Skill acquisition and development, for example, have been extensively researched within multiple but largely separate disciplines in sport science (Pol *et al.*, 2020). Similarly, motor development and psychological development are fundamentally interconnected but have typically been examined as separate concerns, both by researchers and by practitioners (Adolph and Hoch, 2019). The use of multiple but different disciplinary approaches offers a generally valuable approach within coach education, but has resulted in the production of extensive, fragmented evidence that sometimes lacks overall coherence. When coaches learn distinct methodologies, they tend to focus on individual training components and disregard the interconnectedness of these elements (Pol *et al.*, 2020). This has led to paradigmatically distinct understandings of sports programming, planning, and training (Kiely, 2018). Inevitably, knowledge generated in this way is more difficult to adopt and to apply in the constantly changing, interconnected, nuanced, ambiguous, and messy social worlds of athletes and coaches (Jones and Wallace, 2005).

The continued emphasis on discrete, rational ways of knowing keeps pervading coaching practices and institutions. This is an obstacle to improving coach education because it inhibits efforts to build more holistic, ethical, and athlete-centred approaches and limits insights into the complex ways in which people engage and interact with others (De Jaegher, 2019). Coach education needs to be recognised as something that is located within contexts that are ever-changing (Vaughan *et al.*, 2019). Athlete learning also needs to be recognised as something that takes place within complex and social processes (Adolph and Hoch, 2019) in which subjective experiences, emotions, and physical activities are intrinsically connected (Fuchs and Koch, 2014). Importantly, the complexity of these processes means that development or performance outcomes can be achieved via different pathways and means. Discussions about the "quality" of coach education and coaching therefore need to be both science-based and value-based (Hemmestad, Jones and Standal, 2010). Recognising such interconnections and interconnectedness could enable coaches to function more appropriately and effectively in the social contexts of sport.

The challenge of transforming how coaches understand and implement linear models of athlete selection and deselection is reflected in the way researchers and practitioners alike neglect the complex interactions that facilitate and constrain athlete learning and development. The process of selection is difficult due to the need to cater for individual differences in athletes' growth, maturation, and development and because of the nonlinearity of learning, development, and performance (Seifert *et al.*, 2018). Nonlinear and highly variable patterns of elite athlete performance development make it highly likely that the repetitive and standardised progressions and training protocols, stage-based models, and the popular pyramidal concept of athlete development will not meet the needs of individual athletes (Gulbin *et al.*, 2013). New approaches to building and applying knowledge require greater critical reflexivity regarding what coaching practice "does" and how it impacts upon athletes (Denison and Avner, 2011). Empowerment, autonomy, holism, and resilience are popular stated themes in coach development. However, researchers are right to question whether such

Transforming coach education 231

preoccupations are rhetorical if they are not accompanied by more fundamental changes to the models underlying coaching practices and approaches (Denison, Mills and Konoval, 2017). A more diverse knowledge base would allow coaches to make better informed selection decisions.

Sport coaching, athlete development, and performance need to be based on knowledge that is synthesised from across different scientific disciplines (Barker-Ruchti and Purdy, 2021). The key sport science models that inform coach education are still largely multidisciplinary, drawing on distinct and separate scientific disciplines, such as physiology, biomechanics, psychology, motor learning, and sociology (Pol *et al.*, 2020). Consideration is seldom given to variations in the ontological and epistemological assumptions across different, largely independent scientific disciplines (Hausken-Sutter *et al.*, 2021). Transforming coach education will need a deliberate shift away from mono- or multidisciplinary perspectives that are rooted in siloed disciplines and a shift towards transdisciplinary perspectives and understandings (Vaughan *et al.*, 2019). This will require sport science scholars from different disciplines to work together to develop new conceptual, theoretical, methodological, and translational innovations.

## Constraints on coaching knowledge

As noted, knowledge developed and applied in sport has been traditionally based on findings that are rooted in distinct and separated scientific disciplines. This has shaped the way training, sports competitions, and athlete development are perceived and has led to a consensus about what constitutes "the right way" of doing things (Denison *et al.*, 2019). In Western endurance sport, for example, the principles of programming and training praxis have been strongly influenced by positivist knowledge about exercise within the discipline of physiology. This has provided a useful and productive paradigm for sports practitioners; however, it has also been a siloed approach which has limited and constrained the education and vision of coaches and diverted attention away from important non-physiological athlete attributes (Konoval, Denison and Mills, 2019).

Similarly, the hegemonic culture of a lot of male-dominated team sport (e.g., football, ice-hockey) has promoted and prioritised values that are stereotypically associated with the working class, such as modesty, straightforwardness, and hard work. This has led to compromises on the part of athletes in the face of the physical and mental health demands of sport (Manley, Roderick and Parker, 2016) and made many more willing to accept pain and injury as part of their "normal" professional experience (Roderick, 2006). Cultural expectations are also often reproduced and facilitated by the authoritarian leadership of coaches (Kelly and Waddington, 2006). Success, though, can be achieved in other ways. Recent research in Norwegian elite sport, for example, has shown that coaching leadership in sport and performance development that is rooted in cultural values such as democratic involvement, collaboration, and athlete-centred approaches can lead to international success (Hemmestad and Jones, 2019; Erikstad *et al.*, 2020; Hansen *et al.*, 2021).

Traditional sport coaching tends to focus on ways to establish and maintain organisational control, and this has enabled coaches to create a sense of security for themselves as they operate within clearly defined organisational structures and roles (Potrac, Jones and Armour, 2002). These dominant organisational practices in sports programmes implicitly maximise the control of coaches rather than athletes over the training process (Denison *et al.*, 2017). Coaches learn to construct training environments that appear to be successful by their virtue of being orderly and efficient. Similarly, they rely heavily on verbal feedback and instructions that reinforce and prioritise standardised notions of appropriate and "correct" athlete behaviour but tend to give less attention to the individuality of expert player performance. Many talent development systems and stage-based athlete development models restrict athlete development by pre-determining the ways in which athletes "should" be developed (Dowling, Mills and Stodter, 2020). This means that the careers of athletes are prescribed by a definition of moments and milestones that indicate the "right" time for them to progress, excel, or retire from sport (Ronkainen and Ryba, 2017).

Progress monitoring and measurements of time efficiency are important elements of coaching and are not inherently problematic. Technologies that monitor may help to improve coaching and athlete effectiveness, but they may also reduce or negatively alter the social interactions that occur between athletes and coaches. The use of wearable GPS devices, for example, has been shown to coerce professional Rugby League players to comply with potentially unhealthy physical and psychological demands through constant surveillance and to the normalisation of punishment when players have fallen short of prescribed expectations (Jones, Marshall and Denison, 2016). Imbalances in the power dynamics between coaches and athletes can profoundly influence the identities and self-understanding of athletes and their subsequent development if the proscribed institutional norms leave athletes with little agency (Manley *et al.*, 2016). They may also have unforeseen and potentially problematic implications for how players experience their own development (Jones, 2019). How control is exerted and expressed and how knowledge of performance analysis and technologies are used are therefore key factors that can affect whether coaching is either useful or problematic. Deeper and more critical reflections on athlete autonomy and individuality should therefore be central concerns when attempting to develop and reform coach education.

To enable coaches to develop critical, meaningful insights into their own thinking and actions, it will be necessary not only to study sport coaching and athlete development as phenomena in themselves, but also to study the systems of knowledge that produce them. Sports cultures are often closely linked to particular scientific disciplines and the associated praxis (Denison, 2010). These links have emerged within certain historical, cultural, and social settings and are sustained through complex networks of power (Denison *et al.*, 2017). Knowledge, power, and praxis are thus inextricably intertwined (Markula-Denison and Pringle, 2006), and praxis is reinforced in culture and dogma (Cushion and Jones,

2014). Pedagogical practices are therefore also culturally defined by the distinct cultural and organisational settings in which they are located.

Recent empirical research in youth football in Sweden, for instance, has revealed how the pedagogical approaches of coaches and particular player attributes and skills (such as technical and tactical preferences) have been formed through social, cultural, and historical practices (Sullivan *et al.*, 2021). Additionally, in sport coaching, male actors have often been assumed to be innately more knowledgeable and competent than women. As a result, women have typically faced additional barriers when trying to enter the coaching profession (Kilty, 2006). Social, psychological, and pedagogical knowledge have typically received less attention in many coaching cultures (Barker-Ruchti and Purdy, 2021). A potential consequence may have been the "objectification" and "commodification" of athletes, and players being regarded more as products rather than people. The commercialisation of elite sport rooted in economic, not humanistic, ideals and values can be regarded as a manifestation of this problem (O'Gorman *et al.*, 2020).

Probing the power dynamics that are explicitly and implicitly valued in coach education can help to draw attention to the facilitative and constraining effects of underlying current knowledge (Mills and Denison, 2018). Doing so will enable coaches to build a better understanding of what it means to be a better coach. It will also enable knowledge derived from both empirical science and contextual experience to be used in ways that can help to improve sport education, practice, and performance.

## Transforming coach education

Improvements in coach education can be achieved not by making the content more academic, but by focusing instead on how science and knowledge, rooted in pluralism, can be translated into productive and meaningful practice. Innovative coach education should enable coaches to recognise how they are influenced by the ideas and assumptions within their social milieu and to understand how these can impact on their own work and development processes (e.g. Collins, Abraham and Collins, 2012). Coach education should aim to create a culture which is open to the uncertainties inherent in coaching and facilitates teaching in less pre-defined and disciplinary-specific ways. To do this, coaches will need to learn to break free of prescriptive and well-defined approaches, accepting instead the potential learning and development opportunities offered through more flexible, exploratory approaches. They will also need to learn to become less fearful of "not knowing" or "not yet knowing" and about the risks associated with "doing things differently". Successful change will require experimentation with new practices, new training methods, and, hopefully, the emergence of new forms of organisation to facilitate fresher ways of thinking about sport coaching and development.

New approaches will enable better insights into how current praxis is shaped through relations of power. These approaches will also help to achieve profound transformations in coach education and practice. Examples of promising directions for future improvement in coach education include those used in Foucauldian coach learning communities (Kuklick and Gearity, 2019). These communities utilise the concepts of the French social scientist Michel Foucault to better understand how power dynamics work, how to create new and less disciplinary-based practices, and how to address the problems caused by excessive discipline or hyper-structured planning and programming (Kuklick and Gearity, 2019). Similarly, attention should also be given to incremental coaching strategies that attempt to provide more adaptive responses to aspects of practice that, on a day-by-day basis, can be influenced but not fully controlled (Bjørndal and Ronglan, 2019). Strategies to improve coach education could also focus on the science of complex systems (Pol et al., 2020). These draw attention to the need to focus less on prescribed, fixed approaches and instead attempt to understand the properties of systems and the principles that direct their behaviour to then increase the diversity/unpredictability potential of athletes and teams (Pol et al., 2020). An important note is to not limit this approach to a focus on the product of interactions of agents but to incorporate relevant sociocultural conditions (Hausken-Sutter et al., 2021). The application of such approaches will need to be part of a broader shift away from multidisciplinary models of scientific knowledge and towards integrated *transdisciplinary* approaches. We see this as an essential and important first step.

## Acknowledgements

We are grateful to Dr. Hedda H. Berntsen, Dr. Jim Denison, Dr. Brian Gearity, Dr. Joseph P. Mills, Mark O'Sullivan, Dr. Noora Roinkanen, and Dr. James Vaughan for their insightful comments on an earlier draft of the book chapter.

## References

Adolph, K. E. and Hoch, J. E. (2019) 'Motor development: Embodied, embedded, enculturated, and enabling', *Annual Review Psychologie*, 70(1), pp. 141–164. doi: 10.1146/annurev-psych-010418-102836.

Aksum, K. M. *et al.* (2020) 'What do football players look at? An eye-tracking analysis of the visual fixations of players in 11 v 11 elite football match play', *Front Psychology*, 11, 562995. doi: 10.3389/fpsyg.2020.562995.

Bakken, A. (2018) *Ungdata 2018: National results [Ungdata 2018: Nasjonale resultater]*. Available at: http://www.ungdata.no/ (Accessed: 13 June 2021).

Bakken, A. (2019) 'Idrettens posisjon i ungdomstida. Hvem deltar og hvem slutter i ungdomsidretten?', *NOVA Rapport*, Issue. NOVA.

Barker-Ruchti, N. and Purdy, L. G. (2021) 'Education for sustainable development: Teaching deliberation and ethical decision-making in university coach education', *Sports Coaching Review*, pp. 1–20. doi: 10.1080/21640629.2021.1899654.

Bjørndal, C. T. and Ronglan, L. T. (2019) 'Engaging with uncertainty in athlete development – Orchestrating talent development through incremental leadership', *Sport, Education and Society*, 26(1), pp. 104–116. doi: 10.1080/13573322.2019.1695198.

Collins, D. and Bailey, R. (2013) "'Scienciness' and the allure of second-hand strategy in talent identification and development', *International Journal of Sport Policy*, 5(2), pp. 183–191.

Collins, D., Abraham, A. and Collins, R. (2012) 'On vampires and wolves – Exposing and exploring reasons for the differential impact of coach education', *International Journal of Sport Psychology*, 43(3), pp. 255–271.

Cushion, C. J. and Jones, R. L. (2014) 'A Bourdieusian analysis of cultural reproduction: Socialisation and the 'hidden curriculum' in professional football', *Sport Education and Society*, 19(3), pp. 276–298. doi: 10.1080/13573322.2012.666966.

Cushion, C. J., Armour, K. M. and Jones, R. L. (2006) 'Locating the coaching process in practice: Models 'for' and 'of' coaching', *Physical Education and Sport Pedagogy*, 11(1), pp. 83–99. doi: 10.1080/17408980500466995.

De Jaegher, H. (2019) 'Loving and knowing: Reflections for an engaged epistemology', *Phenomenology and the Cognitive Sciences*. doi: 10.1007/s11097-019-09634-5.

Denison, J. (2010) 'Planning, practice and performance: The discursive formation of coaches' knowledge', *Sport Education and Society*, 15(4), pp. 461–478. doi: 10.1080/13573322.2010.514740.

Denison, J. and Avner, Z. (2011) 'Positive coaching: Ethical practices for athlete development', *Quest*, 63(2), pp. 209–227. doi: 10.1080/00336297.2011.10483677.

Denison, J., Mills, J. P. and Konoval, T. (2017) 'Sports' disciplinary legacy and the challenge of 'coaching differently", *Sport Education and Society*, 22(6), pp. 772–783. doi: 10.1080/13573322.2015.1061986.

Denison, J., Jones, L. and Mills, J. P. (2019) 'Becoming a good enough coach', *Sports Coaching Review*, 8(1), pp. 1–6. doi: 10.1080/21640629.2018.1435361.

DiFiori, J. P. *et al.* (2014) 'Overuse injuries and burnout in youth sports: A position statement from the American Medical Society for sports medicine', *British Journal of Sports Medicine*, 48(4), pp. 287–288. doi: 10.1136/bjsports-2013-093299.

Dowling, M., Mills, J. and Stodter, A. (2020) 'Problematizing the adoption and implementation of athlete development 'Models': A Foucauldian-inspired analysis of the long-term athlete development framework', *Journal of Athlete Development and Experience*, 2(3).

Eime, R. M. *et al.* (2013) 'A systematic review of the psychological and social benefits of participation in sport for children and adolescents: Informing development of a conceptual model of health through sport', *International Journal of Behavioral Nutrition and Physical Activity*, 10(1), p. 98. doi: 10.1186/1479-5868-10-98.

Erikstad, M. K. *et al.* (2020) '"As many as possible for as long as possible"—A case study of a soccer team that fosters multiple outcomes', *The Sport Psychologist*, pp. 1–11. doi: 10.1123/tsp.2020-0107.

Fuchs, T. and Koch, S. C. (2014) 'Embodied affectivity: On moving and being moved', *Frontiers in Psychology*, 5. doi: 10.3389/fpsyg.2014.00508.

Gulbin, J. *et al.* (2013) 'Patterns of performance development in elite athletes', *European Journal of Sport Science*, 13(6), pp. 605–614. doi: 10.1080/17461391.2012.756542.

Hansen, P. O. *et al.* (2021) 'Leading and organising national teams: Functions of institutional leadership', *Sports Coaching Review*, pp. 1–22. doi: 10.1080/21640629.2021.1896213.

Hausken-Sutter, S. E. *et al.* (2021) 'Youth sport injury research: A narrative review and the potential of interdisciplinarity', *BMJ Open Sport & Exercise Medicine*, 7(1), p. e000933. doi: 10.1136/bmjsem-2020-000933.

Headrick, J. et al. (2015) 'The dynamics of expertise acquisition in sport: The role of affective learning design', *Psychology of Sport and Exercise*, 16, pp. 83–90. doi: 10.1016/j.psychsport.2014.08.006.

Hemmestad, L. B. and Jones, R. L. (2019) 'Deconstructing high performance Nordic sport: The case study of women's handball (the 'team as method')', *Sport in Society*, 22(4), pp. 671–688. doi: 10.1080/17430437.2017.1389062.

Hemmestad, L. B., Jones, R. L. and Standal, Ø. F. (2010) 'Phronetic social science: A means of better researching and analysing coaching?', *Sport, Education and Society*, 15(4), pp. 447–459. doi:10.1080/13573322.2010.514745.

Johnson, N. et al. (2020) 'U.S. Center for SafeSport: Preventing abuse in sports', *Women in Sport & Physical Activity Journal*, 28(1), pp. 66–71.

Johnston, K. et al. (2018) 'Talent identification in sport: A systematic review', *Sports Medicine*, 48(1), pp. 97–109. doi: 10.1007/s40279-017-0803-2.

Jones, L. (2019) 'Wearable GPS devices in a British Elite Soccer Academy setting: A Foucauldian disciplinary analysis of player development and experience', *Journal of Athlete Development and Experience*, 1(1). doi: 10.25035/jade.01.01.04.

Jones, R. L. and Wallace, M. (2005) 'Another bad day at the training ground: Coping with ambiguity in the coaching context', *Sport Education and Society*, 10(1), pp. 119–134. doi: 10.1080/1357332052000308792.

Jones, L., Marshall, P. and Denison, J. (2016) 'Health and well-being implications surrounding the use of wearable GPS devices in professional rugby league: A Foucauldian disciplinary analysis of the normalised use of a common surveillance aid', *Performance Enhancement & Health*, 5(2), pp. 38–46. doi: 10.1016/j.peh.2016.09.001.

Kelly, S. and Waddington, I. (2006) 'Abuse, intimidation and violence as aspects of managerial control in professional soccer in Britain and Ireland', *International Review for the Sociology of Sport*, 41(2), pp. 147–164. doi: 10.1177/1012690206075417.

Kiely, J. (2018) 'Periodization theory: Confronting an inconvenient truth', *Sports Medicine*, 48(4), pp. 753–764. doi: 10.1007/s40279-017-0823-y.

Kilty, K. (2006) 'Women in coaching', *Sport Psychologist*, 20(2), pp. 222–234. doi: 10.1123/tsp.20.2.222.

Konoval, T., Denison, J. and Mills, J. P. (2019) 'The cyclical relationship between physiology and discipline: One endurance running coach's experiences problematizing disciplinary practices', *Sports Coaching Review*, 8(2), pp. 124–148. doi: 10.1080/21640629.2018.1487632.

Kuklick, C. R. and Gearity, B. T. (2019) 'New movement practices: A Foucauldian learning community to disrupt technologies of discipline', *Sociology of Sport Journal*, 36(4), pp. 289–299. doi: 10.1123/ssj.2018-0158.

Mallett, C. J. and Tinning, R. (2014) 'Philosophy of knowledge', in Nelson, L., Groom, R. and Potrac, P. (eds.) *Research methods in sports coaching*. Oxon: Routledge, pp. 9–17.

Manley, A., Roderick, M. and Parker, A. (2016) 'Disciplinary mechanisms and the discourse of identity: The creation of 'silence' in an elite sports academy', *Culture and Organization*, 22(3), pp. 221-244. doi: 10.1080/14759551.2016.1160092.

Markula-Denison, P. and Pringle, R. (2006) *Foucault, sport and exercise: Power, knowledge and transforming the self.* Oxfordshire: Taylor & Francis.

Mills, J. P. and Denison, J. (2018) 'How power moves: A Foucauldian analysis of (in)effective coaching', *International Review for the Sociology of Sport*, 53(3), pp. 296–312. doi: 10.1177/1012690216654719.

Mills, J. P., Denison, J. and Gearity, B. (2020) 'Breaking coaching's rules: Transforming the body, sport, and performance', *Journal of Sport and Social Issues*, 019372352090322. doi: 10.1177/0193723520903228.

O'Gorman, J. *et al.* (2020) 'Translation, intensification and fabrication: Professional football academy coaches' enactment of the elite player performance plan', *Sport, Education and Society*, pp. 1–17. doi: 10.1080/13573322.2020.1726313.

Pol, R. *et al.* (2020) 'Training or synergizing? Complex systems principles change the understanding of sport processes', *Sports Medicine – Open*, 6(1), p. 28. doi: 10.1186/s40798-020-00256-9.

Potrac, P., Jones, R. and Armour, K. (2002) '"It's all about getting respect": The coaching behaviors of an expert English soccer coach', *Sport Education and Society*, 7(2), pp. 183–202. doi: 10.1080/1357332022000018869.

Roderick, M. (2006) *The work of professional football: A labour of love?* Oxon: Routledge.

Ronkainen, N. J. and Ryba, T. V. (2017) 'Rethinking age in athletic retirement: An existential-narrative perspective', *International Journal of Sport and Exercise Psychology*, 15(2), pp. 146–159. doi: 10.1080/1612197x.2015.1079920.

Seifert, L. *et al.* (2018) 'Skill transfer, expertise and talent development: An ecological dynamics perspective', *Movement & Sport Sciences*, 102(4), pp. 39–49.

Sullivan, M. O. *et al.* (2021) 'Towards a contemporary player learning in development framework for sports practitioners.', *International Journal of Sports Science & Coaching*, 174795412110023. doi: 10.1177/17479541211002335.

Vaughan, J. *et al.* (2019) 'Developing creativity to enhance human potential in sport: A wicked transdisciplinary challenge', *Frontiers in Psychology*, 10.

Vaughan, J. *et al.* (2021) 'Football, culture, skill development and sport coaching: Extending ecological approaches in athlete development using the skilled intentionality framework', *Frontiers in Psychology*, pp. 1–24. doi: 10.3389/fpsyg.2021.635420.

Zehntner, C. and McMahon, J. (2015) 'The impact of a coaching/sporting culture on one coach's identity: How narrative became a useful tool in reconstructing coaching ideologies', *Sports Coaching Review*, 3(2), pp. 145–161. doi: 10.1080/21640629.2015.1051883.

# Index

Pages in *italics* refer to figures and those in **bold** refer to tables.

Active and Health school 46
active lifestyle 2
active living, socio-ecological domains of 39
Adidas 29
adventure therapy 56
All Japan High School Athletic
Federation (AJHSAF) 152
American Youth Soccer Association
(AYSO) 118
Aotearoa NZ's outdoor education *see* New
Zealand, outdoor education in
Arizona Diamondbacks 29
artificial intelligence in sport 30
Association of Summer Olympic
International Federations (ASOIF) 85
athlete's dual careers 6
at-risk jobs 81
audio-visual enhancements 76–77
augmented reality 82
Australia, sport and physical activity in:
Australian Sport Commission (ASC),
role of 127; education strategy 130–132;
physical literacy framework 133; sports
participation among children and
mid-adolescence 127–128

"best practices" in coach education 71–72
big data 77–78
business intelligence in sport 30

Canada, sport development and delivery
in 110–114, **111**, 121; collaborative
approach 113–114; growth of sport
110–111; of Indigenous Peoples 112;
Long-Term Development in Sport
and Physical Activity (LTDSPA)

framework 112–114; National Coaching
Certification Program (NCCP) 114;
outstanding and memorable achievements 110–111; "Own the Podium"
(OTP) high-performance programme
114; Provincial and National Physical
and Health Education (PHE) professional organisations 114; *see also*
México, sport development and delivery
in; United States, sport development
and delivery in
career development learning (CDL) 88;
*see also* work-based learning (WBL);
work-related learning (WRL)
carry-over hypothesis 165
coach assessment 16–18; competency-
based approach 17–18, **18**; cost of 18
coach developer (CD) 12, 14; emerging
role of 15–16; in-practice support 16;
knowledge level 15; knowledge transfer
strategies 15–16; learner-centred
delivery 16; qualifications framework 19;
roles and functions 15; *see also* coach
education and development (CED)
coach education and development (CED)
2, 6, 12, *16*, 228–229; best practices 71–72;
challenges 14; coach as a learner 71;
constraints on knowledge 231–233; in
different contexts 71; gender differences
233; improvements 233–234; internal
learning 13; knowledge transfer and
inputs 13; learner-centred and experiential coach education 69–71; "LEARNS"
framework 70; mediated learning 13;
non-formal and informal education 14;
personal preference and developmental

stage 13–14; programmes 13–14; relationship between physical education and 68; transdisciplinary perspectives 229–231, 234; unmediated learning 13; of youth football coaches 14; *see also* coach developer (CD)

coaching 2, 175; globalisation of 68–69; qualifications 12; workforce 11, 19–20

Commonwealth Sport 199

competence-based training 18, **18**

content-based training 18, **18**

core discipline knowledge 86–87

corruption in sports 33

Coursera 80

Court of Arbitration for Sport 80

Covid-19 pandemic 38, 76, 80

data literacy 30

delivery of sports 12

digital equity 76

digital fandom 31

digitalisation 2

digitalisation of sports 30–31

diversity and inequality in sport 5, 138, 183–184; future directions 190–191; gender inequality 186; in global context 184–185; in physical activity 185; role models and sociocultural stereotypes 187; socio-economic status 186; sport and physical activity offers 186–187

doping 80

Eastern Asia, physical education and school sport in 4, 148, **149–150**; best practices 155; competition in school sport 154–155; context-specific quality PE 153–154, 156; Eastern Asian Alliance of Sport Pedagogy 155; emerging trends and challenges 153–155; future directions 155; higher education institutions, role of 151–152; issue of physical inactivity 153; in Japan 148–149, 154; national and international collaborations 152; School Physical Education Research Association (*Gakutairen*) 155; school sport opportunities 156; in South Korea 149–151, 152, 153; sport federations and associations, role of 152–153; in Taiwan 151, 153, 155; teacher professional development 152; teachers' professional development 154

Eastern Asian Alliance of Sport Pedagogy 152

educational system: in Eastern Asia 148; in Latin America 137–138

Education Outdoors New Zealand (EONZ) 50, 55

EDU:PACT project 5–6, 207, 209–212, *210*

employability: barriers **104**; definition 85; developing 84–90; professional competencies **104**; of sport coaches 105–106; of sport managers 103–105

empowerment and capacity building through sport 187–189; challenges 189; sport educator capacities 189–190

enterprise education 89

entrepreneurship education 89

eSport 31

EU Expert Group on Skills and Human Resources and Development in Sport (XG HR) 100

European athletes 216; EU Guidelines on the Dual Careers of Athletes 216; *see also* high performance athletes (HPA)

European economy 99

European football federations (UEFA) 80

European Handball Federation (EHF) 102

European Institute of Outdoor Adventure Education and Experiential Learning (EOE) 49

European Network of Sport Education (ENSE) 1

European Qualifications Framework (EQF) 99

European Sectoral Social Dialogue Committee for Sports and Active Leisure (ESSDCSL) 103

European Union-funded Europen Sector Skills Alliance for Sport and Physical Activity (ESSA-Sport) project 84

Evita Games 145

experiential learning 51

extended reality 77–78, 82

Fédération Internationale de Football Association (FIFA) 29

Foucauldian coach learning communities 234

German Sport University Cologne 102

globalisation of sports 3, 63–65; global coaching agenda 68–69

## 240 Index

Gold Coast Commonwealth Games, 2018 199
good governance in sports 32–33; *see also* sport management research and education
"The Graeme Dingle Foundation" (Project K) 55

Hauora 56
Hawk-Eye technology 75, 80
health-enhancing physical activity 68
health promotion 4, 163–164; role of sport in 5
"Healthy Settings" movement 164–165
high performance athletes (HPA) 6, 216, 217; biographical analysis of 217; challenges for universities providing dual career of 219–224; dual career opportunities for 217–219; European policies and 218–219; network approach and online learning 221–224, **223**; "White Paper on Sport" 218
Hillary Outdoors 55
Host City Contracts 199
Human Development Index (HDI) 167
Human Development Report 184
human rights in sport education 5, 195; education providers, role of 200–201; examples 198–200; power of sport to promote 196; sport and human rights discourse 196–198

individualisation of lifestyles 5
Instagram 75, 79
institutionalised trust 30
integrity of sport 32–33; *see also* sport management research and education
intercultural communication 31–32
intercultural sport education 6, 188–190, 206–207; future of 212–213; opportunities and challenges of 207–209
internal learning 13
International and European Sport Coaching Frameworks 13
International Coach Developer Framework (ICDF) 15
International Council for Coaching Excellence (ICCE) 69
internationalisation 3
internationalisation and intercultural management of sports 2, 31–32; benefits 31–32; consequences 32; cultural

dimensions 32; *see also* sport management research and education
*International Sport Coaching Journal* (ISCJ) 69

Japan, physical education and school sport in 148–149, 153, 154; *see also* Eastern Asia, physical education and school sport in
Japan Sport Association (JSPO) 152

kaitiakitanga 50, 56
kaupapa Maori 56

Latin America: physical activity and sport participation in 4
Latin America, physical activity and sport participation in 139–144; in Argentina 140–142, 143, 145; challenges 143–144; in Chile 139–140, 142, 143; educational system, role of 137–138; High Competition Sports Programs 141; higher education institutions, role of 141–143; South American Sports Council "CONSUDE," role 141; sports associations, role of 142–143; trends and future developments 144–145; in Venezuela 139, 142
learning analytics 77
learning management systems (LMS) 75
lifelong learning 88–89
Living Labs 2, 45–46; definition 46
Long-Term Coach Development 12

Manaakitanga 56
Massive Open Online Courses (MOOCs) 75, 80–81
mediated learning 13
Mega-Sporting Events Platform for Human Rights 198–201, 203n6
Mercedes-Benz Stadium 29
México, sport development and delivery in 115–117, 121; higher education institutions, role of 142; initiation into sports 116; National Commission of Physical Culture and Sport (CONADE) 115–116; organisation and governance of sport 115–116; physical education class 116; sports training outside school 116–117; *see also* Canada, sport development and delivery in; United States, sport development and delivery in

## Index    241

Ministers and Senior Officials Responsible for Physical Education and Sport (MINEPS) 66
Mysummercamps.com 119; *see also* United States, sport development and delivery in

National Certificate in Educational Achievement (NCEA) 54–55
National Football League games 29
New Zealand, outdoor education in 52–56; adventure tourism activities 53; indigenous culture and 52–53; kaupapa Maori 56; outdoor centres and camps 55–56; in schools 54–56; tertiary providers, role of 53–54; *see also* UK perspective of outdoor education
New Zealand, sport and physical activity participation in 128–129; education strategy 130–132; Sport New Zealand Community Sport Strategy 131–132
Nike's "Designed to Move" 64
Nippon Junior High School Physical Culture Association (NJHSPCA) 152
Nittaidai Coach Developer Academy 69
non-routine learning outcomes 81

Oceania Sport Education Program (OSEP) 130
Open University Analytics (OUA) 77
Organisation for Economic Co-operation and Development (OECD) 137, 199; on developing workers employability 84–85; physical education provision 66
outdoor education 2, 49; in Australasia 50; importance of 56–57; New Zealand perspective 52–56; UK perspective 50–52; youth development 55–56
Outward Bound 55

Pacific region, physical activity and sport participation in 4, 126, 129–130; initiatives to improve sport and physical activity 132–133; key stakeholders 130; Pacific Ending Childhood Obesity Network (ECHO) 132; Pacific Regional Education Framework (PACREF) 2018–2030 132; Sport, Physical Activity and Physical Education (SPAPE) Action Plan 2018–2030 132; "Sporting Schools" initiative 130; surveillance of physical activity 129; "Vitality through Active

Living," Fiji 132; *see also* Australia, sport and physical activity in; New Zealand, sport and physical activity in;
physical activity and health 1, 2; activities and innovations 46; approaches to health behaviour 42; environmental determinants of 41–42; gender differences 167; implications for future education of sport 44–46; importance of 38, 126; individual determinants of 40–41; initiatives 42–43; long-term effects 165–166; moderate-to-vigorous intensity PA (MVPA) 163; pedagogical approaches 165; in school curriculum 4; social determinants of 41; socio-ecological models and approaches 39, 39–40; solutions to promoting 43–44
physical education: in 2035 79–81; changing state and status of 65–66; competing and shared priorities 67–68; curricula 68; future education and training, recommendations 168–169; globalised 66–67; relationship between positive outcomes and 66–67; Walking In ScHools (WISH) study 168
physical literacy 4, 133
Pinterest 75
Pokémon Go app 82
Pop Warner football 118
pre-professional identity (PPI) 90
professional identity 89–90, **91**
professional identity development (PID) 90
professionalisation of sports 3
Program for International Student Assessment (PISA) 64
Public Health England 51

qualifications in sport, European perspectives 3, 99; dimensions 100–101, *101*; employability of sport managers and coaches 103–106, **104**; EU policy 100; future developments and challenges 106–107; sport education and training 100–102; weaknesses in 102
quantified self 78

Real Madrid 32
robotics in sport 30

sedentarism 2; consequences of 38
Shanghai Declaration 164
sitting, health effects of 38–39

## 242  Index

South Korea, physical education and school sport in 149–151, 152, 153; *see also* Eastern Asia, physical education and school sport in
sport education: role digital learning environments 3; technology trends 3; trends 2–3; *see also* technology
sport education delivery 3–4
Sport England 51
sport for development and peace (SDP) agenda 199
sport in North America 121–123. *see also* Canada, sport development and delivery in; United States, sport development and delivery in
sport management research and education 2, 24; degree programmes 25–28, **26–27**; digitalisation 30–31; integrity and good governance 32–33; internationalisation and intercultural management 31–32; NASPE-NASSM Joint Task Force on 25; research methods module 28; sustainability and social responsibility modules 28–30; vocational training 28
sports analytics 30
sports apps 30
sport science programmes 220–221
sports cultures 123, 144, 232
sports governing bodies (SGBs) 195, 201
sports journalism 81
sports participation: benefits 11; in physical education activities 67
sports role models (SRMs) 187
supporting coaches 16
sustainability and social responsibility modules, in sport management curricula 2, 28–30; Adidas's strategy 29; "Sport Sustainability Campaign Evaluation Model" 29–30; *see also* sport management research and education
Sustainable Development Goals (SDG) 4, 6, 28, 164, 201
sustainable society, role of sport 28–29

Taiwan, physical education and school sport in 151, 153, 155; *see also* Eastern Asia, physical education and school sport in
technology: audio-visual enhancements 76–77; for feedback information 81; in higher education 75–78; learning analytics 77; learning management systems (LMS) 75; MOOCs 75, 80–81;

to prevent doping 80; simulation-based education 77–78; social media 75; in sport-related education 3, 78–79, 78–81; *see also* wearable devices, sport- and PA-related
Tokyo 2020 Games 29
Tokyo Organising Committee of the Olympic and Paralympic Games (TOCOG) 29
Toyota: intercultural marketing 32; mobility forms 29
trace data 77
Treaty of Waitangi 52
T-shaped professionals 44–45
T-shaped sport 2, 44–45, 45
Turangawaewae 56

UK perspective of outdoor education 50–52; Active Outdoors market 51; adventure sport coach, role of 51; initiatives 51; Learning Outside the Classroom Manifesto 50; notion of pracademic 52; outdoor activities 50; Outdoor Activity Instructor apprenticeship 52; Sport England strategy 51; *see also* New Zealand, outdoor education in
UNESCO's physical education provision 66, 67
Union of European Football Associations (UEFA) Academy 102
United Nations (UN) Guiding Principles on Business and Human Rights (UNGPs) 195
United States, sport development and delivery in 117–121, 121–122; after-school sport and physical activity programming 118; coaches and coach education 120–121; community-based delivery of sport 118–119; fee-based sports specialisation instructional programmes 119; fee-based summer sports camps 119; interscholastic sports programmes 119; Mysummercamps. com 119; organisation and governance of sport 119–120; Physical Activity Alliance (PAA) specialisation 120; school physical education 118; sports specialisation 119; *see also* Canada, sport development and delivery in; México, sport development and delivery in
United States Department of Health and Human Services (USDHHS) 120

Universal Declaration of Human Rights 203n3
University of Lausanne (Switzerland) 102
unmediated learning 13

virtual reality 77–78, 82
volunteer coaches 19–20

Walking In ScHools (WISH) study 168
wearable devices, sport- and PA-related 5, *174*, 232; in assisting decision-making 177; ethical and privacy issues 178; for gamifying workout experiences 176–177; Garmin Connect 177; for monitoring and improving performance 175; opportunities in sports and PA curricula 178–180; Polar 177; roles 173–178; for smart policy planning 177–178; Strava 177–179; *see also* technology
work-based learning (WBL) 87–88; *see also* career development learning (CDL)
work-related learning (WRL) 87; *see also* career development learning (CDL)
World Economic Forum 84

Young Men's Christian Association (YMCA) 56
youth football in Sweden 233
youth sports dropout 166; factors affecting participation 167–168
youth sports migration 166–167

Printed in the United States
by Baker & Taylor Publisher Services